AF538546

# DETERMINANTS OF ACHIEVEMENT IN ENGLISH

# DETERMINANTS OF ACHIEVEMENT IN ENGLISH

***By***

**Ruchi Dubey**

*M.A. M.Ed. D.Phil.*

*Assistant Professor*

*Department of Education*

*University of Allahabad*

*Allahabad (India)*

**DISCOVERY PUBLISHING HOUSE PVT. LTD.**

**NEW DELHI-110 002**

*Published by:*
**Tilak Wasan**

**DISCOVERY PUBLISHING HOUSE PVT. LTD.**
4383/4B, Ansari Road, Darya Ganj
New Delhi-110 002 (India)
*Phone* : +91-11-23279245, 43596064-65
*Fax* : +91-11-23253475
*E-mail* : discoverypublishinghouse@gmail.com
sales@discoverypublishinggroup.com
parul.wasan@gmail.com
*web* : www.discoverypublishinggroup.com

***First Edition:* 2014**

**ISBN: 978-93-5056-475-2**

**Determinants of Achievement in English**



Printed at:
Aditi Fine Art Press
Delhi

# PREFACE

These days, English language is becoming a forerunner in global communication. It has a special place in the parliament, judiciary, broadcasting, journalism and in the education system. It permeates daily life. Learning English language has become popular for business, commerce and communication throughout the world. It is a major vehicle of modern scientific civilization. As a world language it is used for all branches of learning and for common access of books and journals for people throughout the world. Proficiency in English has been increasingly recognised as a key determinant to professional success. To acquire proficiency in English language one must have mastery of four basic skills-reading, writing, listening and speaking. The students are expected to have a command over English. But it is disheartening to note that despite the importance of English language, the poor performance of students in this subject has continued unabated. Therefore, if one weighs the vital role English language plays in the society against the backdrop of the continuously poor performance of students in the subject, it becomes imperative that further steps need to be taken to address the situation. Various studies have emphasised the influence of numerous factors *viz.*, personal, social, psychological and environmental on students' academic achievement. The book attempts to identify the determinants of achievement in English among students. It is based on author's doctoral dissertation, awarded by the University of Allahabad as a D.Phil. degree in Education. The researcher has made an humble attempt to study the cognitive, motivational and environmental determinants of achievement in English. Cognitive variables include intelligence, emotional intelligence and formal reasoning, motivational variables include academic motivation and causal attributions and environmental variables include classroom learning environment.

The author expresses her heartfelt and sincere gratitude to her esteemed supervisor Prof. K. S. Misra for very kindly illuminating her path throughout with his patience, support and his innate goodness. His encouragement, support, supervision from the initial to the final level enabled her to develop an understanding of the subject. She also take the opportunity to extend her tremendous thanks to all her Teachers for shaping her for what she is. She is indebted to the principals, teachers and students of the schools included in the sample of the study, as without their willing cooperation it would have been impossible to collect the data and pursue the work. She owe her thanks to all the authors and researchers of this field whose published or unpublished material have been used as reference in this study. Lastly, she offer her regards to her near and dear ones for giving their unequivocal support throughout as always for which her mere expression of thanks likewise does not suffice.

**Ruchi Dubey**

# CONTENTS

# CHAPTER 1

# INTRODUCTION

LANGUAGE IS MAN'S finest asset and most basic tool. It would be difficult for men to live together, think or act without the sounds and symbols of language. It is almost impossible to imagine life without language. As the complexity of our civilization increases, the importance of language as tool increases as well.

Webster (1981) while defining language says, "language is audible, articulate human speech as produced by the action of the tongue and adjacent vocal organs." or "any means vocal or otherwise of expressing or communicating feeling or thought".

Language is more than instinctive sounds given in response to environmental conditions. It is a system for interpreting and organizing experience as well as for communicating ideas and feelings. It provides a bond of unity among its speakers. Next to religion, it is one single factor that has contributed to group consciousness (Joseph, 2008).

Language is both a declarative body of knowledge possessed by adult competent body of speakers and a set of procedures (or abilities) by which such knowledge is put to use in a variety of ways in linguistic activities. Language can be viewed primarily as a means of communication among conspecifics (human language being the most developed and sophisticated code), and also as a means of representing and conveying thoughts and intentions, as a symbolic tool or device relating sound and meaning. In this regard, the psychological study of language is at least a two-fold enterprise, for it must address *(i)* a wide array of information types and processing levels involved in understanding and speaking and *(ii)* the intimate connection between the speakers linguistic knowledge and abilities, on one hand and their cognitive and communicative capacities at large, of which linguistic skills are but a subset.

Fully competent users of language are those who had control over the many uses to which language might be put, such individuals are sensitive to what language was possible in terms of grammatical rules, but also to the appropriateness of language in relation to a particular context and to its acceptability in terms of human and social behaviour and the culture of which it was a part (Hutchinson, 1990).

According to Hutchinson (1990), the communicative uses of language are as follows:

1. *Modality* – For expressing degrees of certainity, necessity or conviction.
2. *Moral Discipline and Evaluation* – For expressing approval and disapproval.
3. *Persuasion* – For persuading, suggesting or urging a course of action.
4. *Argument* – For informing or arguing or asserting a point of view.
5. *Rational Inquiry or Exposition* – For exemplifying or defining or expressing implications.
6. *Personal Emotions* – For expressing pleasure, astonishment, shock or annoyance.
7. *Interpersonal Relations* – For expressing degrees of formality or informality and politeness.
8. *Imaginative* – Using language in a creative way.

## THE PURPOSE OF LANGUAGE INSTRUCTION

Language is the most potent vehicle for spreading knowledge in the society across the barriers of literacy (Daudi and Yahya, 2008). Chaturvedi and Mohale (1976) have explained that language plays an important role in education as there can be no education in absence of it and hence it could be regarded as a pre-condition of education. Bernstein (1970) has proved that those who are good in language are good in all other subjects and those who fail in language are likely to fail in all other subjects. He further adds that, language is the foundation of the curriculum because the subjects of the curriculum are taught through the medium of language. According to Abedi (2004), language proficiency is a strong predictor of test performance. The dependence of school achievement on verbal ability not only substantiates the importance of language in school but makes clear the schools' vital responsibility to foster the development of language skills (MacGinite, 1969).

According to Hutchinson (1990), language teaching is largely concerned with transmitting knowledge about how the system of either the native language or a second or subsequent language worked, through drills and exercises which exemplified acceptable ways of constructing phrases and sentences.

Teachers, in the past, considered language to be a static, unchanging subject – as something taught and used only in the English class. There was a 'correct' language, one that was always the same, and one that when learnt was suitable for all times and places. Teachers gave no thought to change, but concentrated on maintaining the purity which they felt was the tradition, that must be upheld. But this is not true, and most of the educators today are aware of the vital nature of language and of how it changes. It is recognised more and more that an acceptable usage in one situation is not necessarily suitable in another; that words and meanings have been added; and that language is functional and fluid, with its principal purpose being to promote communication. Language is now recognised as something alive, changing and along with that culture evolving. Thus, language must be functional for communication actually to occur.

The major purpose of the school is to help children to meet adequately the problems of life, and to find their place in the expanding culture. This may be best done through the language instruction provided at school. The knowledge, habits, attitudes and skills determines the personality of a child and it largely exhibits itself in use of language – the words most frequently employed in writing or speech, the punctuation most needed, the usage of proper stress and intonation which make effective communication possible and handwriting that is legible. Men use language, both to communicate with others and to communicate with himself. Both of these functions are vital to the process of education. Language not only embodies the information that is transmitted to the student but furnishes the organizing patterns that permit him to remember what he experiences, the conceptual substance from which he can build new creations of thought, and the signals with which he can then direct himself (MacGinite, 1969).

**Language Learning Mechanism in Children**

The rate of maturation and the world that constitutes his knowledge are the factors that influence language growth of a child. Limitation in maturity and in experience certainly delimits language growth. Second language learning is a little more complex phenomenon. Besides other factors, certain kinds of direct and indirect inputs influence second language learning. Hill (1967) and McCarthy (1954) pointed to the educative influence of conversation with more mature children and adults on the language development in children.

Second language learning is both a process of creative construction and a skill learning process. When it is said that learning a second language is a process of creative construction, it imply emphasis on certain 'cognitive processing strategies' that the learner bring to task in order to develop internal representation of the second language system. The more convincing view advocates, the use of second language as a performance skill which has a cognitive as well as behavioural aspect. The cognitive aspect involves the internalization of plans for creating appropriate behaviour. For language use these plans are derived mainly from language system. They include grammatical rules and procedures for selecting vocabulary. The behavioural aspect involves the automation of these plans so that they can be converted into fluent performance in real time.

Literacy development includes listening, speaking, reading and writing. These component skills are interrelated since they all involve words. In listening, ideas are received through words while in speaking and writing, ideas are expressed through words and in reading, ideas are communicated through printed words. Language learning must focus on the development of the four skills-listening, speaking, reading and writing in integrated form. This may be termed as whole language approach. Jain (1979) reported that intelligence, English vocabulary, knowledge of grammar, comprehension, spelling, pronunciation, speed and legibility of handwriting, the status of English in the family, extra reading in English and the quality of teacher play a vital role in learning English at the high school stage.

## IMPORTANCE OF LEARNING ENGLISH

The term 'English' has traditionally been used at the secondary and college levels to describe a content, subject or discipline that includes language, literature and composition. Judy (1981) defines 'English' as all uses of language, from informal chatter to formal discussion, from short memos to long examination papers, from the language of television to the language of computers, a programme that is diffused throughout the school, and a way of perceiving, knowing, learning and becoming. Among the languages used in India, English occupies a dignified but delicate position. English has enjoyed and still enjoys a unique place in our school curriculum. It is used as the official language of the country *i.e.*, the language of administration, judiciary and legislature, inter-state and international communication, and trade and commerce. English language occupies a dignified position in the country (Dash, 2004).

English found its way into the warp and woof of the Indian national life. English helps to keep the wheels of the world turn, with its elegance, grace and style. It unfolds the folds of a dark curtain of ignorance. It is as adaptable and transparent as a language that it can take on the tint of any country. Because of the number of people using the language, geographical dispersion and vernacular load, English enjoys a predominant position among the world languages (Jesa, 2005).

English is referred as a 'Living Language', a language that is organic in form and content, growing and transforming with changing times. It has transcended geographical, social and cultural barriers. It is language signifying mobility and uniformity. According to Verma (1987), at the individual level,

English is the language of upward socio-economic mobility; any individual seeking socio-economic advancement at the national level will find ability in English as asset. It is the language of the new global world. Being a highly flexible and fluid language, English adapts itself and also adopts the native environment. The vast repertoire of the English vocabulary is continuously being enriched and enhanced by the varied languages of the world. This unique 'hybrid' quality of the language sustains as well as helps in its global acceptance (Ghanshyam and Chakravarti, 2008). English is the treasure house of world-wide learning and research in literature, life, art, science and technology. The technical importance, the commercial weight and the cultural content of English, explain the world-wide acceptance of the language as the medium of the intellectual exchange (Dash, 2004).

English is the language of preference in this globalised world. The process of globalisation has endowed the English language with an eminence that has eclipsed many other languages with time (Ghanshyam and Chakravarti, 2008).

The growing demands in the horizon of global communication technology necessitate the Indian learners at different levels of learning in formal or informal educational institutions to acquire ease in universal communicative language *i.e.* English in the elite societies to accelerate progress in all fields of development (Sarojini, 2000).

Emphasizing the significance of language as a tool for developing a knowledge society the National Knowledge Commission (2005) has stated: "An understanding of and command over English language is the most important determinant of access to higher education, employment possibilities and social opportunities." Students who are not adequately trained in English as a language are always at a handicap in the world of higher education (Daudi and Yahya, 2008).

The policy of the Government of India toward English has been decided by various Education Commissions and as a result a steady line of thinking has evolved. Being the official language of administration, English got a fillip and relegated the Indian languages to the background. According to the National Knowledge Commission (2005), English is the instrument of building inclusive society and can transform India into a knowledge society.

English is the link language. It works as a link in India. It helps in national integration, and in communication between the state government and the government of the union. It is the greatest unifying link between the Hindi speaking and the non-Hindi speaking people of India. English as a link language connects India with foreign countries as it is a language of international politics, trade, commerce, industry and communication. It is one of the six official languages of the U.N.O. It is the language of the world.

English has been described as a gateway of the world's culture. It is a window to all scientific, technological, legal, socio-cultural and medical progress that is constantly taking place in the world. It is described as a pipe-line for the stream of knowledge in all branches of learning. It is the language of diplomacy and it contains many literary treasures, it gives us an understanding of western thought and culture.

English language has the richest treasure of literature. It is a flexible vehicle of thought. Its literature is wide and varied as life itself, giving the student power to reason and judge with critical balance and equity. English language has been praised for its galaxy of literary talents. It had impressive impact on Indian literature. Because of its literary value, English has been retained in the secondary school curriculum.

To keep pace with the professional advancements which are taking giant leaps, the first and foremost requirement of the job-seekers is to develop professionally and one of the major personality traits in great demand is effective and excellent communication and listening skills. To excel in professional field, one must possess a reasonably good command over English language. It is the key to success; it is the 'bridge' which has to be crossed to reach greener professional pastures.

Computers and internet have literally thrown open the windows to the world. English is the master language in the role of ICT in library, translation and national knowledge network (Singh, 2008a). To inter-connect and correspond globally English is essential. The increasing importance of these new technological advancements has further strengthened the stronghold of English on India as well as on the whole world. India is a fore-runner in the field of software development, and a strong hold on English language has provided millions of Indians to excel in the field.

It is the global language linking the whole world together in one single thread, and provided its speakers with the power to excel, progress and transcend barriers of nation and culture. In India, English has acquired a prominent position. It is the language that has infact unified this diverse country and also given its inhabitants a global mobility.

Acknowledging the importance of English, University Education Commission (1948) reported that, it is a language which is rich in literature-humanistic, scientific and technical; unable to have access to this knowledge, our standard of scholarship would deteriorate and our participation in the world movement of thought would become negligible. English is the only means of preventing our isolation from the world.

The National Research Council (2000) verifies the necessity of time for acquiring academic proficiency in English. It reported that English language learners need to develop not only mastery of conversational English, but also mastery of the spoken and written English necessary to do the academic work.

Thus, it can be concluded that knowledge of English is a valuable asset for all students and a reasonable proficiency in the language is necessary for all those who want to proceed in life. But, inspite of immense importance of English language, the average Indian student is not able to either learn English or communicate in English with a reasonable level of proficiency and fluency. The weakness persists and shall stay as long as the teaching and learning of English will continue in its present form in our schools, colleges and universities.

## TEACHING OF ENGLISH

### Place of English in School Curriculum

A great deal of controversy exists about the place of English in the scheme of studies. Different commissions and conferences attempted to lay down the specific placement of the study of English at different stages of our educational programme. The University Education Comission (1948) opined that the students who are undergoing training at schools must acquire sufficient mastery of English, in order to have access to the treasure of knowledge. The commission recommended that English must be studied in High Schools and in Universities in order that we (people) might keep in touch with the living stream of ever-growing knowledge. The apprehension behind it was that, none of the Indian vernaculars had a larger reach than English and to prevent India from being isolated from the world.

The Secondary Education Commission (1952-53) reported that ".... what was most urgently needed was that our youth acquire knowledge from our sources and contribute their share to its expansion and development. In the attainment of this objective, study of English is bound to play an important part". The commission recommended that during the middle school stage, every child should be taught at least two languages *i.e.* English and Hindi.

Regarding the place of English language in our secondary school curriculum, the Conference of Professors of English of Indian Universities (1953) suggested that – English should continue to occupy an important place in the curriculum of secondary schools. The aim should be the attainment by pupils a good working knowledge of English at the end of the secondary stage. With a view to counteract the present low standard of teaching, English should be taught as a compulsory subject for a period of six years at the secondary stage of 6 periods of 50 minutes each per week.

The Central Advisory Board of Education (CABE) (1957) gave the three language formula and recommended that students at the secondary stage must study three languages *i.e.,* mother tongue or the regional language, Hindi or English, and a modern Indian or a European language. With the application of this formula, some student can read English for 6 years, *i.e.,* from V class and others can read it for 3 years *i.e.,* from VIII - X. But ali students have to study English. This formula gives ample scope to those who are much interested in this language because they can opt it from class V. This formula recommends that English should not be taught at elementary stage. This seems plausible because many teachers are of the view that second language should be taught after pupils develop a good ground in their mother-tongue.

The Kunzru Committee (1959) appointed by the University Grants Commission to report on the question of medium of instruction and the teaching of English, after serious deliberation said that, English must be retained as a properly studied language in our universities even when an Indian language is used as the ordinary medium of teaching.

In connection with the place of English in the secondary school curriculum the Indian Education Commission or Kothari Commission (1964-66) recommends that from V to VII class, two languages will be taught. One of them will be the regional language and the other can be either Hindi or English. From VIII to X class, three languages will be taught *i.e.*, regional language, Hindi or modern Indian language, and English.

The National Policy of Education (1979), recognising the international importance of English recommended that education should be provided in English.

**Aims of Teaching English**

The study of English language has four important aspect, *viz.*, the semantic aspect, the phonetic aspect, the graphic aspect and the phonetic-graphic aspect. The semantic aspect means the understanding of the meaning of words and their relationship in a sentence. It is related to comprehension. The phonetic aspect deals with the spelling and pronunciation. It is the sound aspect. The graphic aspect, which is the writing aspect, deals with the written form of the language. There are two more aspects, the literary aspect leads to ornamentation of a language and the linguistic aspect *i.e.*, the working knowledge of a language. All the four aspects work in co-ordination with each other. They cannot work in isolation. The general aims of teaching English are:

1. To help the pupils to understand what is heard.
2. To help them to understand what is read.
3. To teach them to express ideas in speech.
4. To teach them to express ideas in writing.

Thus, the general aim of teaching English is to develop among the students the 'skill of reproducing' the language, when they speak or write and to develop the receptive skill when they listen to others speaking or when they read what someone has composed. So, the teacher of English has to train the hearing, speaking, reading and writing objective of the pupils. It is known as the linguistic aim of teaching English.

**Difficulties in Teaching English**

Learning a language means learning a skill rather than information, therefore, the teaching should be learner-oriented, not teacher-oriented. The poor performance of the students in English is might be due to various difficulties in teaching and learning faced by the teacher and the student. Among the various difficulties faced by them are – *firstly,* the time available for teaching English is always too short, no matter how generous is the allowance on the time-table for English lessons. *Secondly,* the school environment is not so congenial and permissive to enable the pupils to hear or see or use English. *Thirdly,* the teachers are demotivated and ineffective. Majority of the teachers of English are not professionally equipped to teach English, they are not aware of appropriate methods and not clear about the objectives of teaching English. *Fourthly,* the wide range of learner's ability creates further complications. The teacher has to adjust his teaching accordingly in view of this factor which needs planning and effective execution. Another difficulty in teaching English is related to the text books of English, which are uninteresting for the pupils. Books are drab and dull with lack of attractive reading material. As a result the essential element of pleasure in learning a second language is lost. Dewal (1974) conducted a study on difficulties of teaching English and reported that, the difficulties hampering effective teaching and learning of English are shortage of trained teachers, lack of subject competence in teachers, dearth of good teaching-learning material, lack of individual attention and poor socio-economic background.

Due to these difficulties in teaching English, the learners at all levels commit a large number of errors which is a common problem faced by the teachers, as a result of which students proficiency and achievement in English is also deteriorating. Not realising their own shortcomings, the teachers are often annoyed at the number of errors committed by their learners. A study of error analysis can make it clear to the teachers that no one can learn a language without committing errors. They should realise that errors are a part of learner's learning process and that they should look at errors as a part of language learning, and not something which hinders the process of learning (Kumar, 2007).

Schools, colleges and universities in India, do teach the reading and writing of English language. But, evaluation of student is done only on written English. No fora exist for testing the students in the reading, speaking and listening elements. This is so because these elements do not form classroom schedules; they are neither taught, nor practiced compulsorily and hence not tested (Dhaka, 2008). If a student is good in the written expression of English language he is considered to be a brilliant student, but, majority of students find themselves struggling with English language when it comes to proficiency in communication and listening skills. Dhaka (2008) reported that almost neglible number of student (5.3%) of Engineering could converse in English and almost half of the students could not understand any one speaking to them in English. Students' inability alone is not responsible for such a poor state but there are several deficiencies and causes which need to be addressed by the authorities.

The assessment of language is a multifaceted process (Shipley and McAfee, 1998; Cole, Dale and Thal, 1996; Tomblin, Morris and Spriestersback, 1994; Haynes, Pindzola and Emerick, 1992). In the assessment of language, biological (genetic, heredity), affective (emotion, motivation, attitude, commitment, self-concept/esteem, honesty, trust, resilence), and contextual (socio-economic status, ethnicity, gender, family, demographic environment) mediators (Pressley and McCormick, 1995) and social, educational, and occupational language demands (Larson and Mckinley, 1995; Wallach and Butler, 1994; Lane and Molyneaux, 1992; Weller, Crelley, Watteyne and Herbert, 1992; Wallach and Miller, 1988) must be considered (Farmer, 2000).

## FACTORS INFLUENCING ACHIEVEMENT IN ENGLISH

Academic talent may be best understood from a societal perspective in which characteristics of the individual and characteristics of the environment both contribute to the expression of talent. The academic performance of students is influenced by a set of intellectual and non-intellectual factors, working in dynamic interaction. Among the intellectual factors are scholastic ability, aptitude, academic attainments, etc. and the non-intellectual factors include personality traits, motivation, study habits and the like. Achievement in English is influenced by various factors. Mohan (2006) stated that English score is positively related to language proficiency. According to Sucaromana (2004), factors that may influence achievement in English are emotional intelligence, family encouragement for learning English, study habits, level of engagement and attitude towards studying English. Sarojini (2000) reported that poor language skills of the in-service English teachers have been influencing the school pupils learning skills of English language. Sinha (1998) attributes difficulties in learning English by V standard students to low awareness of syllables, short attention span and comprehension problems. Factors like appropriate study habits and low test anxiety contribute to better achievement in English. (Verma, 1996a, 1996b).

Achievement in English is also influenced by intelligence (Dubey, 2010a; Kaur, 1992; Chandy, 1991; Kaile, 1988; Joshi, 1984; Brahmabhatt, 1983 and Jain, 1979), general mental ability (Srivastava, 1995), socio-economic status (Hakuta *et al.* 2000; Khan, 1996; Thejovathi, 1995; Chandy, 1991; Singh, 1989; Chandra, 1988; Joshi, 1984; Bramabhatt, 1983; Kakkar, 1975), interest (Tachibana, Matsukawa and Zhong, 1996; Sankarappan, 1992; Singh, 1989; Kakkar, 1975), anxiety (Hemamalini, 2010; Verma, 1996a; Sibia, 1989;

Brahmabhatt, 1983), extensive reading (Meera and Remya, 2010; Constantino, Lee and Krashen, 1997; Mason and Krashen, 1997) and pupils' attitude towards English (Fakeye, 2010; Mazumdar, 1992; Mohan, 1991; Budhdev and Ravina, 1989; Chandra, 1988; Wethington, 1970). Emeke and Adeoye (2009) reported that students' achievement in English is effected by emotional intelligence and self-efficacy training.

Chandy (1991) found positive relationship between achievement in English and physical study facilities, family stability, family climate, punishment and study habits. Studies have revealed that students with high proficiency in vocabulary, spelling, stylistic transformation, derivational structures, applied grammar and contextual meaning were superior in proficiency in English (Dey, 1991). Chandra (1988) reported that proficiency in written English at +2 level is correlated with knowledge of grammar, reading comprehension, vocabulary, occupational status of the parents, use of English outside the formal educational settings, educational qualifications of the members of the family and learning habits. Achievement in the areas of comprehension, composition and pronunciation, in English is influenced by the cultural and economic background and intelligence of students. Intelligence of students also influences achievement in the areas of spelling, applied grammar and vocabulary in English (Khare, 1986). Growth of English language ability is also influenced by caste, personality and administrative control of an institution (Joshi, 1984). According to Pandey (1982), the most important factors related to low achievement in English are lack of guidance at home, lack of environment of speaking English, lack of training to English language teachers and that teachers are not oriented in the modern techniques of teaching of English. Jain (1979) reported that English vocabulary, knowledge of grammar, comprehension, spelling, pronunciation, speed and legibility of handwriting, the status of English in the family, extra reading in English and the quality of teacher play a vital role in learning English language at the high school stage.

Achievement in English is also influenced by other factors like literacy level of parents (Kumar and Ambedkar, 2005; Sankarappan, 1992), parental motivation, parental encouragement (Chou, 2005; Chandy, 1991; Mohan, 1991), students' motivation (Mohan, 1991), language competence and rule learning (Gupta, 1990), morale (Dube, 1989), creativity (Meera and Remya, 2010; Upadhyaya, 2000; Kaile, 1988), medium of instruction (Clement and Singh, 1993), locality of school (Balasubramanian, 1994), study habits (Verma, 1996b, 1996c; Abdullahi, 1996), medium of achool (Shobhna, 2004), school adjustment (Gudadur, 2009), n-achievement and emotional stability (Brahmabhatt, 1983) of students. Self-concept also emerged as an important factor influencing achievement in English. In this context Areepattamannil and Freeman (2008) reported that verbal self-concept and school self-concept were the best predictors of English GPA.

Thus, it can be concluded that achievement in English has a complex functional dependence on genetic, personal and environmental factors. The former take care of inheritance and intelligence, personal factors may include personality, interest, attitude, aptitude, study habits, anxiety, academic motivation, language competence and creativity, and the latter includes everything ranging from socio-economic status to role of parents.

## THEORETICAL FRAMEWORK

It is generally agreed that scientific knowledge of the language and the psychological and social factors involved is necessary for successful foreign language teaching. This knowledge can be gained through the various language acquisition theories.

### Language Acquisition Theories

#### *Behaviourism and Operant Conditioning of Language*

The Behaviourist school of psychology aims at a functional explanation of language learning. The behaviourist conceives language learning as conditioned verbal behaviour consisting of a series of stimulus-response bonds. The core of language learning is the formation of a set of language habits which consists of conditioned responses. These habits can be formed by making the learner spend a major part of his time in practicing the pattern. Thus, repetition is the key for the formation of language habit (Mukalel, 2003). According to Skinner (1957), imitation plays a role in language acquisition. In Skinner's view, language development is based on operant conditioning, because the environment (consequences) teaches a person to operate on the environment with words. The response (relating to language learning), if reinforced, is strengthened, repeated or occurs again. Thus, the child makes a sound, utters a word or a sentence.

#### *Cognitive Theory*

The cognitive schools of psychology aim at a functional explanation of language learning. The cognitive interpretation of language learning rests upon the neuro-psychological bases of thought. For cognitive psychology, language learning is a 'meaningful process', unlike the behaviourists who explain language learning as a mechanistic process. This theory is parallel to transformational generative grammar, which considers language-learning as a rule-governed behaviour involving the cognitive faculties of man; rather than a conditioning process.

#### *Language Development and Cognition*

According to Piaget (1926), language is a symptom of existing cognitive structures of the child. Language acquisition varies depending upon the stage of cognitive development. During the sensori motor period (age 0-2 years), language is almost absent until the final months of the period. During pre-operational period (age 2-7 years) egocentric and socialised speech are noticed.

In the concrete operation period, their understanding is limited to concrete objects, *i.e.*, children use language in relation to concrete objects. They cannot use language for abstract ideas. During the formal operation period, the children's language is free from the concrete objects. In this stage, children develop the verbal ability to express abstract ideas.

***Structuralist Model***

According to the structuralist model, language is determined entirely by the environment and the child strives 'to learn the language exactly as his environment, speaks it' (Leopold, 1948). The language acquisition process involves simple imitation and selective reinforcement (Saville-Troike, 1982). The structuralist model assumes that, language is a structured system of components.

***Theory of Transformational Grammar***

Noam Chomsky, the propounder of the theory of transformation grammar considers language learning as a rule-governed behaviour rather than a conditioning process. Chomsky (1959-65) said that learners not only respond to stimuli, they transform stimuli according to the rules of grammar stored in their heads. The transformation consists of sequencing words to invent sentences and of generalising grammatical rules to apply them to new vocabulary. Learners use their own bags of tricks to confront language and manipulate language to suit their needs. According to Chomsky, learners possess an innate competence for language acquisition, this innate capacity to acquire language is the result of his unique human biological inheritance, *i.e.*, Language Acquisition Device (LAD). Chomsky states that no one acquires a language by learning all the possible sentences of that language. Instead of learning billions of sentences, a child unconsciously acquires a grammar that can generate an infinite number of sentences in his own native language. The person's ability to generate new grammatically correct sentences is called the generative transformational grammar.

The basic assumption of this 'nativist' model is that rich and impoverished environment can affect the rate of development of language among children (Bates, 1976). Brown and Fraser (1963) are also of the view that child language development is a process of rule formation and discovering universal features (Slobin, 1970). For Chomsky, all humans have the inborn inclination to learn and master a language. In contrast to this, Skinner counts on the environment, and not on some inherent predisposition in language acquisition.

Thus, it can be said that, reward or punishment, and practice and imitation influence language development and learners do use innate tendencies to learn and create language.

***Bernstein's Theory***

Bernstein (1961), in his thesis about language differences among social classes, suggested that there are two general types of language, one that of the lower class and the other of the middle social class. The first, a restricted code, which does not follow standard English grammar, is simple, rigid and easily predictable; the second, an elaborated code, is more flexible, offers more alternatives and is less predictable. Bernstein (1971) argued that language and social class are forces that restrict the achievement of students from low socio-economic backgrounds. He argued that the language use of middle-class families tends to be rich and elaborate in qualities and implies sets of logical operations that help children who live in such environments to have better school achievement (DeMarrais and LeCompte, 1995). Conversely, because students from low-income backgrounds live in less enriched family environment, their family environment limit their perception and language development, which in turn affects their achievement (Bernstein, 1971).

***Cognitive Code Method***

Applied linguists believe that learners must understand what they are learning and they must be allowed to make use of their cognitive skills in order to help them to achieve comprehension of grammatical structure. Rules can provide a short cut to learning. Formation of concepts results from verbalising grammatical relations. Pattern drills create language demanding situations. Sequencing and grading of linguistic items begin with a 'base' and acquire transformations.

Carrol's model (1963, 1974) of school learning can be applied with success in learning a foreign language. The model consists of five elements:

1. The learner's aptitude (as a function of time needed to achieve success).
2. The learner's general intelligence.
3. The learner's perseverance (time allowed by the learner).
4. The quality of instruction (sequence order).
5. The opportunity for learning (time allowed by the school).

Oller (1980) claimed that there is a general factor of language proficiency that exhausts most of the reliable variance on various subtasks of listening, speaking, reading and writing. He equates this with spearman's 'g', and proposes that putative measures of intelligence are essentially equivalent to measures of language proficiency. Intelligence (as defined by scores on tests) is simply a reflection of underlying general language ability.

***Attribution Theory***

Attributions are inferences about the causes of success and failure. Among the most prevalent inferred causes of success and failure are ability, effort, task difficulty or ease, luck, mood and help or hindrance from others (Graham, 2003).

Weiner's Model (1971) states that, an incoming stimulus viewed as a source of information, is encoded into the belief system that gives it a meaning. The subsequent response is then guided by the intervening structure of thought. It is based upon the assumption that beliefs about the causes of success and failure mediate between antecedent stimulus-organism transaction and ensuing achievement behaviour. According to the model, individuals utilise four elements of ascription both to predict and interpret the outcome of an achievement related event. These four causal elements are – *(i)* Ability (A), *(ii)* Effort (E), *(iii)* Task difficulty (T) and *(iv)* Luck (L). Thus, Outcome (O) of an achievement related event is said to be a function of these four factors.

$$O = f(A, E, T, L)$$

In attempting to explain the outcome (success and failure) of an achievement related event, the individual assesses his own or the performers' ability level, the amount of effort that was expended, the difficulty of the task and the magnitude and direction of perceived luck.

Other Attribution theorists have also suggested that individuals tend to attribute the causes of their success and failure in achievement situations to four major factors: *(i)* their ability, *(ii)* the amount of effort expended; *(iii)* the difficulty of the task and *(iv)* luck (Weiner, 1972; Weiner, Kukla, Frieze, Reed, Rest and Rosenbaum, 1971). According to Weiner (1979) and Frieze (1976), these causes can be classified along three dimensions related to certain psychological consequences. These dimensions include stability, locus and control. The stability dimension refers to how fixed or variable a cause is overtime and is linked to one's future expectancy of success and failure. Causes differ in locus, or whether the cause is internal or external to the person and is linked to certain self-esteem affects such as competence, pride and guilt. The control dimension refers to whether or not a cause is under one's perceived control and is linked to the evaluation and helping behaviour of others. To of the four components in the model (ability and effort) describe qualities of the person undertaking the activity, while the remaining two (task difficulty and luck) are properties external to the person or environment factors. Further, two of the elements (ability and task difficulty) are somewhat enduring, whereas magnitude of the two remaining components (effort and luck) is relatively variable. Two of the causal factors in the model (ability and effort) are under one's control while the remaining two (task difficulty and luck) are uncontrollable on the part of the individual.

Such a dimensional classification allows one to examine the properties of different causal attributions and to predict possible affective reactions and expectancy changes which might, in turn, lead to certain achievement behaviours.

Attributions of success and failure to causes which are internal on the locus dimension can lead to increased feelings of pride, shame, competence and other effects of self esteem (Weiner, 1979; Weiner, Russell and Lerman, 1978). Several studies comparing the attributional pattern of high and low achievers found that high achievers were more likely to perceive internal factors, particularly effort, as being important to their achievement outcomes, while low achievers were likely to make external attributions (Pearl, Brayon and Donahue, 1980; Barnett and Kaiser, 1978; Crandal, Katkovsky and Crandall, 1975).

In a success situation, people feel maximum pride when they attribute their performance to either ability or effort *i.e.,* to internal causes. Such internal attributions and their related affects can further lead to certain achievement behaviours including the tendency to initiate future achievement activities, intensity of motivation, and preference for tasks of intermediate difficulty (Bar-Tal, 1978; Weiner, 1972; Weiner *et al.* 1972). Attribution of success to good luck or the ease of the task produces considerably less pride. Failures attributed to the difficulty of the task or to bad luck results in little shame since no personal responsibility is taken for failure.

The stability dimension affects cognitive changes in expectancy following success or failure. When attributions are made to unstable factors, such as effort and luck, one's future expectancy is maintained or shows less change than when attributions are made to stable causes, such as ability and task difficulty (Weiner, 1979; Weiner, 1972; Weiner *et al.* 1972). This is because unstable attributions suggest to the person that future outcomes may be different since the present outcome was due to factors which are likely to change. In contrast, stable attributions suggest that future outcomes will probably remain the same, which increases with one's future expectancy of success and failure. When success is perceived as caused by good luck, the resulting expectancy is that failure might occur in future since luck is believed to be an unstable external factor. Corresponding expectation are found for attributions to bad luck in situation of failure. Attribution to lack of effort (an internal unstable cause) in failure results in higher expectancy for future success than attribution to stable causes. Failure attributed to lack of ability results in low expectancy for future success since one assumes that one's ability cannot increase greatly, therefore, future performance will show little improvement. Also because ability is a stable cause, success attributed to ability results in high expectancy for future success. Accordingly, attributions for success to ease of task (stable cause) results in high expectancy for success and attributions of failure to difficulty of the task results in low expectancy for success.

The control dimension relates to how others perceive one's personal responsibility of the person's behaviour, and their sentiment or feeling towards him (Weiner, 1979). In failure situations, it is seen that, if others perceive the cause to be under one's personal control, they are less likely to offer help, tend to make more negative evaluations of the behaviour, and have more negative feelings towards the person (Weiner, 1979). The controllability dimension is related to a number of interpersonal affects, such as pity and anger; pity and sympathy are experienced toward others whose failures are caused by uncontrollable factors. In contrast, anger is elicted when others' failure are due to causes within their control. These emotional reactions also can serve as indirect attributional cues *i.e.,* they provide information about the cause of achievement. If a teacher expresses pity and sympathy following student failure, that student tends to make low ability attribution. Hence, pity from others can undermine beliefs about ability (Graham, 2003).

The causes people believe to be responsible for their (and other's) success and failures determine the way in which they subsequently behave. Those who believe that their failures are caused by a variable and controllable causes are more likely to make a positive response to the failure, in attempting to overcome it, than are those who believe that the same degree of failure is caused by stable or uncontrollable factors (Rogers, 1990).

In achievement domains, and particularly school contexts, there appears a set of causes of success and failure – ability, immediate and long-term effort, task characteristics, intrinsic motivation, teacher's competence, mood and luck. In particular, in achievement settings, ability and effort are the dominant perceived causes of performance; that is success is attributed to high ability and/or effort, and failure to low ability and lack of trying (Weiner, 1992). There is evidence showing that ability and effort attribution may differ across academic subject areas, and for ability attributions this may be related to level of achievement in that area (Marsh, Cairns, Relich, Barnes and Debus, 1982). Kanoy, Johnson and Kanoy (1980), Weiner, (1979), Nicholls (1978) and Sherman (1977) believe that attributions is closely tied to one's own perceptions of academic competence.

***Achievement Motivation Theory***

Psychology has been applied to education but so far no systematic theory of academic motivation has been formulated. The work of some researchers does offer possibilities of evolving postulates that would help in the teaching-learning process. An important approach in this direction is the theory of achievement motivation formulated by J.W. Atkinson (1966).

Achievement motivation refers to a pattern of actions and feelings connected to striving to achieve some internalised standard of excellence in performance (Vidler, 1977). Achievement oriented behaviour is seen to be a function of a number of factors including the motive to succeed, the motive to avoid failure, the perceived probability of success and the incentive value of success (Paul, 1982).

Atkinson (1957, 1964) elaborated the theory of achievement motivation. His theory implies that in situations where probability of success or failure is very high, individual's motive to achieve success and motive to avoid failure has little or no effect.

The assumptions of Atkinson's theory are:

1. The theory is appropriate in achievement oriented situation, that is, in situations in which the person feels himself responsible for the outcomes to be measured against some prescribed standards. In other words, it is appropriate in situations which require both skill and competence.
2. The theory assumes that achievement situations will be governed by two opposite motives – a motive to approach success and a motive to avoid failure. Both will be enduring parts of a subjects personality and their relative strengths will differ from person to person. This means that the theory regards both the personal and situational factors as important.
3. The theory assumes that the incentive value of success and incentive value of failure (Is, If) directly depend upon the expectancy factor (Ps, Pf), subjective probability of success and subjective probability of failure.

The theory predicts that achievement-oriented subjects will be more motivated towards moderately difficult tasks than failure-threatened subjects. When applied to education, this would mean that achievement-oriented subjects will be more inclined towards challenge.

Achievement-oriented subjects have not necessarily shown their best performance at intermediate level of success and failure threatened subjects have only occasionally shown deteriorated performance at this level. This conflicting result as shown by the studies of Klinger (1966), Smith (1964), Karabenick and Youssef (1968) and Atkinson (1967) can be explained on the basis of two reasons. *Firstly*, prediction of performance involves many complex factors and so Atkinson theory does not give consistent results. *Secondly*, the tendency to persist can have an eventual or long range effect on education outcomes. The above discussion leads us to conclude that Atkinson's theory of achievement motivation accurately predicts differences among achievement-oriented and failure-threatened subjects towards moderate or intermediate success levels. The theory is full of applications to academic motivation (Srivastava, 1974).

***Person Environment Fit Theory***

This theory was propounded by Lazarus (1966). It indicates that discrepancies between what a person desires or expects from the environment and what he actually gets make him feel stressed.

This stress is caused due to emotional burnout which he faces due to the non fulfillment of his expectation from the environment. In the adolescence, if the student perceive inhibitive learning environment then his motivation for learning is adversely affected. Thus, emotional instability, stress and demotivation lead to low academic achievement.

## ORIGIN AND STATEMENT OF THE PROBLEM

In the present scenario, English has gained immense importance as it is referred as a 'living language' (Ghanshyam and Chakravarti, 2008). It is essential for survival in the present globalised world. It is a way of perceiving, knowing, learning and becoming. This international link language has the potential for binding together countries of conflicting linguistive loyalties. It is the window to the outside world. It is the library language and the language of Science, literature, research and technology. Knowledge of English helps a person to become citizen of the world. It is only through English that one can establish social, economic, cultural and political relations with other countries. For business, commerce, internet and communication knowledge of English has become mandatory. National Knowledge Commission (2005) has recognised English as an instrument that can transform India into a knowledge society. According to Dhaka (2008), good command over English language is essential in order to keep pace with the professional advancements and to excel in professional field. Thus, it is very essential for the upcoming generation to have good command and proficiency in English in order to have the power to excel and progress.

Inspite of immense importance and globalised acceptance of necessity of knowledge of English language, the average Indian student is not able to either learn English or communicate in English to a reasonable level of proficiency and fluency. The weakness persists and it shall stay as long as the teaching and learning of English will continue in its present form in our school, colleges and universities. Weaknesses related to the personal factors of the learner and his environment also play a crucial role. According to Neugebauer (2008), in the deficit model approach to instruction of English, students' burdens and obstacles to learning are predominantly viewed as deficiencies within an individual child rather than as inadequacies in the child's environment or life circumstances (Harry, Klinger, Cramer and Sturges, 2007; Goldenberg, Rueda and August, 2006; Valenzuela, 1999). English language learners are to blame for falling behind due to their poor motivation, because they exhibit problematic behaviour, or because they altogether lack socially appropriate behaviour or academic capacities (Suarez-Orozco and Suarez-Orozco, 2001; Valenzuela, 1999). Many English language learners are highly dedicated to learning English, and often are highly motivated to achieve academically (Suarez-Orozco and Suarez-Orozco, 2001). Bose (2002) is of the view that learning of a language and the acquisition of certain amount of proficiency depend not so much on the number of years it is studied but very much on the motivation of the students, the types of teachers, methods of teaching adopted and instructional material designed.

In Skinner's (1957) view, language development is based on operant conditioning, because the environment teaches a person to operate on the environment with words. According to Leopard (1948), language is determined exactly by the environment. Bernstein's (1961) view of restricted and elaborated code, as two types of language used by the lower and middle social class signifies the fact that environment does influence language learning of the learner. This environment can be of family or school. This indicates that environmental factors play an important role in language acquisition. The cognitive interpretation of language learning rests upon the neuro-psychological bases of thought. This emphasises the importance of cognitive factors in language proficiency. Piaget (1926) is also of the view that, language acquisition varies depending upon the stage of cognitive development. Cognitive skills help the learner to achieve comprehension of grammatical structure (Jesa, 2005). Intelligence also plays an important role in language learning.

Concern for achievement is a universal phenomenon and achievement in English has become significant due to the fact that importance of English has been widely recognised and accepted. Research evidences had shown that achievement in English among student is positively related to intelligence, interest, pupils' attitude towards English, study habits, family climate, parental factors, motivation, emotional intelligence, emotional stability, creativity, language competence, socio-economic status and anxiety. Proficiency in English also depends upon proficiency in vocabulary, spelling, knowledge of grammar, and reading comprehension. Thus, it can be said that, achievement in English has a functional dependence on genetic, personal, cognitive, motivational, linguistic, psychological, social and environmental factors.

Psychologists believe that motivation is a necessary ingredient for learning (Biehler and Snowman, 1986). The issues of motivation of students in education and its impact on academic performance are considered as an important aspect of effective learning. According to Green-Demers, Legault, Pelletier and Pelletier (2008), high student motivation is beneficial. Academic motivation has been associated with increased time spent on studying, lower tardiness, absenteeism (Yelle, Green-Demers and Pelletier, 2005) and better academic performance (Johnston, 2006; Reeve, Bolt and Cai, 1999; Deci, Vallerand, Pellitier and Ryan, 1991). Roebken (2007), Steinberg (2006), and Morris, Brooke and May (2003) also reported that achievement motivation is a key determinant of academic performance. In the absence of sufficient motivation to learn, satisfactory learning is unlikely to take place (Fontana, 1981). Evidence of academic motivation can be seen in the amount of goals set and achieved, positive classroom climate and utilisation of cooperative learning strategies (Phillips and Steinkomp, 1995). Skaalvik and Skaalvik (2006), Skaalvik and Skaalvik (2004), Broussard and Garrison (2004), Sandra (2002), Eppler and Harju (1997), Johnson (1996), Niebuhr (1995), and Parkerson, Schiller, Lomax and Walberg (1984) found significant relationship between academic performance and motivation. Research evidence has shown that academic/achievement motivation is positively related to achievement in Mathematics (Tella, 2007; Baskaran, 1991), Physics (Ellekkakumar and Elankathirselvan, 2001), Arts (Sharma, 2008), and Law (Hills, 1958). However, Sidhu and Singh (2005), and Rajput (1984) found no effect of achievement motivation on scholastic achievement in learning of concepts of Physics and Mathematics respectively. Motives and drives play a very important role in learning a second language. Girad (1977) points out that motivation is a basic factor in language learning and no other principle is as important as motivation because a student motivated to learn the language can himself manage to learn the language, some how or the other. Thus, the amount of effort a student puts in learning a language ensures good results. Gesinde (2000) posits that the urge to achieve varies from one individual to another, while for some individuals need for achievement is very high whereas for others it may be very low.

Emphasing the role of environment, Feldman (1982) observed that, even if the individual has an exceptional level of talent, this talent will not develop if the individual's environmental circumstances do not stimulate the growth of talent. Girija and Bhadra (1976) opined that environmental factors seemed to exert considerable influence on the performance of students. Family environment, classroom environment and social environment can influence achievement in English. What takes place in classroom is fundamentally important for the future well being of children (Tripathi, 2009). According to Singh (2008b), specific classroom environment is needed for bringing about desirable changes in the behaviour of the students. The classroom has long been recognised as a critical milieu for students' educational achievement (Fraser and Walberg, 1991; Anderson and Burns, 1989; Borich, 1988; Walberg, 1968). Dart, Burnett, Boulton-Lewis, Campbell, Smith and McCrindle (1999) reported that deep approaches to learning were significantly related to classroom environments which were perceived to be highly personalised and encouraging. Researches on classroom environment have indicated positive associations between the nature of the classroom environment and pupils' attitudinal and achievement outcomes (Wong and Fraser, 1997; Goh, Young and Fraser, 1995; McRobbie and Fraser, 1993; Fraser and O'Brien 1985). Reymond and Jeffrey (1993) reported that perception of classroom environment affects the achievement of high school students. Shanmughadas (2004) opined that achievement in Social Sciences is varied by classroom climate. Santha (1998) found that classroom climate had a significant effect on achievement in Physics. Madhubala (1990) reported that different classroom behaviour of students like listening attentively, discussing points, accepting help and teacher behaviour responding to students' questions and management of teacher directed activities were positively related to the achievement in Economics. Gyanani and Agarwal (1998) revealed significant main effect of classroom climate on achievement of B.Ed students. However, no relationship was found between achievement in Mathematics and different dimensions of classroom climate in the studies done by Yadav (2006), Zareen (2001), and Goh and Fraser (1997). Parmane (1999) found significant relationship between achievement in Algebra and prejudice, disinterest, inattention, imperceptions, anxiety, unrewarding experience and unfulfilled curiosity as identified by the students as psychological barriers during classroom. When a language other than English is used in the home and children are limited in English proficiency, they do poorly in school (Chalfont, 2000). Teachers' behaviour in the classroom is associated with pupils' performance (Rogers, 1990).

In academic field, students with high IQ perform better than the students with low IQ. Similar were the views of Ho, Bennett and Cox (2008) who reported that academic achievement is consistent with intellectual ability. According to Terman (1916), there were vast individual differences in human mental endowment which affected peoples' ability to profit from schooling. He proposed that some children are feeble minded, therefore they are unable to be high achievers. In the same tradition, various researchers have attempted to explain differences in student achievement by arguing that they are caused by genetic deficiencies (Hernstein and Murray, 1994; Hernstein, 1973; Jensen, 1969). Advocates of this theory equate low educational achievement with innate limitations. They propose that differences in achievement are the results of genetic variations in intelligence. According to Eysenck (1979), intelligence of the child is a predictor of educational achievement. There is ample evidence to support the view that intelligent children do better in school achievement (Rastogi, 1974; Rao, 1971; Sinha, 1970, Kakkar, 1970; Joshi and Passi, 1968; Pathak, 1962). Several studies have reported the relationship of high IQ with achievement in Science (Palta Singh, 2008; Singh and Dwivedi, 1993; Sudhir and Murleedharan, 1987), Mathematics (Aswal, 2001) and English reading scores (Garfinkel and Tabor, 1991). However, Sidhu and Singh (2005) reported no significant effect of intelligence on scholastic achievement of students in learning of concepts in Physics. Language learning capacity is highly related to intelligence. Intelligence plays a greater role in comprehension of a language. Reflective thinking and reasoning enable the learner to grasp the meanings and comprehend the language (Bose, 2002). Relating intelligence to second language learning, in the past it was conceived that the greatest barrier to second language learning seemed to boil down to a matter of memory, in the sense that if a student could remember something he or she was exposed to, he or she would be a successful language learner because intelligence was traditionally defined and measured in terms of linguistic and logical-mathematical abilities. It has also been found that there is something which makes a less intelligent person successful and hinders a well-qualified person from making it to the top, and this is emotional intelligence (Codaty, 2008). Thus, success depends upon intelligence and ability to control emotions. IQ alone is no more the measure of success. It only accounts for 20 per cent and the rest goes to emotional and social intelligence, and luck (Goleman, 1995). Emotional intelligence is comprised of emotional reasoning about our feelings and emotions. It can help to channelize the feelings of adolescents in constructive direction because feelings affect motivation, learning, memory, attention, concentration, oral expression, written expression, academic success and important domains of education (Kusche and Greenberg, 1994). According to Sabath (2010), success in academic activities involves a certain amount of emotional balance. Learning in school is a progressive and planned activity. Ray (1996) stated, "Research has shown that critical thinking skills learned in the context of social emotional training, transfer easily to an academic content, but the opposite is not true: critical thinking skills learned in an academic context do not transfer naturally to a social-emotional context. This explains why some children who have strong analytical skills in terms of Mathematics or Science continue to make unsafe or injurious decisions in the social realm, while kids with strong social-emotional abilities do better in school than their less emotionally literate classmates with higher IQ's". Emotional intelligence has come to be viewed as an important predictor of one's ability to succeed in the classroom (Parker, Summerfeldt, Hogan and Majeski, 2004; Zeidner, Mathews and Roberts, 2004). Emotional intelligence has been found to be positively related to achievement in Environmental Studies (Srivastava, 2007), Mathematics (Adeyemo and Adetona, 2007), Science (Bhalla, 2010), Biology (Pandey, 2008), Fine Arts (Singh, 2006a) and English self-efficacy (Elias *et al.* 2008). However, Dubey (2008b) found that emotional intelligence is not related to achievement in Ancient History, Physics, Chemistry, Zoology and Botany. Petrides *et al.* (2004a) reported that emotional intelligence had no influence on performance in Mathematics and Science. The findings of the study done by Pandey (2008) prove that emotional intelligence is not related to achievement in History, Education and Music. Grace (2004) also reported that emotional intelligence is not a significant predictor of GPA. Another factor that influences students' academic achievement is his reasoning ability. Reasoning ability had been found to have a positive influence on achievement in Mathematics (Srivastava, 2005; Tiwari, 1986), Commerce (Muthumanickam, 1992), Life Sciences (Chhikara, 1985), Chemistry (Singh, 1986a). Achievement in Mathematics had been also found to be positively related to abstract reasoning (Ngailiankim, 1991) and numerical reasoning (Katiyar, 1979). According to Piaget (1958), during adolescence, formal reasoning ability develops. Since formal reasoning refers to hypothetical, deductive, reflective and combinatorial thinking. It may also effect students' achievement in English. Research evidence had shown that formal reasoning is positively related to achievement in Environmental Studies (Dubey, 2007), Science (Commons, Miller and Kuhn, 1979; Lawson *et al.* 1975), Molecular Genetics

(Zeitoun, 1988), Biology (Bano, 1995), Physics (Griffith, 1985), Mathematics (Fowler and Watford, 2000; Commons, Miller and Kuhn, 1979; Cloutier and Goldschmid, 1976), Psychology (Fowler and Watford, 2000) and Chemistry (Varquez and deAnglat, 2009). Formal reasoning abilities have been identified as essential ability for success in advanced Science and Mathematics courses (Adey and Shayer, 1994; Lawson, 1985, 1982; Linn, 1982; DeCarcer, Gabel and Staver, 1978). According to Mwamwenda (2005), those who have attained proportional and combinatorial reasoning outperformed in Educational Psychology than those who had not attained formal operations.

Human beings generally take personal responsibility for success and blame external factors for their failure (Miller and Ross, 1975). Students attribute their academic success to their ability and effort and their failure or low achievement in academic arena to task difficulty and luck because it makes them feel proud in front of others and also helps them to escape guilt and shame for low achievement. Several studies comparing the attribution patterns of high and low achievers found that high achievers were more likely to perceive internal factors, particularly effort, as being important to their achievement outcomes, while low achievers were more likely to make external attributions (Pearl, Bryan and Donahue, 1980; Barnett and Kaiser, 1978; Crandal, Katkovsky and Crandall, 1965). The causal belief which an individual has about his performance affects his expectation about academic performance (Weiner, 1979; Bar-Tal, 1978; Weiner, 1972). It has been found that children high on need for achievement perceived that effort was an important determinant of performance while those low on need for achievement, had perceived that outcome was only weakly influenced by hardwork (Murray and Mednick, 1975; Weiner and Potepan, 1970). There is evidence showing the above said attribution pattern across different subjects. Sharma (2006) found that Ist division B. Ed., students attributed their performance to internal factors (effort and ability) while IInd division B.Ed., students attributed their performance to external factors (chance and task difficulty). Boruchovitch (2004) found that effort id the most important attribution for success and failure in Mathematics. Gupta (1994) reported that effort attribution is positively related to achievement in Mathematics, Science and Social Studies. The study conducted by Brown and Rogers (1991) revealed that students who succeeded in Psychology believed that ability played a more important role in determining their performance than those who failed. The results of the study by Raviv and Bar-Tal (1980) showed that in case of success, pupils' tended to attribute the outcome in Mathematics more to internal than to external causes and more to stable than to unstable causes. Performance in Chemistry test were found to be positively related to attribution to high ability and negatively related to attribution to good luck (Kovenklioglu and Greenhaus, 1978).

The author could came across few studies where an attempt has been made to investigate intelligence, emotional intelligence, formal reasoning, academic motivation, causal attributions and classroom environment as the determinants of achievement in English at the high school stage. So, the author felt the need for further exploration and following questions arose in the mind of the author:

1. Does gender difference exist with regard to intelligence, emotional intelligence, formal reasoning, academic motivation, causal attributions, perception of classroom environment and achievement in English?
2. Does any relationship exist between intelligence and achievement in English?
3. Does any relationship exist between emotional intelligence and achievement in English?
4. Does any relationship exist between formal reasoning and achievement in English?
5. Does nay relationship exist between academic motivation and achievement in English?
6. Does any relationship exist between causal attributions and achievement in English?
7. Does any relationship exist between classroom environment and achievement in English?
8. Do students with high, moderate or low intelligence differ from one another on achievement in English?
9. Do students with high, moderate or low emotional intelligence differ from one another on achievement in English?
10. Do students with high, moderate or low formal reasoning differ from one another on achievement in English?
11. Do students with high, moderate or low academic motivation differ from one another on achievement in English?
12. Do students differing with respect to causal attributions for success or failure in English achievement differ from one another on achievement in English?
13. Do students perceiving high, moderate or low stimulation in classroom environment differ from one another on achievement in English.
14. Do intelligence, emotional intelligence, formal reasoning, academic motivation, causal attribution and classroom environment contribute to prediction of achievement in English?

The present study was intended to answer the above mentioned questions.

The problem for the present study may be stated as 'Cognitive, Motivational and Environmental Determinants of Achievement in English.'

## OBJECTIVES OF THE STUDY

### Main Objectives

The present study was conducted to achieve the following main objectives:

1. To study the relationship between intelligence and achievement in English.
2. To study the relationship between emotional intelligence and achievement in English.
3. To study the relationship between formal reasoning and achievement in English.
4. To study the relationship between academic motivation and achievement in English.
5. To study the relationship between causal attribution[*1] and achievement in English.
6. To study the relationship between classroom environment[*2] and achievement in English.
7. To find out whether students with high, moderate and low intelligence differ from one another in their achievement in English.
8. To find out whether students with high, moderate and low emotional intelligence differ from one another in their achievement in English.
9. To find out whether students with high moderate and low formal reasoning differ from one another in their achievement in English.
10. To find out whether students with high, moderate and low academic motivation differ from one another in their achievement in English.
11. To find out whether students differing with respect to causal attributions differ in their achievement in English.[*3]
12. To find out whether students perceiving high moderate and low stimulation in classroom environment differ in their achievement in English.[*]
13. To find out the extent to which intelligence, emotional intelligence, formal reasoning, academic motivation, causal attributions and classroom environment can predict achievement in English.

### Subsidiary Objectives

In the process of accomplishing the above mentioned objectives, following subsidiary objectives have also been realised:

1. To develop a Causal Attribution Scale.
2. To develop an English Language Achievement Test.
3. To compare male and female students on:

(a) Intelligence.
(b) Emotional intelligence.
(c) Formal reasoning.
(d) Academic motivation.
(e) Causal attribution.
(f) Classroom environment.
(g) Achievement in English.

## HYPOTHESES

To achieve the above mentioned objectives, the following hypotheses were formulated and tested:

1. There is no significant relationship between intelligence and achievement in English.
2. There is no significant relationship between emotional intelligence and achievement in English.
3. There is no significant relationship between formal reasoning and achievement in English.
4. There is no significant relationship between academic motivation and achievement in English.
5. There is no significant relationship between causal attributions and achievement in English.
6. There is no significant relationship between classroom environment and achievement in English.
7. Students with high, moderate or low intelligence do not differ from one another in their achievement in English.
8. Student with high, moderate or low emotional intelligence do not differ from one another in their achievement in English.
9. Student with high, moderate or low formal reasoning do not differ from one another in their achievement in English.
10. Students with high, moderate or low academic motivation do not differ from one another in their achievement in English.
11. Students differing with respect to causal attributions do not differ from one another in their achievement in English.
12. Students perceiving different amount of stimulation in classroom environment do not differ from one another in their achievement in English.
13. Intelligence, emotional intelligence, formal reasoning, academic motivation, causal attribution and classroom environment do not significantly contribute to achievement in English.
14. Male and female students do not differ from one another on:

(a) Intelligence.
(b) Emotional intelligence.
(c) Formal reasoning.
(d) Academic motivation.
(e) Causal attributions.
(f) Classroom environment.
(g) Achievement in English.

**DEFINITIONS OF THE TERMS USED**

Many technical terms have been used in the present study and it is necessary to define them so that further discussion may be understood in proper context.

- *Achievement in English* – According to Hubley (2003), achievement is the measure of knowledge and skills that individuals learn in a relatively well-defined area through formal or informal educational experiences. It encompasses students' ability and performance in English Language Achievement Test.
- *Intelligence* – According to Cattell, intelligence is of two types – fluid intelligence and crystallized intelligence. Cattell *et al.*, (1966) classify mental factors into two broad groups, those which reflect biological endowment, are described as fluid intelligence, and those which reflect experiential-educative-acculturative influences, are described as crystallized intelligence. Cattell (1971) proposed a hierarchical model of intelligence in which 'g' was divided into two components, fluid intelligence and crystallized intelligence. Fluid intelligence (Gf) is the ability to apply cognitions to novel problems, to acquire new informations, and to induce new relationships among known informations. This type of intelligence is considered abstract and culture-free. Crystallized intelligence (Gc) includes skills and knowledge acquired across the lifespan that enable individuals to apply proven problem-solving skills to familiar challenges. This form of intelligence is acquired and relies heavily on culture and experience. Fluid intelligence is measured by Cattell's Culture Fair Test.
- *Emotional Intelligence* – According to Misra (2007), "Emotional intelligence is the ability to be aware of emotions, to understand emotions and to manage emotions". Emotional intelligence refers to emotional reasoning. It points to the individual's ability to express, understand, manage, regulate and control emotions of oneself and of others.
- *Formal Reasoning* – It refers to hypothetical, deductive, reflective and combinatorial thinking. Piaget *et al.* (1958) ascribes that, adolescent who has adopted formal thinking is capable of reasoning and of arriving at conclusions without assistance from things actually present. In the

formal operations period the person is able to test hypothesis and draw inferences, objects no longer need to be present to enable a person reason about them. Since symbolic representations can be employed, it is possible for the person to combine objects, ideas and events that otherwise would seem disconnected or impossible, to arrive at a reasonable solution. Propositions rather than concrete objects can be acted upon and symbols without referential meaning can be manipulated. Reversibility in thinking in the form of negation and reciprocity becomes functional. Formal operations provide the underpinnings of scientific thought, in which one must formulate and test hypotheses systematically and in which all possible alternative outcomes are considered (DiVesta, 1982). Another characteristic of formal thought involves the ability to remove oneself from the immediate context of a problem in order to get an additional perspective. The most socially significant characteristics of formal thought is the metacognitive ability to thinking about thinking *i.e.,* the ability to reflect on thought process itself. Formal thought is characterized by a relative freedom from the immediate constraints of a problem, which results in flexibility (Torres, 2000). In general, the adolescent achieves the capability of critical evaluation of one's own thinking, theory construction, and capacity of abstraction (Peck and Richek, 1969).

- *Academic Motivation* – Academic motivation is a concept that has been introduced to explain some of the differences in school attainment of children with similar measured abilities. The concept of academic motivation has been borrowed from the studies of Entwistle (1968), and Finger and Schlesser (1965). On the basis of their investigations the academic motivation has been defined as one's determination to succeed in academic studies (Srivastava, 1974). The various factors of academic motivation are academic aspiration, attitude towards school and study habits.

Aspiration refers to one's desire or ambition, especially to aim at high things, to mount up and involves striving to achieve success in difficult tasks and circumstances. Academic aspiration means a student's aims, goals, hopes, targets that he sets for himself in the field or activity of academic achievement.

Attitude refers to "a readiness to react toward or against some situation, person, or thing, in a particular manner, for example, with love or hate or fear or resentment, to a particular degree of intensity" (Cronbach, 1954). Attitude towards school means a mental set or emotional readiness to react favourably to educationally significant situations in the school environment so as to make the best utilisation of all school facilities and resources, having a deep care and appreciation of them and to make use of all the provided opportunities for one's growth and development and the service of society. A favourable attitude towards school involves deep interest and close attention and hearty participation in school activities, possessing sentiments of love and regard for the school.

Study habits have been defined and described by different persons in various ways. According to Sorenson (1954), "Study habits basically consist of effective methods of study". According to Armstrong (1956) "study is the total of all the habits, determined purposes and enforced practices that the individual uses in order to learn". Study habits involve governing one's will, setting up high and right purposes, and concentrating one's energies, one's powers and capacities towards their realisation. It would mean keeping regular hours, maintaining congenial atmosphere for study, deep absorption, proper working schedule, planning of work, following the laws of learning, thorough quest for supplementary material, practicing preciseness of oral and written-expression. In short, study habits serve as motives for academic achievement.

In other words it can be said that when all these three things combined together helps the individual in his determination to get good success in academic activities. The combination will be called academic motivation.

- *Causal Attributions* – Attributions are the inferences about the causes of success and failure (Graham, 2003). Attribution refers to causal perception of success and failure at achievement tasks. The causal categories in this study are limited to effort, ability, luck, task difficulty, spiritual and support.
- *Classroom Environment* – The classroom conditions, processes and psychological stimuli which influence the educational achievement of the child, constitute educational environment (Dave, 1963). It refers to those forces in the environment of the learner which have the potentiality to contribute to academic development of the learner. It consists of psycho-social conditions that characterize the overall interpersonal feelings existing within it. They affect the learning of students (Misra, 2001). Learning climate is influenced by teacher-student interaction in the classroom.

There are 18 dimensions of learning environment of classroom-cohesiveness, diversity, formality, speed, facilitation, friction, goal direction, favouritism, difficulty, apathy, democratic orientation, cliqueness, disorganization, competition, creative stimulation, encouragement, involvement and conformity. Their operational definitions are as follows:

1. *Cohesiveness* – It refers to tendency of class members to remain friendly to each other.
2. *Diversity* – It indicates existence of variety in the classroom.

3. *Formality* – It indicates paying attention to rules, forms, expectations and conventions.
4. *Speed* – It refers to students' or teachers' behaviour to do thing in a short time.
5. *Facilitation* – It points to existence of situations which make learning to do things easy.
6. *Friction* – It points to occurrence of difference of opinion leading to argumentation and quarrelling.
7. *Goal Direction* – It refers to understanding and acceptance of achievable and appropriate goals of the class and performance of goal oriented behaviours.
8. *Favouritism* – It refers to practice of favouring persons unequally.
9. *Difficulty* – It refers to existence of things or ideas that are hard to understand or execute.
10. *Apathy* – It indicates absence of sympathy or interest and existence of indifference of persons involved in teaching-learning process towards each other.
11. *Democratic Orientation* – It indicates that class members treat each other as equals.
12. *Cliqueness* – It indicates tendency of class members to form clique *i.e.*, a group of persons united by common interests, members of which support each other and shut others from their company.
13. *Disorganization* – It points to upset working of the class.
14. *Competition* – It refers to occurrence of activities in which students compete.
15. *Creative Stimulation* – It refers to teachers' activities to provide conditions and opportunities to stimulate creative thinking.
16. *Encouragement* – It implies teachers' behaviour to stimulate learning of students by encouraging their behaviour.
17. *Involvement* – It refers to teachers' behaviour to structure and monitor students' learning.
18. *Conformity* – It indicates students' actions which are in agreement with what is accepted or required by their teachers.

## DELIMITATIONS OF THE STUDY

Keeping in view the limited resources, time, feasibility, facilities at the disposal of the investigator, the present study was confined to the following parameters:

1. Population for the present study consists of students who are studying in class XI in Allahabad city.
2. Data has been collected from the students of U.P. Board Hindi medium schools.

3. Cognitive determinants included in the study are intelligence, emotional intelligence and formal reasoning.
4. Motivational determinants in the study comprised of academic motivation and causal attributions.
5. Environmental determinants are comprised of 18 dimensions of classroom environment as measured by Misra's Learning Environment Inventory.
6. Only achievement in English language has been measured. Items in the 'English Language Achievement Test' belong to content areas namely pronoun, adjective, noun, verb, adverb, preposition, spelling, tenses, sentence, article, translation, word-formation, active/passive voice, direct/indirect speech.
7. Dimensionality/Factorial structure of Causal Attribution Scale could not be ascertained. Spiritual dimension of Causal Attribution Scale is loaded with religiousity.

## FOOTNOTES

*1. This objective was achieved with reference to 6 causal dimensions *i.e.*, task difficulty, ability, effort, luck, spiritual and support.

*2. This objective was achieved with reference to each of the 18 dimensions of classroom environment *i.e.*, cohesiveness, diversity, formality, speed, facilitation, friction, goal direction, favouritism, difficulty, apathy, democratic, cliqueness, disorganization, competition, creative stimulation, encouragement, involvement and conformity.

*3. This objective was achieved with reference to each of the 6 dimensions.

* This objective was achieved with reference to each of the 18 dimensions.

CHAPTER

2

# REVIEW OF RELATED STUDIES

RESEARCH TAKES ADVANTAGE of the knowledge which has accumulated in the past as a result of constant human endeavor. Past gives birth to the present and decides about the future. This is the reason why review of past literature is important for research work. Research can never be undertaken in isolation of the work which has already been done on the problem, which are directly or indirectly related to the study proposed by the researcher. There exists a continuum between the old theories and the new ones. A careful review of research journals, books, dissertations, thesis and other sources of information on the problem to be investigated is one of the important steps in the planning of research work. The past is to be discussed to view a problem in a proper perspective so that the researcher may streamline the efforts to solve the problem. Through the review of related literature new thoughts and curiosities arise, misconceptions are removed and possibility of repetition is removed. After becoming aware of the strengths and weaknesses of various researches, the researcher does not repeat those mistakes (Helan, 1996). According to Ramal (1996), any research related written work is not considered appropriate unless and until it includes discussion of review of research of related works. Keeping in view the objectives of the present study, numerous studies pertaining to the relationship of achievement in English with intelligence, emotional intelligence, formal reasoning, academic motivation, causal attribution and classroom environment were reviewed. Since the author came across very few studies pertaining to the relationship between achievement in English and other independent variables, the author has included the studies related to achievement in language and academic achievement in general with reference to the above mentioned independent variables.

The author has organized the studies into the following groups –

1. Studies on achievement in relation to intelligence.
2. Studies on achievement in relation to emotional intelligence.
3. Studies on achievement in relation to formal reasoning.
4. Studies on achievement in relation to academic motivation.
5. Studies on achievement in relation to causal attribution.
6. Studies on achievement in relation to classroom environment.
7. Review of tools related to causal attribution.
8. Review of tools related to English language achievement test.

The review of related studies is being presented in this chapter.

## STUDIES ON ACHIEVEMENT IN RELATION TO INTELLIGENCE

### Studies on Intelligence and Achievement in English

Dubey (2010a) tried to examine achievement in language in relation to intelligence. The sample for the study consisted of 90 students. 'Cattell's Culture Fair Intelligence Test' of A. K. S. Cattell and R. B. S. Cattell was used as a tool to measure intelligence. Marks obtained by the students in class XII examination served as an index of achievement. Findings of the study revealed positive relationship between intelligence and achievement in English; and students with high intelligence were found to have high achievement in English as compared to the students with low intelligence.

Saricaolu and Arikan (2009) investigated the relationship between intelligence type and students' success in grammar, listening and writing English as a foreign language. Preparatory class students (N=144) attending Erciyes University's School of Foreign Languages participated in the study and the data was collected through the Multiple Intelligence Inventory for Adults of Armstrong (1994). Analysis of the data revealed negative relationships between students' test score in grammar and bodily-kinesthetic, spatial and intrapersonal intelligence.

Deary, Strand, Smith and Fernandes (2007) conducted a longitudinal study on more than 70,000 students and reported existence of positive correlation (r=.67) between intelligence and achievement in English and general intelligence contributed 48 per cent variance in success in English.

Tourani (2006) found that for students of class IX, achievement in English was found to be independent of intelligence when pre-achievement in English was taken as a covariate.

Verma (1996d) examined whether achievement in English is influenced by intellectual ability. The sample for the study consisted of 500 class X students. Group General Mental Ability Test by Jalota was used as a tool for data collection. Achievement marks were noted from the official records of the school. The major findings of the study were – intellectual ability had a significant main effect on achievement of students in English; and high intellectual ability students had substantially higher achievement in English than their low intellectual ability counterparts.

Balasubramanian (1993) attempted to study how far intelligence is related to pupil's academic achievement in English. The sample for the study comprised of 320 boys and 260 girls studying in class XII. The findings of the study was that intelligence of pupils positively influence their academic achievement in English.

Omoluabi (1993) conducted a study on 240 students in Nigeria and found that although students in class 2-5 had a higher mean score on intelligence as measured by Culture Fair Intelligence Test, their mean scores in English were average.

Srivastava (1992) tried to examine whether students' achievement in English can be predicted with the help of non-verbal intelligence tests. The sample for the study consisted of 645 high school students. D. A. Pidgeon Non-Verbal Intelligence Test and the Revised Minnesota Paper Form Board Test were used as tools for the study. The findings of the study revealed significant correlation between scores on non-verbal tests and achievement in English. It was also found that intelligence can predict students achievement in English.

Kaur (1992) conducted a study on relationship between intelligence and academic achievement in different subjects among X graders. The sample comprised of 600 class X students (300 boys and 300 girls) of Patiala district of Punjab. R. K. Tandon's 'Samuhik Mansik Yogyata Pariksha' was used to measure intelligence of students. Marks obtained by the students in class IX annual examination served as an index of academic achievement. It was found that for male and female students, intelligence was positively related with achievement in all the subjects including English, Hindi and Punjabi.

Chandy (1991) attempted to identify the pupil related variables that result in poor achievement in English among 1040 students (533 boys and 507 girls). The tools used for the study were Non-Verbal Test of Intelligence and English Achievement Test. The findings of the study were – there exists positive relationship between intelligence and achievement in English for total sample and sub-samples (boys and girls of forward and backward community groups); intelligence explained maximum variance in achievement in English; and intelligence accounted for 48 per cent of the variance in English achievement.

Singh (1989) conducted a study on 908 students of class X to find out the degree of relationship between intelligence and achievement in English. Mental Ability Test by A.C. Joshi and Achievement Test in English were used as tools for the study. It was found that achievement in English is positively related to intelligence; and English achievement of boys and girls is influenced by intelligence.

Kaile (1988) conducted a study with the objective to study the relationship between intelligence and achievement in mother tongue and foreign language and to examine the relative potential of intelligence in prediction of scholastic achievement in mother tongue and foreign language. The sample for the study comprised of 712 class X students of Punjab. Jalota and Singh's Group Test of General Mental ability was used to measure intelligence. Marks obtained by students in Punjabi (Mother tongue) and English (Foreign language) in matric examination, were considered as measures of achievement. It was reported that intelligence predicted achievement in English and Punjabi; significant differences did not exist between the mean achievement scores in Punjabi and English of over-achievers and under-achievers as identified on the basis of intelligence.

Patel (1987) attempted to study the relationship between English and intelligence in the case of SC, ST and advantaged children. The sample comprised of 270 students with an age between 13-15 years. Cattle's Culture Fair Test of intelligence was used to measure intelligence. It was found that English is positively related with intelligence among SC group; and academic achievement in English can be predicted by intelligence in all the three groups.

Khare (1986) studied the effect of intelligence on the performance of students in English on a sample of 553 students selected through stratified random sampling method. Seven achievement tests (for seven different dimensions of English) were constructed by the investigator. R. K. Tandon's 'Samoohik Mansik Yogyata Parikshan' (1970) was used to measure intelligence. It was found that intelligence is an important factor in achievement in the areas of comprehension, composition, pronunciation, spelling, vocabulary and applied grammar.

Joshi (1984) studied the relationship between intelligence and English language abilities. The sample comprised of 720 students. The data were collected administering Raven's Progressive Matrices and Sharma's English Language Ability Test. It was found that – growth status of language ability is a function of structural factors operating within *i.e.,* intelligence; and there exists significant relationship between intelligence and growth of various English language abilities.

Brahmabhatt (1983) studied the relationship of various psychosocial factors affecting achievement in English language. The sample comprised of 130 students of class VII each in the experimental and the control group. Intelligence Test of K. G. Desai was used to measure intelligence. It was found that intelligence when paired with pre-achievement in English shared high correlation with achievement in English.

Work by Barton, Dielman and Cattell (1972) involved the examination of relationships among measures of culture fair intelligence and grades in school. It was found that value of correlation between intelligence and English achievement for 6th and 7th grade students were .45 and .53 respectively.

**Studies on Intelligence and Achievement in Language**

Dubey (2010a) conducted a study on 90 undergraduate students and reported that intelligence as measured by Cattell's Culture Fair Intelligence Test is positively related to achievement in Hindi.

Srivastava (1995) estimates the predictive value of two non-verbal tests and two verbal tests for success in literary subjects (Hindi, English, Sanskrit) in the high school examination. The two non-verbal tests were D. A. Pidgeon Non-Verbal Tests and Revised MPF-B Test and the two verbal tests were the Bureau of Psychology Test-23 and BPT-13. The sample comprised of 645 students from 6 districts of U.P. Correlational and regression analysis revealed that all the tests had the potential of predicting success in literary subjects in the high school examination.

Jain (1995) investigated the relationship of achievement in Sanskrit with intelligence among 400 students of class X. Standard Progressive Matrices Test by J. C. Raven had been used to measure intelligence of the students. Sanskrit marks obtained by the students in CBSE examination served as an index of achievement in Sanskrit. Intelligence appeared to have a positive relationship with scholastic achievement in Sanskrit. But, intelligence did not emerge as a significant contributor of the variance of scholastic achievement in Sanskrit.

Srivastava (1992) examined whether students' achievement in literary subjects (Hindi and Sanskrit) can be predicted with the help of non-verbal intelligence tests. 645 high school students were assessed on D. A. Pidgeon Non-Verbal Intelligence Test and the Revised Minnesota Paper Form Board Test. Scores on both non-verbal tests were significantly correlated with marks in Sanskrit and Hindi. Since non-verbal tests predicted students' success in literary subjects they can be used as predictors of students' achievement in Hindi and Sanskrit.

Ramamani (1990) conducted a study on students of class IV and found that intelligence had significant effect on the scores in the language proficiency and achievement tests. He also found that non-verbal intelligence appeared to be more important variable affecting the academic performance.

Haq (1988) found that male over achievers in Hindi had higher intelligence than female students.

Patel (1987) found that intelligence is positively related with achievement in Oriya. Intelligence can predict achievement in Oriya in case of general, scheduled cast and scheduled tribe students. It can also predict achievement in Hindi and Sanskrit among general and ST students.

Gaur (1982) studied the relationship of intelligence with reading ability, comprehension and vocabulary of students in Hindi. The sample comprised of 500 students. Intelligence Test, Comprehensions Test and Vocabulary Test prepared by the researcher were used. It was found that intelligence was significantly related to speed of reading, comprehension and vocabulary of students.

Cattell and Butcher (1968) obtained culture fair intelligence scores and various measures of achievement in school on both urban (N=153) and rural (N=124) samples of high school children. They found that correlation between intelligence and language and spelling for urban students were .48 and .40 respectively and for rural students were .25 and .22 respectively.

**Studies on Intelligence and Academic Achievement**

Dhall and Thukral (2010) investigated the relationship between intelligence and academic achievement among 1000 students of class IX of Punjab. Group Test of General Mental ability by R. K. Tondon (1971) was used as a tool for the study. Academic achievement was measured from the results of VIII class annual examination. The results revealed positive relationship between intelligence and academic achievement among both boys (r=.637) and girls (r=.437).

Nikose (2010) aimed to find out the extent of relationship between intelligence and academic achievement among 300 tribal secondary school students studying in VII and IX class P. S. M. Intelligence Test was used as a tool for the study. The aggregate marks of the annual examination was taken as an index of academic achievement. The findings of the study revealed positive relationship between intelligence and academic achievement.

Palta Singh (2008) tried to examine the relationship between intelligence and achievement among 180 students of class IX. Jalota's Group Test of General Mental Ability was used to measure intelligence of the students. Annual examination marks of the students were considered as an index of scholastic achievement. The findings of the study revealed that there exists positive relationship between intelligence and scholastic achievement scores.

Naderi, Abdullah, Hamid and Sharir (2008) examined intelligence as a predictor of academic achievement among undergraduate students. Participants of the study were 105 male and 48 female students. Cattell's Culture Fair Intelligence Test was used as a tool for the study. Cumulative grade point average was taken as a proxy of achievement. The findings revealed lower correlation between intelligence and cumulative grade point average. The study fails to support intelligence as a predictor of student's academic achievement.

Dubey (2008a) attempted to study the relationship between intelligence and academic achievement of socially deprived students. The sample comprised of 52 male B.A.-I students of University of Allahabad. 'Culture Fair Intelligence Test' prepared by R. B. Cattell and A. K. S. Cattell was used as a tool for data collection. Marks obtained by students in U. P. Board intermediate examination was considered as a measure of achievement. It was found that intelligence is positively related to achievement among non-socially deprived students but it is not related to achievement among highly and moderately socially deprived students.

Laidra, Pullman and Allik (2007) investigated predictors of academic achievement in a sample of 3618 students (1746 boys and 1872 girls) in Estonia. Intelligence as measured by Raven's Standard Progressive Matrices was found to be the best predictor of students' GPA in all grades.

Deary, Strand, Smith and Fernandes (2007) conducted a longitudinal study on more than 70,000 children and found that correlation between intelligence trait and educational achievement was .81.

Singh (2007) found that there exists positive correlation between academic achievement and intelligence among B. A., students. Students with high intelligence level have high academic achievement as compared to students with low intelligence.

Fahim and Pishghadam (2007) sought to find out whether intelligence have any role in the academic achievement of 508 university students majoring in English language literature. Wechsler's Adult Intelligence Scale was used to measure intelligence of the students. Students GPA of second year were taken as an index of achievement. The result revealed that academic achievement did not correlate much with IQ but was strongly associated with verbal intelligence which is a subsection of IQ test.

Anandmani (2006) attempted to study general intelligence in relation to achievement among IX class students. The sample for the study comprised of 100 student of class IX. General Mental Ability Test prepared by M. C. Joshi was used to measure general intelligence. The findings of the study revealed that boys achievement is positively related general intelligence, while for girls, general intelligence is not related to achievement.

Varma (2003) studied the relationship between academic achievement and intelligence among 600 Arts and Science stream students from intermediate schools of Firozabad. Group Intelligence Test by S. S. Jalota was used as a tool for the study. Marks obtained by the students in the high school examination were taken as a measure of achievement. The findings of the study revealed positive correlation between intelligence and academic achievement.

Behera (2002) attempted to study intelligence in relation to academic achievement among 374 senior secondary vocational stream students of +2 level of Chandigarh city. Standard Progressive Matrices by Raven and final examination marks as an index of academic achievement were used for data collection. It was found that intelligence is positively related to academic achievement, significant difference existed between high and low intelligence group of students with respect to academic achievement; and boys with high intelligence were found to have high academic achievement in comparison to their counterparts with low intelligence.

Shah (2002) conducted a study on 1040 students of standard VIII, IX and X. The data were collected by administering Desai-Bhatt Verbal-Non-Verbal Group Intelligence Test and for the educational achievement of the students, their scores in the annual examination were used. The finding of the study revealed significant difference among the IQs of the students of high, average and low educational achievement.

Mackintosh's (1998) survey reckoned that there is a correlation between 0.4 and 0.7 between IQ scores and school performance grades.

Pradhan (1997) studied the effect of intelligence on the scholastic achievement on 90 school girls. Students of grades 6 and 7 were administered Raven's Coloured Progressive Matrices Test. Scholastic achievement record was taken as an index of achievement. Result indicated a significant relationship between scholastic achievement and intelligence.

Mavi and Patel (1997) attempted to study academic achievement among 525 tribal and 195 non-tribal students of class IX. Raven's Progressive Matrices was used as a tool for data collection. Total scores of students in class VIII served as an index of academic achievement. It was found that, there exists positive relationship between academic achievement and intelligence.

Chitra, Thiagarajan and Krishnan (1995) conducted a study on 104 Scheduled Caste girl students and 100 non SC girl students pursuing higher secondary course. The objective of the study was to examine the relationship between intelligence and academic achievement of the students. Intelligence was measured through Culture Fair Intelligence test (Form A) by Cattell and Cattell. It was found that significant relationship exists between intelligence and academic achievement among SC students.

Singh and Verma (1995) tried to study the effect of intelligence on scholastic success of class XI students. The sample for the study comprised of 400 students. Raven's Standard Progressive Matrices was used to collect the data. The study revealed that there exist positive relationship between intelligence and scholastic success of both rural and urban students.

Venugopal (1994) investigated the influence of intelligence on achievement among pupils at the middle school level. The sample for the study comprised of 300 pupils covering 210 boys and 90 girls. Tools used for the study were Guilford's Intelligence Test and Achievement Test developed by the investigator. The study revealed relationship between achievement and intelligence.

Charles (1993) reported that verbal intelligence is highly correlated with students' performance at the SSC examination.

Agarwal (1993) tried to examine psychosocial factors of academic achievement among 800 students of class XI. Group Mental Ability Test by R. K. Tondon was used to measure intelligence of the students. Marks obtained by the students in class X examination were used as a measure of academic achievement. It was found that academic achievement has positive correlation with intelligence; and intelligence contributes in deciding achievement.

Omoluabi (1993) investigated why some students performed outstandingly in school examination but poorly on intelligence tests and vice-versa. 240 students in Nigeria were assessed on the Culture Fair Intelligence Test (CFIT). Their class examination results were taken as an index for aggregate scores. Although students in class 2-5 had a higher mean score on the CFIT, their aggregate score in school examination was lower. A positive but non-significant relationship was seen between performances on intelligence tests and school examinations.

Gupta, Mukerjee and Chatterji (1993) found that intelligence is most closely related to academic achievement among 1453 subjects of class X. Raven's Standard Progressive Matrices was used as a tool for the study.

Garg and Chaturvedi (1992) assess the contribution of intelligence in determining academic achievement. A sample of 179 rural and 356 urban school students completed Jalota's Intelligence Test, the scores of which are regressed with their class X examination marks. The independent contribution of IQ to academic performance was found to be 63.1 per cent.

Namrata (1992) found that high achievers were intellectually superior where as low achievers tended to be intellectually inferior.

Garg (1992) compared failed and passed students in relation to intelligence. The sample consisted of 200 failed and 200 passed students selected randomly from 27 schools of the 5 districts of Garhwal region. The finding was that, the passed students were more intelligent than the failed students.

Kumar (1989) conducted a study on 1024 secondary school students of Aligarh district. The tools used in the study were General Intelligence Test by R. K. Tandon and marks obtained by the students in English, Hindi, Mathematics, Science and Social Studies were considered as measures of scholastic achievement. It was found that – intelligence is significantly related to scholastic achievement; and scholastic achievement can be predicted by intelligence through multiple linear regression equation.

Sharma (1988) conducted a study on 1200 student of class XII to find out the association of intelligence with scholastic achievement. The tools used in the study were Verbal, Non-Verbal Mixed Type Group Test of Intelligence developed by P. N. Mehrotra and U. P. Board Examination marks of class XII were considered as measures of achievement. It was reported that, verbal intelligence, non-verbal intelligence and intelligence were positively related with scholastic achievement among students of all the streams.

Das (1986) attempted to establish regression equation for academic achievement in relation to intelligence. The sample comprised of 820 students of class X of Assam state. The tools used for the study were – Bora's Group Verbal Examination of General Intelligence Test and scores of HSLC examination. It was found that intelligence is a powerful predictor of academic achievement, contributing 40.26 per cent of total variance.

Kumar (1986) found that regression co-efficients reveal that intelligence made a remarkable contribution to the success of boys and girls at the under-graduate examination.

Misra (1986) found that intelligence is positively related to academic performance and it positively affects the academic performance of the students.

Mitra (1985) found that intelligence is the most significant correlate of achievement irrespective of sex. Intelligence accounted 3/5th of the variance in the prediction of academic achievement.

Dixit (1985) conducted a comparative study of intelligence and academic achievement of boys and girls studying in class IX and XI. The sample for the study consisted of 800 students of class IX and XI. Jalota's Group General Mental Ability Test was used to get an idea about their mental ability and marks obtained by them in the annual examination were taken as a criterion of academic achievement. The findings of the study were – there is no difference in the academic achievement of intellectually very superior and superior boys and girls of class IX and XI; at all other intellectual levels, the academic achievement of the girls of class IX and XI were superior to that of boys; there is high correlation between intelligence and academic achievement among boys; and there is average correlation between intelligence and academic achievement among girls.

Sween (1984) attempted to investigate the effect of intelligence on performance of students. The sample comprised of 192 students randomly selected from 25 schools of Chandigarh city. The tools used for the study were Jalotas General Mental Ability Test. The finding of the study revealed that students with high intelligence scored significantly better than students with low intelligence.

In a review of a number of investigations in the US, Parkerson, Schiller, Lomax and Walberg (1984) concluded that the correlation between intelligence and educational achievement are in the range of 0.6 - 0.7.

Lynn, Hampson and Magee (1983) in a study on the determinants of educational achievement among 700 adolescents in Northern Ireland found that intelligence correlated 0.64 with educational achievement measured by CSE examination.

Singh (1983) investigated the achievement of mentally superior child in relation to intelligence. P. N. Mehrotra's Group Test of Intelligence was used to identify superior and average groups. The sample consisted of 450 students. It was found that there exists positive relationship between intelligence and achievement for the superior group but a negative relationship for the average group.

Shanmagusundaram (1983) reported that high achievers at undergraduate level had high intelligence than the low achievers.

In a study of Japanese 11-year old children, it has been found by Kashiwagi, Azuma and Miyake (1982) that the verbal IQ of the Weschsler Test was correlated .58 with a composite score of educational achievement consisting of Arithmetic, Language, Social Studies and Science, while the Weschsler non-verbal IQ correlated only .29 with educational achievement.

Aruna (1981) examined the relationship of intelligence with academic achievement of SC and ST students. The sample consisted of entire SC and ST students of class VII of Chitradurga district. The tools used for the study were Achievement Test Battery constructed and standardized for this purpose and Fremaiatha's Non-Verbal Group Test of Intelligence. It was found that, there exists significant correlation (r=.44) between intelligence and academic achievement of SC and ST students.

Shivappa (1980) found that intelligence measured through non-verbal test of intelligence is a positive correlate of academic achievement among high school pupils and it makes maximum contribution in predicting academic achievement.

Girja (1980) found that intelligence measured through progressive matrices potentially contribute to GPA – the first year college achievement scores.

Singh (1976) found that among undergraduate students academic achievement is positively related to intelligence as measured by the Standard Progressive Matrices.

Dhami (1974) conducted a study on IX and X standard students. The tools used were Intelligence Test by Jalota and Singh, the index of scholastic achievement was determined from the average of the percentage of marks secured in the middle standard examination, the annual examination and other house tests for two years. The major finding was that intelligence contributed substantially to success in scholastic achievement.

Makhija (1973) as a result of his study stated that, intelligence has positive influence on scholastic achievement of first year male students.

Reddy (1973) found that intelligence is a prominent predictor of academic achievement among first year degree college students.

Kanderian (1969) tested 6th grade students in Iraq on the Culture Fair Intelligence Test and teacher-made tests of school achievement and found a significant positive correlation (r =.29).

Miles (1954) found that high IQ children tend to do better in school especially in verbally originated subjects.

Besides these, Srivastava (1992), Kaur (1991), Chadha and Chandra (1990), Devi (1990), Dixit (1989), Kumar (1989), Sood (1988), Bhusari (1988), Mehrotra (1986), Srivastava (1980), Sinha (1967) and Tupas (1926) had also found that there is positive relationship between academic achievement and intelligence.

## STUDIES ON ACHIEVEMENT IN RELATION TO EMOTIONAL INTELLIGENCE

### Studies on Emotional Intelligence and Achievement in English

Adeoye (2010) investigated the impact of emotional intelligence training on academic achievement in English Language among students of Senior Secondary Schools. The sample consisted of 270 participants drawn from nine co-educational schools across three selected educational zones. Simple random sampling technique was used to select three schools from each zone among those that met the inclusion criteria set for the study. A pre-test, post-test, control group quasi-experimental design was adopted. The findings of the study revealed that there exists positive relationship between emotional intelligence as measured by Emotional Intelligence Training Package (EIPTA), and achievement in English as measured by English Language Achievement Test (r=0.73).

Dubey (2010a) conducted a study on 90 students to examine the relationship between emotional intelligence and achievement in language. 'Test of Emotional Intelligence' developed by K. S. Misra was used to measure emotional intelligence of students. Marks obtained by the students in U. P. Board intermediate examination was taken as an index of achievement. The results revealed that emotional intelligence is positively related to achievement in English. The results also revealed that students with high emotional intelligence had high achievement in English in comparison to their counterparts with low emotional intelligence.

Emeke and Adeoye (2009) investigated the effect of emotional intelligence training on the English achievement on 270 Nigerian secondary school students. Emotional Intelligence Training Package and English Language Achievement Test were used as tools for data collection. Data analysis revealed that participants exposed to emotional intelligence training performed better in English language achievement test.

Pandey (2008) tried to examine the relationship between emotional intelligence and academic achievement among +2 level 160 students. Emotional intelligence was measured with the help of Test of Emotional Intelligence of K. S. Misra. The findings of the study indicated that emotional intelligence is not related to achievement in English among Arts stream girls while it is positively related to achievement in English among boys of Arts and Science stream and girls of Science stream.

Rouhani (2008) conducted a study in which short literary readings were used in a cognitive-affective reading based course to see how they affect emotional intelligence. Mayer, Salovey and Caruso (2002) Emotional Intelligence Test (2002) was administered on 70 Iranian EFL undergraduate students in a pre-test post-test quasi-experimental design. The results revealed that the cognitive-affective reading-based course in which literary readings were used significantly improved the subjects' emotional intelligence scores.

Dubey (2008b) attempted to study the relationship between emotional intelligence and achievement in English among undergraduate students. The sample comprised of 42 students of B. A.-III. Test of Emotional Intelligence (Student Form) developed by K. S. Misra was used as a tool. B. A. II marks of the students in English served as an index of achievement. It was found that emotional intelligence is not related to achievement in English.

Sucaromana (2004) conducted a study on 273 lower-secondary school students of Thailand. The focus of the study was to investigate the relationship between emotional intelligence and achievement in English. Result suggests that emotional intelligence has a direct effect on Thai student's achievement in English. In addition, it suggests that emotional intelligence affects achievement in English indirectly through family encouragement, study habits and levels of encouragement.

**Studies on Emotional Intelligence and Achievement in Language**

Dubey (2010a) conducted a study on 90 undergraduate students and reported that emotional intelligence as measured by Misra's test of Emotional Intelligence is not related to achievement in Hindi.

Pishghadam (2009) examined the role of emotional intelligence in second language learning among 508 second year students of four universities of Iran. Emotional Intelligence Inventory was used as a tool for the study. The findings of the study revealed that second language learning was strongly associated with several dimensions of emotional intelligence.

Pandey (2008) examined the relationship between emotional intelligence and academic achievement in Hindi among +2 level 160 students. Emotional intelligence was measured with the help of Test of Emotional Intelligence of K. S. Misra. The finding of the study revealed positive relationship between emotional intelligence and achievement in Hindi among students of both Arts and Science stream.

Pishghadam (2007) examined the relationship between EQ and second language success among 528 Iranian University students in Tehran. Emotional intelligence scores were correlated with the students' GPA and the scores that they obtained at the end of second year at the university in listening, reading, speaking and writing. The results indicated that second language skills and GPA strongly correlated with intrapersonal skills in the EQ test.

Using Bar-On's Emotional Quotient Inventory (EQ-i) and a revised version of the Oxford's Strategy Inventory for Language (SILL), Aghasafari (2006) in a correlational design investigated the relationship between EQ and second language learning strategies among 100 sophomore participants at Islamic Azad University in Iran. The results indicated that there exists positive relationship between overall EQ and language learning strategies.

**Studies on Emotional Intelligence and Academic Achievement**

Alam (2010) examined the relationship between emotional intelligence and academic success on a sample of 250 adolescents (125 boys and 125 girls) from different kendriya Vidyalayas of Hyderabad city. Emotional Intelligence Inventory by S. K. Mangal and S. Mangal was used as a tool for the study. The aggregate marks of the students in the annual examination of class X served as an index of academic success. The findings of the study revealed positive relationship between emotional intelligence and academic achievement for total sample (r=.201) and for boys (r=.238) and girls (r=.275).

Bano (2010) tried to find out the relationship between emotional intelligence and academic performance among 600 class XI students and found that academic performance of high emotionally intelligent student is high as compared to low emotionally intelligent students.

Sabath (2010) investigated the relationship between emotional intelligence and academic performance of 50 final year students of Government Women's College, Sabalpur and found positive relationship between emotional intelligence and academic performance.

Lal, Sharma and Sharma (2010) tried to examine emotional intelligence in relation to academic achievement among scheduled caste students. The sample for the study consisted of 584 class XI students. Mangal Emotional Intelligence Inventory was used as a tool for the study and examination record was taken as an index of academic achievement. The findings revealed that male SC students of Arts and Science stream and female SC students of Science stream, with high emotional intelligence are academically superior to their counterparts with low emotional intelligence.

Olatoye, Akintunde and Yakasai (2010) conducted a study on 235 students and reported that there is no relationship between emotional intelligence and cumulative grade point average (r= -.178).

Salami and Ogundokun (2009) examined the predictive effects of emotional intelligence on academic performance of students. Participants were 485 secondary school students randomly selected from 10 co-educational secondary schools in Oyo State (male = 258 and female = 226). The research instruments used for data collection were – Emotional Intelligence Behaviour Inventory, Mathematics Achievement Test and English Language Achievement Test. The findings indicated linear correlation between academic performance and emotional intelligence (r=.714). It was also found that emotional intelligence was a potent predictor of academic performance of students.

Hassan, Sulaiman and Ishak (2009) conducted a study on 223 secondary school students to examine the relationship between emotional intelligence and academic achievement. Emotional intelligence was assessed through self-report measure of emotional intelligence adapted from Schutte Self-report of Emotional Intelligence. The results of the study indicated that emotional intelligence is positively related to academic achievement (r=.78) and among male (r=.79) and female students (r=.76).

Berenson, Boyles and Weaver (2008) examined the intrinsic factor of emotional intelligence to determine the extent to which they predict GPA among students attending community college. The finding revealed that emotional intelligence emerged as the most significant predictor of GPA.

Pandey (2008) conducted a study on relationship between emotional intelligence and academic achievement among 160 +2 level students of both Arts and Science stream. Test of Emotional Intelligence developed by K. S. Misra was used to measure emotional intelligence of students. Marks obtained by the students served as an index of academic achievement. The findings of the study revealed that among Arts stream girls, emotional intelligence is not related to total academic achievement while among Arts stream boys and Science stream boys and girls, emotional intelligence has been found to be positively related with total achievement.

Downey, Mountstephen, Lloyd, Hansen and Stough (2008) examined the relationship between emotional intelligence and scholastic achievement in Australian adolescents. The sample consisted of 209 secondary school students (86 male and 123 female). Academic success was found to be associated with higher levels of total emotional intelligence. Regression analysis revealed that emotional intelligence differentially predicted secondary school subject grades.

Holt (2008) tried to determine how emotional intelligence among undergraduate students is related to academic achievement. The findings of the study indicated significant positive relationship between students GPA and four emotional intelligence abilities *viz.*; emotional management task (r=.226), social management task (r=.297), managing emotions (r=.290) and emotional reasoning (r=.222).

Dubey (2008b) conducted a study on emotional intelligence and achievement among undergraduate students. The sample comprised of 162 undergraduate students of B. A.-III of Arts and Science stream. Test of Emotional Intelligence (Student Form) developed by K. S. Misra was used as a tool for data collection. Marks obtained by students in B. A.-II examination were considered as measures of achievement. The findings of the study revealed no significant relationship between emotional intelligence and achievement among students of arts and science stream; and no significant difference in achievement among students of Art and Science Stream with high and low level of emotional intelligence.

Elias, Mahyuddin, Abdullah, Roslan, Noonlin and Fauzee (2008) conducted a study on 688 secondary school students and found positive correlation between EQ and academic achievement (r= .195).

Singh (2008c) attempted to study the relationship between emotional intelligence and achievement. The sample consisted of 100 female students of class XI. Test of Emotional Intelligence (Student Form) developed by K. S. Misra was used for measuring emotional intelligence. Marks obtained by students in the High School examination of U. P. Board were considered as measures of achievement. The findings of the study revealed that emotional intelligence is positively related to achievement among general students but it is not related to achievement among SC students; female students with high emotional intelligence achieve better than students with low emotional intelligence in case of general category; and there is no significant difference in the achievement of high and low emotionally intelligent scheduled caste female students.

Dubey (2008a) attempted to study the relationship between emotional intelligence and academic achievement of socially deprived students. The sample comprised of 52 male B. A.-I students of University of Allahabad. Test of Emotional Intelligence (Student Form) developed by K. S. Misra was used for measuring emotional intelligence. Marks obtained by students in U. P. Board intermediate examination were considered as measures of achievement. It was found that emotional intelligence is not related to achievement among highly, moderately and non-socially deprived male students.

Adeyemo (2007) examined the moderating influence of emotional intelligence on the link between academic self-efficacy and achievement among university students. The participants in the study were 300 undergraduate students of the University if Ibadan, Nigeria. Emotional Intelligence Questionnaire constructed by Schutte *et al.* (1998) was used to measure the emotional intelligence while student's first semester result was used as a measure of academic achievement. The result demonstrated that emotional intelligence is positively related to academic achievement (r= .33).

Abdullah (2007) investigated the relationship between emotional intelligence and academic achievement of students. A sample of 297 students of first semester served as participants of the study. Every respondent was asked to complete a set of questionnaires which measures emotional intelligence. Marks obtained by the students in the mid-semester examination were taken as an index of achievement. Results indicated that self-motivation dimension of emotional intelligence explain the variance in academic achievement.

Fahim and Pishghadam (2007) conducted a study on 508 university students (134 male and 374 female) and found that academic achievement is strongly associated with several dimensions of emotional intelligence (intrapersonal, stress management and general mood competencies) as measured by Bar-On Emotional Quotient Inventory.

Marquez, Martin and Brackett (2006) conducted a study on 77 high school students. Mayer-Salovey-Caruso Emotional Intelligence Test was used to measure emotional intelligence of students. Students' academic grades obtained from school record served as an index of academic achievement. Findings revealed that emotional intelligence scores among adolescents correlated with their academic achievement.

Emeke, Adeoye and Torubeli (2006) using 600 adolescents from four senior secondary schools found that emotional intelligence significantly correlates with improvement in academic achievement of the participants.

Anandmani (2006) attempted to study the relationship between emotional intelligence and achievement among boys and girls. The sample for the study comprised of 100 students of class IX. Emotional Intelligence Questionnaire developed by K. S. Misra was used to measure emotional intelligence of students. It was found that emotional intelligence is not related to achievement among both boy and girls.

Phillips (2005) found no significant relationship between scores on emotional intelligence and scores on the student end-of-course evaluation.

Austin, Evans, Goldwater and Potter (2005) conducted a study on emotional intelligence and exam performance. Participants were a sample of 156 first year medical students. The findings of the study provide limited evidence for link between emotional intelligence and academic performance.

Bastian, Burns and Nettelbeck (2005) tried to investigate the relationship between emotional intelligence and academic achievement. The study was conducted on 246 first-year tertiary students. Statistical analysis showed that correlations between emotional intelligence and academic achievement were small and not statistically significant.

Besharat *et al.* (2005) examined the impact of emotional intelligence on academic success in a sample of 220 Iranian University students in Isfahan. They reported that EQ was positively correlated with academic success.

Sibia, Mishra and Srivastava (2005) tried to examine the relationship between emotional intelligence and academic achievement. A total of 340 students participated in the study. The Emotional Intelligence Test prepared by the investigator was used to measure their emotional intelligence. Significant correlation was found between regulation and management of emotion component of emotional intelligence and academic achievement. However, no relationship was reported between emotional intelligence and academic achievement.

Drago (2004) attempted to explore the relationship between emotional intelligence and academic achievement in non-traditional college students.

Mayer, Salovey, Caruso Emotional Intelligence Test (MSCEIT) was used to measure emotional intelligence of the students. Student's GPA served an index of academic achievement. Results of the study indicated that emotional intelligence is significantly related to student's GPA scores. It suggests that academic achievement is related to students' ability to recognise, use and manage their emotions.

Parker *et al.* (2004) examined the relationship between emotional intelligence and academic achievement in high school. Students attending high school in Alabama completed the Emotional Quotient Inventory. At the end of the academic year the EQ-i data were matched with students' academic records for the year. Findings of the study revealed that academic success was strongly associated with several dimensions of emotional intelligence.

Supporting the effect of trait emotional intelligence on academic performance, Petrides *et al.* (2004a) reported that emotional intelligence was significantly related to scholastic achievement among 659 students with its effects having noteworthy implications for low IQ pupils. It was further reported that it moderated the effect of IQ on English performance.

Manhas (2004) in her study on adolescents studying in higher secondary schools of Jammu region found a positive significant correlation between emotional intelligence and academic achievement.

Study by Bar-On (2003) indicates existence of significant relationship between emotional intelligence and academic achievement. Their results show that emotional-social intelligence can predict who will perform well in school and who will not.

Vela (2003) found that there is significant correlation between emotional intelligence skills and academic achievement of 1st year college students. It was also found that students' emotional intelligence can better predict academic achievement.

Nelson and Nelson (2003) administered Personal Achievement Skills System (PASS) on 165 freshmen students in order to measure their emotional intelligence. After four years the researcher compared students' PASS scores with their GPA and found that emotional intelligence skills such as time management, goal achievement and assertive communication correlated with academic success.

Using the Bar-On Emotional Quotient Inventory, Lori (2003) conducted a study to determine the extent to which the presence of specific emotional intelligence attributes predicted the GPA of community college students. The findings of the study revealed no correlation between emotional intelligence score and student GPA.

Shanwal (2003) explored that academic achievement showed positive correlation with one of the component of emotional intelligence.

Lewis (2003) found no correlation between academic resilience and emotional intelligence.

Brackett and Mayer (2003) found positive relationship (=.21) between emotional intelligence measured through MSCIET and high school rank.

O'Connor and Little (2003) reported positive relationship (r=.23) between cumulative GPA and emotional intelligence measured through Bar-On's Emotional Quotient Inventory.

Barchard (2003) studied the ability of emotional intelligence to predict academic achievement in a sample of undergraduate psychology students, using year-end grades as the criterion. The predictive validity of emotional intelligence was compared with the predictive validity of traditional cognitive abilities and the Big Five dimensions of personality. Only some measures of emotional intelligence predicted academic success, and none of these measures showed incremental predictive validity for academic success over and above cognitive and personality variables. It was concluded that the overlap between many emotional intelligence measures and traditional measures of intelligence and personality limits their incremental predictive validity in this context. A correlation of .20 between MCEIT scores and GPA has been reported.

Vander-Zee *et al.* (2002) studied the relationship of emotional intelligence with academic intelligence. The objective of the study was to examine the relationship of self and other rating of emotional intelligence with academic intelligence as well as the incremental validity of emotional intelligence in predicting academic and social success. The sample for the study comprised of 116 students between the age group of 18-32 years. It was concluded that, academic intelligence is inconsistently related to emotional intelligence revealing both positive and negative inter relations. Emotional intelligence can predict academic success.

Parker (2002) reported that academic success (staying in University) was strongly associated with emotional intelligence. Emotional intelligence scores were able to correctly identify the majority of students who would return for their second year. Emotional intelligence scores were even better at identifying those students who would abandon post secondary education altogether in comparison to transferring to another institution.

Parker *et al.* (2001) found that academic success was strongly associated with several dimensions of emotional intelligence.

Gautam (2000) in her study on a sample of 200 students of class XI found a high positive relationship between emotional intelligence and academic achievement.

Newsome, Day and Catano (2000) examined whether emotional intelligence (EQ-i) would account for variance in academic achievement scores after controlling for individual scores on measure of cognitive ability. They found that neither the EQ-i factor scores, nor the total EQ-i score was significantly related to academic achievement. No support was found for claims of emotional intelligence's ability to predict academic achievement.

Bar-On (2000), using his own measure, found correlations ranging from .06 - .12 (positive but not significant) between emotional intelligence and academic achievement.

Chico (1999) did not found any relationship between emotional intelligence scores and GPA.

Koh (1999) in his study explored the relationship between emotional intelligence and academic achievement among 341 respondents. There were two self-report instruments used to measure emotional intelligence – the Emotional Quotient Inventory (Tapia, 1998) and the EQR (self-developed). Academic achievement was measured by the grades of the first semester examination. Findings of the study revealed that there exists significant correlation between emotional intelligence scores and the grades of the first semester examination. All the five dimensions of emotional intelligence (self-awareness, self-regulation, empathy, motivation and social skills) were found to have significant correlations with grades of the first semester examination.

Schutte *et al.* (1998) conducted a study on a sample of 63 stduents and reported that there exists positive relationship (r=.32) between emotional intelligence as measured by Schutte Emotional Intelligence Scale and academic grade.

Goleman (1998) revealed high positive correlation between emotional intelligence and achievement.

Academic performance of University students is positively related to emotional intelligence (Stewart, 1998).

Lepage and Pamela (1997) reported that academic achievement is positively related to emotional intelligence.

## STUDIES ON ACHIEVEMENT IN RELATION TO FORMAL REASONING

Since the author could came across very few studies pertaining to relationship between formal reasoning and academic achievement, studies pertaining to relationship between different forms of reasoning and academic achievement have also been reviewed.

### Studies on Formal Reasoning and Achievement in English

Dubey (2010a) conducted a study on 90 students to examine achievement in language in relation to formal reasoning. Test of Formal Reasoning developed by L. K. Oad and K. S. Misra was used as a tool for the study. Marks obtained by the students in class XII examination served as an index of achievement. The findings of the study highlights that formal reasoning is not related to achievement in English; and students with high and low formal reasoning do not differ from one another on achievement in English.

**Studies on Formal Reasoning and Achievement in Language**

Dubey (2010a) reported that formal reasoning as measured by Test of Formal reasoning of L. K. Oad and K. S. Misra is not related to achievement in Hindi.

Cloutier and Goldschmid (1976) conducted a study on a sample of 117 children and reported that school achievement in French is significantly related to formal reasoning.

**Studies on Formal Reasoning and Academic Achievement**

Dubey (2008a) attempted to study the relationship between formal reasoning and academic achievement among socially deprived students. The sample comprised of 52 male students of B. A.-I of University of Allahabad. Test of Formal Reasoning developed by L. K. Oad and K. S. Misra was used as a tool for measuring formal reasoning and marks obtained by students in U. P. Board intermediate examination were considered as measures of achievement. It was found that formal reasoning is not related to achievement among highly, moderately and non-socially deprived students.

Misra (1999) conducted a study on 60 female students of class VIII and found that formal reasoning score is related to achievement (r = .46). He further stated that formal reasoning can predict achievement.

Ramachandran (1990) attempted to find out the relationship between academic performance and reasoning. The sample comprised of 500 students of class XI. The tools used were Verbal and Numerical Reasoning Test developed by K. K. Pillai and school marks register. It was found that there is positive and significant correlation between academic performance and total reasoning.

Gupta (1990) attempted to assess the contribution of memory to the performance of college students in the intermediate Arts and Science examinations. The sample comprised of 280 male and female students. The tool used was Verbal Reasoning Test. It was found that a major portion of the performance in college examination was accounted to factors of verbal and non-verbal reasoning.

Strahan and O'Sullivan (1988) conducted a study on the influence of cognitive reasoning on achievement test scores in the middle grades. The purpose of the study was to examine how middle school student's cognitive reasoning level (*e.g.,* concrete *vs.* formal reasoning ability) contributed to the variability of their achievement test performance. Performance of 213 middle grades students on a test of formal reasoning was analysed in comparison with scores on tests of achievement and scholastic aptitude. Results support cognitive reasoning as a significant correlate of achievement test performance when considered alone and when controlling for scholastic aptitude. Results suggest that performance on reasoning test is related to performance on achievement tests in a fashion different from performance on scholastic aptitude tests.

French (1965) found a significant correlation between measures of reasoning and freshman year grades.

## STUDIES ON ACHIEVEMENT IN RELATION TO ACADEMIC MOTIVATION

This section embodies a review of few researches pertaining to relationship between academic/achievement motivation and achievement.

### Studies on Academic Motivation and Achievement in English

Dubey (2010c) tried to examine academic motivation of high and low achievers in English among 100 students of class XI. Academic Motivation Inventory of J. P. Srivastava and English Language Achievement Test prepared by the investigator were used as tools for the study. The findings of the study revealed that – students with high achievement in English had higher academic motivation than the students with low achievement in English.

Dubey (2010b) conducted a study on impact of academic motivation on achievement in English. Academic Motivation Inventory of J. P. Srivastava and English Language Achievement Test of the investigator were administered on a sample of 110 class XI students of Allahabad city. Product moment co-efficients of correlation and ANOVA were used for the analysis of the data. The results revealed positive relationship between academic motivation and achievement in English and as compared to students with low academic motivation, students with high and moderate academic motivation have high achievement in English.

Tourani (2006) found that achievement in English is independent of achievement motivation when pre-achievement in English is taken as a co-variate. She further reported that students with high level of achievement motivation have a strong desire for significant accomplishment, for mastering skills or ideas, for control and for rapidly attaining high standards.

Mohan (1991) investigated the role of motivation in English language acquisition. The sample comprised of 546 senior secondary school students. The tools used were English Achievement Test (EAT) and English Language Attitude and Motivation Questionnaire (ELAMQ). The study revealed that some aspects of motivation showed significant correlation with some aspects of English learning.

### Studies on Academic Motivation and Achievement in Language

Patel (1987) found that achievement motivation is positively related with total achievement in case of scheduled caste and advantage students. Achievement motivation can predict total achievement in case of advantaged and scheduled tribe student and in Oriya, Sanskrit and Hindi in case of advantaged students.

Tripathi (1986) attempted to study the relationship between achievement motivation and academic attainment. The sample consisted of 500 high school students. It was found that boys' scores on achievement motivation are significantly correlated with achievement in Hindi. It was also found that achievement motivation of boys and girls highly correlated with achievement.

Prakash (1981) attempted to study the effect of achievement motivation on the performance in a linear programme on Hindi vocabulary. The sample consisted of 324 students of class IX. Achievement Motivation Test (Rao's Hindi version) was used to identify the students of three levels of achievement motivation. The findings of the investigation were – the performance of high achievement motivation group was higher than that of average and low achievement motivation groups; and the average academic motivation subjects had higher achievement than the low achievement motivation subjects.

**Studies on Academic Motivation and Academic Achievement**

Meenakshi (2003) in her research project revealed that pupils with high achievement motivation scored 50 per cent more marks as compared to pupil with low achievement motivation.

Varma (2003) tried to examine the relationship between academic achievement and achievement motivation among 600 Arts and Science stream students of Intermediate level. Achievement motivation was measured with the help of Achievement Motivation Test by V. P. Bhargava. High school marks of the students were taken as an index of achievement. The study revealed that there is negative relationship between academic achievement and achievement motivation among Arts and female students.

Behera (2002) conducted a study on 374 senior secondary vocational stream students of +2 level of Chandigarh city. Achievement Motivation Scale by Deo and Mohan and final examination marks as an index of academic achievement was used for data collection. The findings of the study revealed that significant difference existed between high and low achievement motivation group in respect of academic achievement; achievement motivation is positively related to academic achievement; and girls with high achievement motivation had higher academic achievement than low achievement motivation group.

Yuthim (2001) conducted a study on 240 students of class IX to evaluate academic achievement in Bloom's taxonomic categories in relation to achievement motivation. Achievement Motivation Test by Deo and Mohan was used as a tool for the study. The findings revealed that the mean score of academic achievement of high achievement motivation group is higher in every taxonomic category and also in the total academic achievement than that of low achievement motivation group.

Mahapatra (1998) conducted a study on 200 students. Achievement Motivation Questionnaire by Argyle and Robinson was used to measure achievement motivation of students. It was found that achievement motivation enhance the achievement level of students.

Pramod (1996) investigated the relationship between achievement motivation and academic performance. The sample for the study comprised of 300 students (150 boys and 150 girls) of class XI. Prayag Mehta's Achievement Motivation Inventory was used as a tool to measure achievement motivation of the students. It was found that there exists linear relationship between scholastic performance and achievement motivation. Achievement motivation was also found to be the most dominating influencing factor on academic performance.

Benno (1995) conducted a study to investigate the relationship between achievement motivation and academic achievement. The sample for the study comprised of 604 scheduled caste students of class X. Achievement Motivation Inventory by Prayag Mehta and Academic Achievement Test constructed by the investigator were used as a tools for the study. The findings of the study were that significant differences were found on academic achievement between scheduled caste students grouped on the basis on achievement motivation, and achievement motivation has been found to be a significant predictor of academic achievement.

Sarode (1995) attempted to study the impact of academic motivation on academic achievement among 398 male and 165 female higher secondary students. Jack Frymier's Academic Motivation Scale was used to measure the academic motivation of the students. Statistical analysis of the data revealed that academic motivation exerted influence on academic achievement in case of students of Science stream and male students of Arts stream; while it exerted no influence on students of Commerce stream and female students of Arts stream; higher academic motivation show significant difference in academic achievement than students with low academic motivation.

Agarwal (1993) tried to examine factors of academic achievement among class XI students. Academic Motivation Inventory of J. P. Srivastava was used to measure academic motivation of the students. Marks obtained by the students in class X was taken as an index of achievement. The findings of the study revealed that academic achievement is positively related to academic motivation.

Kulshrestha (1993) conducted a study to examine the relationship of educational achievement with achievement motivation among adolescents. The sample for the study consisted of 400 students of class XI of Mathura city. Achievement Motivation Test of V. P. Bhargava was used to measure the achievement motivation of the students. High school marks of the students were taken as a measure of educational achievement. Statistical analysis of the data revealed negative relationship between achievement and achievement motivation among male and female students of Arts and Science stream.

Meena Rani (1992) attempted to find out the difference in scholastic achievement of advantaged and disadvantaged students having different levels of academic motivation. The sample comprised of 500 girls students of class XI of Allahabad city. Academic Motivation Inventory by Srivastava and Maheshwari was used as a tool for the study. High school marks (total) were taken as an index of achievement. It was found that – at three different levels (high, average and low) of academic motivation, the subjects identified as advantaged and disadvantaged when compared to their scholastic achievement, showed a uniform pattern of result.

Radha Rani (1992) conducted a study on a sample of 500 boys and girls of Science and Arts stream, to find out the relationship between academic achievement and achievement motivation. Achievement Motivation Test developed D. G. Rao was used as a tool for data collection and achievement marks of high school examination was taken as an index of academic achievement. The finding of the study revealed that there exist positive relationship between academic achievement and achievement motivation among both boys and girls.

Harikrishnan (1992) attempted to examine academic achievement in relation to achievement motivation. The sample for the study comprised of 300 students. The tool used in the study was Achievement Motivation Inventory of Prayag Mehta. Marks obtained by the students in school served as an index of academic achievement. It was found that the achievement is not related to achievement motivation.

Singhal (1991) examines the relationship between academic achievement and academic motivation among 200 grade IX students. Results indicate existence of positive relationship between academic achievement and academic motivation.

Devanesan (1990) studied the relationship between achievement motivation and scholastic achievement among 300 higher secondary students. Prayag Mehta's Achievement Motivation Inventory was used as a tool for the study. It was reported that there exists positive relationship between achievement motivation and scholastic achievement of higher secondary students.

Tripathy (1990) conducted a study on academic performance of tribal and non-tribal high school students in relation to their academic motivation. The objective of the study was – to study the relationship between academic performance and academic motivation among tribals and non-tribals; and to compare the relationship between academic performance and academic motivation in tribal and non-tribal groups. The sample comprised of 800 class IX students of tribals and non-tribal groups of Orissa. Academic Motivation Inventory by Mock and Doyle was used as a tool. It was found that there is no relationship between academic performance and academic motivation; academic performance is positively related to academic motivation among tribal high achievers and low achievers; and academic performance is significantly and positively related with academic motivation of non-tribal students.

Ramasamy (1988) attempted to investigate the relationship between academic achievement and achievement motivation among high and low achievers. The tools used for the study were SSLC Public Examination marks and Rao's Achievement Motivation Test. The collected data were treated using correlation. Academic achievement was found to be positively related to achievement motivation, among high and low achieving boys and girls.

Buch (1988) studied the school performance of primary school children in the context of motivation and revealed that school performance is significantly related to achievement motivation.

Mitra (1985) studied the relationship between achievement motivation and academic performance among students of class IV-VII. Questionnaire on achievement motivation constructed by Durgadas Bhattacharya was used. Students' annual examination marks were taken as measures of academic performance. It was found that achievement motivation is positively and significantly correlated with academic achievement for both the sexes. Achievement motivation accounted for 3/5th of the variance in academic achievement.

Shanmugasundaram (1983) assessed the influence of achievement motivation on the academic achievement of undergraduate students. The sample consisted on 620 students from 20 colleges under the jurisdiction of Madras University. The data were analysed with the help of mean, SD, CR, partial correlation, multiple correlations and multiple regressions. It was found that high achievers had higher achievement motivation than low achievers.

Gandhi (1982) found that achievement motive is significantly and positively related to academic achievement of high school students of both the sexes; and academic achievement of high school boys and girls is significantly affected by their being high, average or low on achievement motive.

Sharma (1981) found that poor academic motivation contributed to underachievement.

Desai (1979) attempted to study the relationship between pupils' academic motivation and academic achievement. The sample consisted of 1,555 pupils. The tools used for data collection were – Junior Index Motivation of Frymier, and Academic Achievement Rating Scale constructed by the investigator. The major finding of the investigation was that pupil's academic motivation is positively related to their academic achievement.

Bridgeman and Shipman (1978), in a longitudinal study of disadvantaged children have shown that achievement motivation scores, as measured by

Gumpgookies Test (Adkins, Payne and Ballif, 1972) in the year prior to entering Ist grade, contributed significantly to predictions of achievement in 3rd grade.

Abrol (1977) found significant and positive correlation of moderate value between achievement motivation measured through Achievement Motivation Test of Mehta and scholastic achievement taken from school records among students of class X.

Srivastava (1974) attempted to conduct a study on the effect of academic motivation on the academic achievement of boys. The objectives of the study were – to find out how for academic motivation effects scholastic achievement; and to find out how far academic motivation contributes to the prediction of academic achievement. The sample for the study comprised of 1131 boys of class X. Test of Academic Motivation prepared by the investigator was used to measure academic motivation. Achievement Test in General Hindi, General Science, Social Studies and Mathematics by R. P. Bhatnagar were used as measures of academic achievement. The findings of the study were – academic achievement is positively related to academic motivation. (r = .22); academic motivation of the tenth class students highly influences their academic achievement; and achievement motivation can predict academic achievement.

Mehta (1968) tried to examine achievement motivation in relation to academic performance on the population of IX class in Rajasthan. He found that need achievement showed positive correlation with the total performance at the school annual examination as well as with the performance in individual subjects.

Studies by Sinha (1967) and Lavin (1967) revealed positive relationship between achievement motivation and academic achievement among class X and college students respectively.

Besides these, Meijer (2004), Alam (2001), John (1996), Gottfried (1990), Veekarchavan and Bhattacharya (1989), Ahluwalia (1985), Tiwari (1984), Parkerson, Schiller, Lomax and Walberg (1984), Singh (1976), Schlesser and Finger (1965), and McClelland (1956) have also reported positive relationship between achievement/academic motivation and academic achievement.

## STUDIES ON ACHIEVEMENT IN RELATION TO CAUSAL ATTRIBUTION

### Studies on Causal Attribution and Achievement in English

Dubey (2009b) tried to examine the relationship between causal attributions and achievement in English among 70 male and 84 female class XI students. English Language Achievement Test and Causal Attribution scale developed by the investigator were used as tools for data collection in the study. The findings of the study revealed that achievement in English is positively related to ability and effort attribution for both male and female students; task difficulty was positively related to achievement in English among male students; and achievement in English was not related with luck, spiritual and support attribution among both male and female students.

Chou (2005) investigated the impact of parental support on English proficiency. A sample of 285 freshmen and senior year college students from Taiwan served as participants of the study. The findings of the study revealed that students who perceive more parental support got higher mean scores on English proficiency.

Chan and Youlden (1995) conducted a study to examine attributional pattern for achievement in English among 1859 students. Causal Attribution Scale developed by Chan was used as a tool for the study. Achievement measures for English were based on students' end of the year result in English. The results indicated that students were most likely to attribute success to effort, than to ability and least likely to luck.

**Studies on Causal Attribution and Achievement in Language**

Moreano (2004) conducted a study to examine the relationship between causal attribution for success and failure and academic achievement among 284 primary school (V and VI grades) students in Lima. The Sydney Attribution Scale was applied on them and language grades were assumed as an index of academic achievement. The results revealed that grades in language correlated with all the factors of causal attribution.

In the study by O'Sullivan and Howe (1996) relations between children's reading achievement and their causal attribution were investigated. A total of 513 students of grades 3, 6 and 9 participated. Students independently rated the importance of seven variables (effort, intellectual ability, liking for reading, the teacher, help at home, difficulty of reading material and luck) for their good and poor reading outcomes. The major findings were that at each grade student's attributions were reliably related to their reading achievement on the Gates-MacGinite Reading Comprehension Test, with attributions to ability, liking for reading and help at home especially critical; as students' grade in school increased they focused more on themselves and less on others as causal determinants of their reading performance.

Gupta (1994) attempted to study the relationship between causal attribution and academic achievement of gifted children in Hindi. The sample comprised of 3246 students of U. P. The tools used for data collection were – Short form of Sydney Attribution Scale (SAS) (Hindi Adaptation) and Hindi Achievement Test by L. N. Dubey. It was found that academic achievement of gifted students is positively and significantly correlated with causal attribution of their achievement outcome in Hindi. Effort attribution is significantly and positively related with achievement of gifted students in Hindi. The relationship is retained in above average achievers (AAA) group also. In Hindi, the AAA and BAA do not perceive effort as a causal explanation for their achievement outcome in different way. Achievement outcome is positively and significantly related to ability attribution. External attribution made by gifted students is positively and significantly related with achievement in Hindi.

Heibert, Winograd and Danner (1984) assessed the attribution of children of low and high reading achievement in III and VI grade. Children were asked to rate the degree to which each of six causes [*(i)*ability, *(ii)* luck, *(iii)* task difficulty, *(iv)* paying attention, *(v)* studying and *(vi)* assistance from others] was responsible for the success or failure in reading. The study revealed that achievement interacted with low achieving III graders give higher ratings to causes more clearly beyond their control than high achieving III graders whereas low and high achieving sixth graders did not differ.

Pearl *et al*. (1980) compared children's achievement levels with the kinds of attributions they made in reading achievement. They asked under achieveing and control children in grades 1-8, to rate the importance of effort, ability, task difficulty and luck in reading situations. Results showed that achievers (control group) had a greater tendency to attribute failure to lack of effort and also showed more internal feelings of control over success.

**Studies on Causal Attribution and Academic Achievement**

Lei (2009) conducted a study on 1400 students of University of Yantai and reported that in the success situation, college students mainly attribute the examination results to teaching quality and persistent diligence etc. while factors like luck and help from others are not considered as the main causes for success in examination; conversely in the failure situation, they tend to attribute the results to poor improvisation, difficult degree of test papers and bad luck while factors like poor teaching quality, lack of hardwork are not regarded as the main causes for poor performance in examination.

Jha (2008) conducted a study to examine the attribution pattern among undergraduate university students in the context of academic achievement. The sample for the study comprised of 128 students of Science and non-Science streams of University of Allahabad. The study revealed that there exists significant difference in attribution pattern among students in the context of academic achievement.

Sharma (2008) found that ability has the greatest direct effect on academic achievement of adolescents.

According to WEAC (2005), higher achieving students are likely to attribute their success in high school to hard work and ability.

Valle Arias *et al*. (1999) reported that students attribute low performance to ability and luck.

Siana *et al*. (1998) focusing on 985 secondary schools students in London and England, found that Asian students of both the sexes rated parents and friends as more important in contributing to academic success. This means that support attribution is given importance.

Shukla (1994) conducted a study on 80 (40 male and 40 female) postgraduate students. Attribution Scale by Girishwar Mishra was used as a tool for data collection. The major findings of the study were – in success condition, both male and female students attributed more to all internal factors *i.e.,* self-responsibility, effort, behaviour, memory, motivation and interest in comparison to failure condition; female subjects attributed their success/failure in a significant way on the following six attributional categories – *(i)* self-responsibility, *(ii)* effort, *(iii)* behaviour, *(iv)* memory, *(v)* motivation and *(vi)* interest; male subjects attributed their outcome (success/failure) more to their effort, behaviour, memory, motivation and interest in a significant way.

Pan (1993) reported that Chinese emphasise ability and effort equally as two major causes of success and failure. He further stated that high achievers attributed their success strongly to ability and intelligence rather than effort.

Gama and deJesus (1991) assessed the impact of the experience of academic success and failure on the causal attribution patterns of 147 Brazilian elementary school students. Among the V graders successful students' predominant attributional pattern was internal.

Peterson and Barrett (1987) administered Academic Attributional Style Questionnaire and reported that students who make internal, stable and global attributions for negative events tend to do more poorly in classes.

Taliulii and Gama (1986) reported that Brazilian elementary students attribute their performance to four causal factors – *(i)* ability, *(ii)* effort, *(iii)* task difficulty and *(iv)* luck. He further reported that most of the students attributed their success to effort.

Beharwal (1986) found that high achievement oriented subjects' perceived ability and internality as responsible for their outcome whereas low achievement oriented subjects considered fate and externality to be the potential causes that affected their outcome. High achievement oriented subjects attributed success to ability and fate and failure to lack of this.

Rao and Murthy (1984) conducted a study on 540 undergraduate students belonging to Banglore city. The results of the study indicated that high achievers were internal *i.e.,* they attribute their success to their ability and effort.

Marsh (1984) investigated a sample of 559 fifth grade students. Measures were collected to assess multiple dimension of self attribution for causes of academic outcomes and academic achievement. It was found that overall students who attribute academic success to ability and effort, and who do not attribute failure to lack of ability, and to a lesser extent not to lack of effort were found to have better academic achievement (based on test scores).

Marsh *et al*. (1982) looked at the stability of effort and ability attributions across different academic content areas using Sydney Attribution Scale. They compared effort attributions for reading success and failure versus Mathematics success and failure for 248 5th grade students similar comparisons were made for ability attributions. Their results suggested that attributions do not generalise across academic content areas, but this was primarily evidenced for ability attributions.

Kovacs (1981) explored attributions of 138 community college students about their academic success and failure. It was found that females rated their comprehension of the material, study, skill and effort higher than males.

Watkins and Astilla (1980) examined causal attributions for success and failure by 246 Filipino college students. They found that they ascribed possible success more to internal rather than to external sources.

Bernstein, Stephan and Davis (1979), and Kovenglioglu and Greenhouse (1978) reported that attributions to internal causes were more likely to occur following successful academic outcomes; whereas external causes were more likely to be called upon to explain academic failure. In these studies, college subjects who did well on a course examination were more likely to endorse attributions such as ability and effort, than student who perceived their own or others behaviour as a failure. On the hand, students who failed, emphasised bad luck or the difficulty of the test as being important causes for the outcome.

Arkin and Maruvama (1979) investigated causal attribution for achievement and their effects on task selection. The sample comprised of 240 students. It was found that – college students attributed their own performance and the performance of average students to ability, task preparation and luck; successful students perceived internal factors as more important causes and unsuccessful students perceived external factors as more important causes of their own performance than the performance of average students; and successful students saw internal and stable factors as more important causes of other's outcome (as well as their own) than did the unsuccessful students.

Jindal (1976) conducted a study on a sample of 40 college students of Haryana and reported that successful students were more likely to attribute their success to their own (*i.e.,* internal factors) than failing students.

Frieze (1976) conducted a study in which college subjects were given the opportunity to provide their own explanations of imagined academic outcomes in a free response format. Analyses of free responses demonstrated that success was attributed more often than failure, to ability (an internal stable cause) whereas failure was attributed more often to being in a bad mood (an internal unstable cause) Stability appeared to be a more important attributional dimension than locus of control in differentiating causes for success and failure.

Bailey, Helm and Goldstone (1975) studied attribution and expectations of undergraduate students for performance in a college examination. Among students who succeeded, expected and actual performance were positively related to attribution to high ability and negatively related to attribution to good luck. Among students who experienced failure, expected performance was positively related with attribution to low effort and negatively related with attribution to low ability.

Feather (1969) investigated attribution behaviour under conditions where differences in subject's expectation were achieved either by selection or by experimental manipulation. It was found that subjects who were initially confident of passing a test (achievement) tended to attribute success to ability (internal attribution). Thus, unexpected outcomes were attributed to external factors and expected outcomes to stable internal factors.

Crandal *et al.* (1965) found that achievement among young girls was positively correlated with internal attributions for success. For older boys, achievement was positively correlated with internal attributions for failure.

## STUDIES ON ACHIEVEMENT IN RELATION TO CLASSROOM ENVIRONMENT

Research indicates that classroom climate affects not only how much is learned, but how long learning lasts and how much future learning there is likely to be (Anderson, 1982; Ehman, 1980; Brookover, Schweitzer and Schneider, 1978). Negative, sullen or passive emotional climates usually dampen enthusiasm for current learning and decrease ambition for future learning. Conversely, warm, stimulating interpersonal classroom relations not only facilitate current learning but also foster positive attitudes towards future learning (Hamachek, 1990).

### Studies on Classroom Environment and Achievement in English

Dubey (2010d) conducted a study on 100 students of class XI studying in U. P. Board affiliated schools of Allahabad city. The objectives of the study were – to study the relationship between learning environment and achievement in English; and to find out whether students perceiving different amounts of stimulation in learning environment differ from one another on their achievement in English. Learning Environment Inventory developed by K. S. Misra and English Language Achievement Test prepared by the investigator were used as tools for data collection. The findings of the study were – achievement in English has been found to be positively related to goal direction and competition dimensions of learning environment; achievement in English is not related to to cohesiveness, diversity, speed, friction, facilitation, formality, favouritism, difficulty, apathy, democratic orientation, cliqueness, disorganization, creative stimulation, encouragement, involvement and conformity dimensions of learning environment; students perceiving high goal direction in learning environment have high achievement in English in comparison to their counterparts perceiving low or moderate goal direction; as compared to students perceiving moderate level of competition in learning environment, students perceiving high level of competition have high achievement in English; students perceiving different amounts of cliquenesss, cohesiveness, diversity, formality, speed, facilitation, friction, favouritism, difficulty, apathy, democratic orientation, disorganization, creative stimulation and conformity in learning environment do not differ from on another in their achievement in English.

Urdan (2004) employed survey methods and hierarchical linear modeling analytic methods with a sample of high school students and the study revealed that both at individual level and classroom level goal structure perceptions were associated with students' achievement in English.

Baek and Choi (2002) conducted a study to investigate the relationship between students' perception of classroom environment and their academic achievement among 1012 X and XI grade students of Korea. The Korean Classroom Enviornment Scale was used to measure psychosocial characteristics of the classroom environment. It was found that the seven subscales in the KCES (*i.e.*, involvement, affiliation, completion, task orientation, order and organization, rule clarity, and teacher control) had a significant correlation with students' academic achievement measured through English achievement test. It was also found that classroom environment was a good predictor of students' academic achievement.

Balasubramanian (1989) attempted to study the classroom climate in relation to pupils' achievement in English at higher secondary stage. The sample for the study comprised of 37 male and 15 female post-graduate teachers teaching English at standard XII. The sample comprised of 1025 male and 975 female students of class XII. It was found that indirect influence patterns of teacher's classroom behaviour influenced better classroom climate and ultimately resulted in better academic achievement in English, while direct influence patterns of teachers' classroom behaviour caused poor classroom climate and low level of achievement in English.

**Studies on Classroom Environment and Achievement in Language**

Chatterji (1987) conducted a study on the effect of total learning environment on the language development of students and found that the total learning environment had a significant effect on the language development.

**Studies on Classroom Environment and Academic Achievement**

Allen and Fraser (2007) conducted a study on 320 students of class IV and V. Learning Environment Questionnaire and Standford Achievement Test were used as tools for the study. Findings of the study revealed that different dimensions of learning environment *i.e.*, cohesiveness, teacher support, involvement, task orientation, equity and investigation were not related to achievement.

Avinashilingam and Sharma (2005) conducted a study on 91 undergraduate students and found that classroom factor plays a major role in affecting students' academic performance.

Marjoribanks (2003) examined 4382 females and 3940 males and found that learning environment is associated with educational attainment.

Ladson-Billings (1994) argued that achievement of students is increased significantly when inequality in student treatment is minimized.

Singhal (1991) examined the relationship between academic achievement and nine dimensions of classroom social climate among 200 students of ninth grade. Results indicate a significant positive relationship between academic achievement and classroom climate variables such as affiliation, teacher-support, task orientation, competition and innovation. Academic achievement was found to be negatively correlated with teacher control and had no correlation with involvement, order and organization, and rule clarity dimensions of social climate.

Padhi (1991) conducted a study to determine the relationship between classroom environment and academic achievement of the students. The sample comprised of 636 class IX students. The tools used for the study was Individualised Classroom Environment Questionnaire, long form developed by Rentoul and Fraser, and school marks were considered as the academic achievement in different school subjects. The finding of the study was that, the correlation between the classroom environment and academic achievement was not significant.

Dhar (1989) found that effect of school environment was significant on academic achievement of Arts and Science stream students.

Dubey (1989) studied the effect of school environment on achievement. He used a self made tool for measuring school environment. The main finding of the study was – school environment had differential effect on academic achievement; and enriched school environment is significantly better than poor school environment for academic achievement.

Byrne, Hattie and Fraser (1986) studied the effect of actual classroom environment on achievement. They concluded that co-operation within the classroom promotes higher achievement.

Doctor (1984) conducted a study on classroom climate and achievement of pupils. The sample covered 30 classes and 1279 pupils. Classroom Climate Scale was used to measure the classroom climate. It was found that classroom climate had consistency with academic achievement and academic achievement was dependent on classroom climate.

Upadhyaya (1984) conducted a study on class VIII students to assess the effect of classroom environment on learning and attainment. The Classroom Environment Scale developed by Moos and Trickett and standardised achievement tests of all the subjects were used as tools for data collection. The major finding of the study were – each of three aspects of classroom environment-interpersonal relationship, goal orientation, and system maintenance and change, was significantly correlated to academic achievement; of the three dimensions comprising interpersonal relationship, involvement and affiliation were positively correlated with achievement while teacher support was not; task orientation and competition, the two dimensions of the aspect-goal orientation, were highly correlated with academic achievement; order and organization, a dimension of system maintenance, which implied polite and orderly student behaviour in the classroom as well as out of class activities were not related to academic achievement; the only dimension negatively correlated with academic achievement was rule clarity, a dimension of system maintenance, teacher control signifying the strictness of the teacher in implementing and enforcing rules and magnitude of punishment on violation of rules was positively correlated with academic achievement; and there was no relationship between examination marks and classroom environment except as regards goal orientation; however competition was not related to the examination marks.

Zaidi (1984) studied the relationship between achievement and learning environment. The sample consisted of 100 girls studying in class XI. Learning Environment Inventory of Anderson and Walberg as adopted by K. S. Misra, was used for measuring learning environment. Marks obtained by students in half-yearly examination were considered as achievement scores. It was found that achievement is positively related with seven dimensions of learning environment *viz.*, cohesiveness, speed, goal direction, democratic orientation, competitiveness and satisfaction; difficulty, apathy and disorganization were negatively related with achievement; and diversity, formality, friction, favouritism and cliqueness had a non significant relationship with academic achievement.

GCPI (1981) conducted a study on 10 schools of Allahabad. Information was collected from principals and teachers. It was found that encouragement to students is significantly effective in improving the examination results.

Haertel, Walberg and Haertel (1981) using classroom environment studies revealed students perceptions of classroom environment as a critical factor in determining students' achievement. They analysed 12 studies with data involving 823 classes and approximately 1700 students. Their findings clearly supported strong association between student learning outcomes and psychosocial characteristics of their classrooms. They concluded that gains in learning outcomes were consistently associated with classrooms which were perceived as having greater cohesiveness, satisfaction, goal direction, organization and less friction.

Hirunwal (1980) found that classroom climate bore a positive relationship with the academic achievement of class IX pupils.

Desai (1979) attempted to study the relationship between classroom climate and academic achievement. The sample consisted of 1,555 students of secondary schools. The tools used were Classroom Climate Scale of Thelen and Academic Achievement Rating Scale constructed by the investigator. It was found that level of classroom climate is positively related to their academic achievement.

Tripathi (1978) attempted to study the relationship between academic achievement and disruptive classroom behaviour. The sample consisted of 506 male intermediate class students. Classroom behaviour was measured through observation and intermediate marks were taken as an index of academic achievement. It was found that academic achievement and disruptive classroom behaviour yielded a significant negative correlation.

Verma (1977) attempted to investigate the relationship between socio-emotional climate of the classroom and academic achievement of pupils. The sample consisted of 1,294 students of secondary schools. The tools used for the study were Teacher Classroom Behaviour Sociometric Test and Attainment Test in Social Studies and General Science. It was found that socio-emotional climate of the classroom predicted and influenced the pupils' academic achievement.

Rathbone (1972) found that open classroom facilitates child centred learning.

**REVIEW OF TOOLS RELATED TO CAUSAL ATTRIBUTION**

Although a great deal of research based on Weiner's *et al.* (1971) model of causal attribution for success and failure have been published in 1970s, relatively little attention has been given to the question of how causal attribution should best be measured (Deaux and Farris, 1977).

There are a number of commonly used techniques for assessing causal attribution *viz.*, open ended responses, independent rating, ipsative ratings, paired comparisons, choice of one major cause, bi-polar rating, ratio scale and direct measures of causal dimensions. Each of these methods has its own advantages and disadvantages in terms of practical considerations.

O' Sullivan and Howe (1996) developed causal rating scale for measuring causal attribution about reading. It included seven causal variables *i.e.*, effort, intellectual ability, liking for reading, the teacher, help at home, difficulty of reading material and luck.

Henry and Campbell (1995) developed a measure of attributional style for academic events. It contains 20 items, equally divided between positive and negative events. The measure displayed adequate good reliability and also predicted academic performance.

Gupta (1994) constructed a five-point rating attribution scale to cover success and failure for four content areas *i.e.*, Mathematics, Science, Social

Studies and Hindi. The causal categories which were attributed for success and failure were – task difficulty, ability, effort and luck. The scale has 48 items. Test-retest reliability of the scale was .61 and .58 at an interval of 7 and 14 days respectively. The obtained score for ability, effort and external factors for success and failure conditions were correlated with obtained scores in success and failure situations on attribution scale. The six co-efficients of correlation, three for success and three for failure were .72, .53, .48, .60 .51 and .49. They indicate validity co-efficients of the conditions of the attribution scale for each category.

Peternson and Barrett (1987) developed the Academic Attributional Style Questionnaire AASQ which uses the same format as ASQ (Attributional Style Questionnaire) and contains descriptions of 12 negative events that occur in academic settings. The measure has high internal consistency.

Sharma and Tripathi (1986) measured teacher's attribution for students' performance on a five-point rating scale. Each of the attributive categories were rated on a five-point rating scale, ranging from 'very little' to 'very much' through 'considerable'. In one study by Sharma and Tripathi (1986) the attributive categories were task difficulty, ability, effort, chance and family of the student and in another study an additional attributive category, quality of teaching in school was added. In another study by the same authors children were asked to express the causality for each attributive category: effort, chance, ability and luck on a five-point rating scale, ranging from 'very much' to 'very little'.

Misra and Misra (1986) developed an Attributional Questionnaire to obtain causal attributions for performance in the half yearly examination of first year intermediate class. It contains four items related to the dimension of mental ability, luck, preparation for examination at home and difficulty level of the course of studies. It is a five-point rating scale ranging from 'very less' to 'very much'.

Beharwal (1986) developed structured response measure requiring subjects to give their percentage ratings on five causal categories (ability, effort, luck, home environment and self confidence) while determining their success and failure on an anagram task. The reliability estimate for the measure was based on judges and experts' agreement and subjects' giving rank to a cause for explaining success/failure of subjects. Face validity has been established.

Ronis *et al.* (1983) distinguished between two different methods of measuring causal stability. Indirect method ascertains the subjects' attributions for success and failure to dominant causes such as ability, effort, task difficulty and luck. Then, an apriori classification scheme (from Weiner *et al.* 1971) is used to derive a stability index. This index is a resultant of ascriptions to unstable causes (effort plus luck) subtracted from ascriptions to stable causes (ability plus task difficulty). Ronis *et al.* (1983) advocated a 'direct' or 'perceived' technique of assessment. In the perceived technique, causal stability is assessed straight forwardly by asking whether success or failure was due to something unchanging and stable over time or something changing and unstable over time.

**REVIEW OF TOOLS RELATED TO ENGLISH ACHIEVEMENT TEST**

Testing of English as a foreign language is less well developed (Carroll, 1969). The assessment of language is a multifaceted process (Shipley and McAfee, 1998; Cole, Dale and Thal, 1996; Tomblin, Morris and Spriestersbach, 1994; Haynes, Pindzola and Emerick, 1992).

Salami and Ogundokun (2009) constructed a 20-item multiple choice English Language Achievement Test with four options per item. In this test some of the test items were constructed by the researchers with the assistance of an expert in the field of English language, while few of them were selected from the past West African Examination council questions based on syllabus for SS2 classes. Expert validity was established. The internal consistency reliability coefficient (Cronbach's alpha) for the scale was reported .75. The test-retest reliability measure of the test was .76.

In order to measure students' academic achievement in English, high school teachers who have taught English for more than five years, developed two English Achievement Tests. One was for 10th grade students and the other was for 11th grade students. Each test comprised of 25 multiple-choice items (Baek, 2001; Baek *et al.* 1998). To check the reliability of these English Achievement Test, Cronbach's alpha co-efficients were used (.84 for English test 10th grade and .80 for English test for 11th grade). Correlation co-efficients between these tests and standardised achievement tests, which were developed by Korea Institute of Curriculum and Evaluation, were used to identy the concurrent validity of these instruments. The values of coefficient of correlation were .64 for both 10th grade and 11th grade tests.

Chawla (1992) standardised a multiple choice vocabulary test of English Language. It consisted of 22 multiple-choice items selected on the basis of difficulty value and discrimination index. The standard deviation of scores and time taken in the test was 5.56 and 8.70 minutes respectively.

Dey (1991) attempted to standardise a proficiency test in English for class X. The areas included in the test were vocabulary, spelling, stylistic transformation and alteration, derivational structures, applied grammar and contextual meaning.

Khan (1989) constructed and standardised a diagnostic test in English for standard VIII with regard to structures.

Dube (1989) constructed an achievement test in English for high school students.

Khare (1986) constructed seven achievement tests for different dimensions of English in order to measure learning outcomes of students taught through traditional and structural approach.

Zaidi (1986) constructed a Language Achievement Test for students of class V. It consists of 30 items with difficulty value ranging from 20-70 per cent and discrimination index ranging from .4 - .67. Split-half reliability was .68. Concurrent validity was calculated and the test was validated against the school marks. Content validity was also established.

Patil (1985) constructed an achievement test to measure overall language ability of the Arts graduates. The test included items of vocabulary, associative recognition, translation of contextualized words etc. The test had four parallel forms – A, B, C and D and all the four forms were highly inter correlated.

Gupta (1983) prepared and standardised four linguistic skills test in English for standard X – *(a)* a test on reading and understanding *(b)* a test on hearing and understanding *(c)* a test on speaking correctly *(d)* a test on writing correctly. The last test had two parts – a spelling test and a test on grammar and composition. The reliability, validity and decile norms of the tests were estimated.

Singh (1978) constructed a battery of objective tests for the assessment of proficiency in writing English composition. The battery consisted of seven tests on spelling, punctuation, vocabulary (phrases), vocabulary (words), paragraph organization, applied grammar and handwriting.

Visvesvaran (1975) attempted to construct an achievement test in English based on the teaching units of standards VI, VII and VIII.

Deshpande (1972) and Misra (1970) standardised achievements test in English for class VIII-X for students in Assam and Maharashtra respectively.

Chatterji and Mukherjee (1970) developed a test of English knowledge and comprehension at the higher secondary level. It covered English usage, word meaning, grammar, spelling and comprehension. The reliability co-efficients estimated for different subtests by using KR 21 formula ranged between .53 - .81.

Buch, Patel and Kotwal (1960) standardised achievement tests in English for class VIII, IX and X. The test retest reliability co-efficients ranged between .88 - .96.

Rangaswamy and Feroze (1957) standardized an achievement test in English for the middle stage students of Coimbatore district of Tamil Nadu. The test included subtests related to language usage, spellings, punctuation capitalisation, reading, vocabulary and comprehension.

## ANALYSIS OF THE FINDINGS OF STUDIES REVIEWED

Analysis of various studies has revealed that, there exists positive relationship between intelligence and achievement in English. (Dubey, 2010a;

Kaur, 1992; Chandy, 1991; Singh, 1989), intelligence and academic achievement (Dhall and Thukral, 2010; Palta Singh, 2008; Deary, Strand, Smith and Fernandes, 2007; Singh, 2007; Varma, 2003; Behera, 2002; Mackintosh, 1998; Mavi and Patel, 1997; Singh and Verma, 1995; Agarwal, 1993; Gupta, Mukerjee and Chatterjee, 1993; Kumar, 1989; Sharma, 1988; Misra, 1986; Parkerson, Schiller, Lomax and Walberg, 1984; Lynn, Hampson and Magee, 1983; Shivappa, 1980 Singh, 1976). However, Dubey (2008a) and Omuluabi (1993) found that there is no relationship between intelligence and academic achievement.

Findings of Laidra, Pullman and Allik (2007), Agarwal (1993), Garg and Chaturvedi (1992), Srivastave (1992), Kaile (1988), Das (1986), Mitra (1985), Shivappa (1980), Vogel (1976) and Reddy (1973) establish the fact that intelligence is a predictor of academic achievement. However, findings of Naderi, Abdullah, Hamid and Sharir (2008) fail to support intelligence as a predictor of academic achievement.

Achievement in English was not found to be related with emotional intelligence (Dubey, 2008b). However, Dubey (2010a) and Pandey (2008) found positive relationship between emotional intelligence and achievement in English. Sucaromana (2004) reported that emotional intelligence affects achievement in English indirectly. Studies by Alam (2010), Sabath (2010), Salami and Ogundokun (2009), Hassan, Sulaiman and Ishak (2009), Adeyemo (2007), Besharat *et al.* (2005), Parker *et al.* (2004), Manhas (2004), Bar-On (2003), Vela (2003), Shanwal (2003), O'Connor and Little (2003), Gautam (2000), Schutte *et al.* (1998), Goleman (1998), Lepage and Pamela (1997) indicate existence of positive relationship between emotional intelligence and academic achievement. Schutte *et al.* (1998) found that there is negative relationship between emotional intelligence and academic achievement. However, studies of Pandey (2008), Dubey (2007), Anandmani (2006), Phillips (2005), Bastian, Burns and Nettelbeck (2005), Sibia, Mishra and Srivastava (2005), Lori (2003), Newsome, Day and Catano (2000) and Chico (1999) indicate existence of no relationship between the two.

Salami and Ogundokun (2009), Berenson, Boyles and Weaver (2008), Downey, Mountstephen, Lloyd, Hansen and Stough (2008), Parket *et al.* (2004), Bar-On (2003), Vela (2003) reported that emotional intelligence can predict academic achievement. While studies by Grace (2004) and Newsome, Day and Catano (2000) indicate that emotional intelligence cannot predict the same.

Analysis of the findings revealed that formal reasoning is not related to achievement in English (Dubey, 2010a). Dubey (2008a) found that formal reasoning is not related to academic achievement among students. While Mishra (1999) reported that formal reasoning is related to achievement. Studies by Ramachandran (1990), and Strahan and O' Sullivan (1988) revealed that academic achievement is related to reasoning ability.

Analyses of the studies pertaining to relationship between academic motivation and achievement have revealed that there exists positive relationship between the two. Dubey (2010b) reported positive relationship between academic motivation and achievement in English. Achievement was found to be related with achievement motivation (Behera, 2002; Agarwal, 1993; Radha Rani, 1992; Singal, 1991; Devanesan, 1990; Ramasamy, 1988; Buch, 1988; Tripathi, 1986; Mitra, 1985; Abral, 1977; Sinha, 1967; Lavin, 1967; Schlesser and Finger 1965; Ghahbazi, 1956). Contrary to this, Varma (2003), and Kulshrestha (1993) revealed negative relationship between academic achievement and academic motivation. However, studies by Harikrishnan (1992) and Tripathi (1990) indicate existence of no relationship between achievement and achievement motivation.

Findings of Benno (1995), Patel (1987), Bridgeman and Shipman (1978) and Srivastava (1974) establish the fact that achievement/academic motivation can predict achievement.

Analysis of the finding conducted in the field of causal attribution and achievement has revealed that students generally attribute their success to internal factor (ability and effort) (Soric, 2009; Sharma, 2006; WEAC, 2005; O'Sullivan and Howe, 1996; Shukla, 1994; Gama and deJesus, 1991; Misra, 1983; Power and Douglas, 1984; Kumari 1982) and their failure to external factors (task difficulty and luck) (Lei, 2009; Misra, 1982; Bernstein. Stephan and Davis, 1979; Kovenlioglu and Greenhause, 1978; Freize and Weiner, 1971). Sharma (2008) found that ability has the direct effect on academic achievement. Dubey (2009) reported positive relationship ability, effort, task difficulty attributions and achievement in English and no relationship between luck, spiritual and support attributions. Chan and Youlden (1995) reported that students attribute success in English to effort.

Analysis of the studies pertaining to relationship between classroom environment and academic achievement has revealed that, some dimensions of classroom environment are related to academic achievement of students. Dubey (2010d) reported that achievement in English is positively related to goal direction and competition dimensions of learning environment. Urdan (2004) also found that goal structure of classroom is associated with achievement in English. Baek and Choi (2002) found that involvement, affiliation, competition, task orientation, order, organization, rule clarity and teacher control dimensions of classroom environment are related to students achievement in English. Chatterji (1987) found significant effect of total learning environment on language development. Marjoribanks (2003) reported that learning environment is associated with educational attainment. Byrne, Hattie and Fraser (1986) concluded that co-operation within the classroom promotes achievement. Upadhyaya (1984) found that three aspects of classroom environment *i.e.*, interpersonal relationship, goal orientation and system maintenance and change are related to academic achievement. Zaidi (1984) reported that seven dimensions of learning environment are positively and three dimensions are negatively related to achievement.

For measuring causal attribution for academic performance in total as well as in specifc subjects, Causal Attribution Rating Scale and Questionnaire have been developed. O' Sullivan and Howe (1996) developed Causal Rating Scale for measuring causal attribution about reading. Gupta (1994) constructed Rating Scale to cover success and failure in Mathematics, Science, Social Studies and Hindi. Peterson and Barrett (1987) and Misra and Misra (1986) developed Academic Attribution Questionnaire.

Some language skills based achievement tests have been developed in English. In the English language various test for class VI-XI has been constructed. Significant work has been done by Salami and Ogundokun (2009), Baek *et al.* (2001), Baek *et al.* (1998), Chawla (1992), Zaidi (1986), Khare (1986), Patil (1985), Gupta (1983), Singh (1978), Visvesvaran (1975), Despande (1972), Chatterji *et al.* (1970) and Buch *et al.* (1960).

**LINKAGE BETWEEN PREVIOUS RESEARCHES AND THE PRESENT STUDY**

The analysis of the review of the researches presented in the proceeding pages shows that:

1. There exists positive relationship between intelligence and achievement in English.
2. There is no conclusive evidence about the relationship between emotional intelligence and achievement in English.
3. Few studies revealed the relationship between formal reasoning and academic achievement in general and formal reasoning and achievement in English.
4. Studies indicate existence of positive relationship between academic/ achievement motivation and academic achievement, but it is yet to be established in relation to achievement in English.
5. Studies on relationship between achievement in English and causal attribution do not provide conclusive evidence.
6. Few studies have revealed relationship between classroom environment and academic achievement in general. The relationship between achievement in English subject and various dimensions of classroom environment is yet to be explored.

Relationship of achievement in English language with intelligence, emotional intelligence, formal reasoning, academic motivation, causal attributions, and classroom environment among higher secondary (XI) students needs exploration. Therefore, the author has made a humble attempt to study the cognitive, motivational and environmental determinants of achievement in English.

# CHAPTER 3

# RESEARCH DESIGN

THE WELL PLANNED and goal oriented educational research requires proper research design. While conducting research we adopt systematic and sophisticated techniques of thinking and reasoning, utilising specialised tools, procedures and statistical analysis in order to obtain a more precise and accurate solution for a problem. Research design is a plan, structure and strategy of investigation conceived so as to obtain answers to research questions and to control variance (Kerlinger, 1973). It is the blue print of the detailed procedures of testing the hypothesis and analysing the obtained data. It enables the researcher to answer research questions as validly, objectively, accurately and economically as possible. It provides an overview of the total layout including consideration of how the work has to be executed. It consists of the information about the research work in view of framework of study, sampling, tools to be used for collecting necessary data, controls to be exercised and statistical techniques to be used for analysing the data. This chapter provides a description of the research design.

## METHOD OF STUDY

The nature of problem determines the appropriateness of the method to be used in any research work. The present research attempts to study achievement in English among students in relation to intelligence, emotional intelligence, formal reasoning, academic motivation, causal attribution and classroom environment. Causal comparative and correlational survey method of descriptive research have been used to conduct the present study.

## POPULATION AND SAMPLE

The population of this study comprises of male and female students studying in class XI in U. P. Board schools of Allahabad city. To begin with, the investigator prepared a list of U. P. Board schools in Allahabad city. By using the table of random numbers, the author selected three boys' and three girls' schools. They are Bharat Scouts and Guide Inter College, Colonelganj Inter College, Sadan Lal Sawal Das Inter College, D. P. Girls Inter College, St. Anthony's Inter College and Hindu Mahila Inter College. The author went to these schools and randomly selected one section of XI class from each school. All students studying in that section were included in the sample. Thus, cluster sampling was adopted to select the sample for the present study. The distribution of the sample subjects has been shown in the Table 3.1.

**Table 3.1: Distribution of students selected as sample subjects**

| Name of the School | No. of Male | No. of Female |
|---|---|---|
| 1. Bharat Scouts and Guide Inter College | 70 | |
| 2. Colonelganj Inter College | 75 | |
| 3. Sadan Lal Sawal Das Inter College | 82 | |
| 4. D. P. Girls Inter College | | 57 |
| 5. St. Anthony's Convent | | 84 |
| 6. Hindu Mahila Inter College | | 71 |
| **Total Sample Size** | **227** | **212** |

## VARIABLES IN THE STUDY

The present study attempts to explore achievement in English among students in relation to intelligence, emotional intelligence, formal reasoning, academic motivation, causal attribution and classroom environment. The independent variables are intelligence, emotional intelligence, formal reasoning, academic motivation, causal attribution and classroom environment and the dependent variable is achievement in English.

## TOOLS USED

Collection of reliable and valid data about various variables is necessary for carrying out research investigation. Suitable tools pave the way for the accomplishment of the objectives of a study and the collection of pertinent data. The selection of tools for a particular study depends upon various considerations such as objectives of the study, the amount of time at the disposal of the researcher, availability of suitable tools for data collection, personal competence of the researcher, techniques of scoring and interpretation etc. The criteria for selection of tools are illustrated in Fig. 3.1.

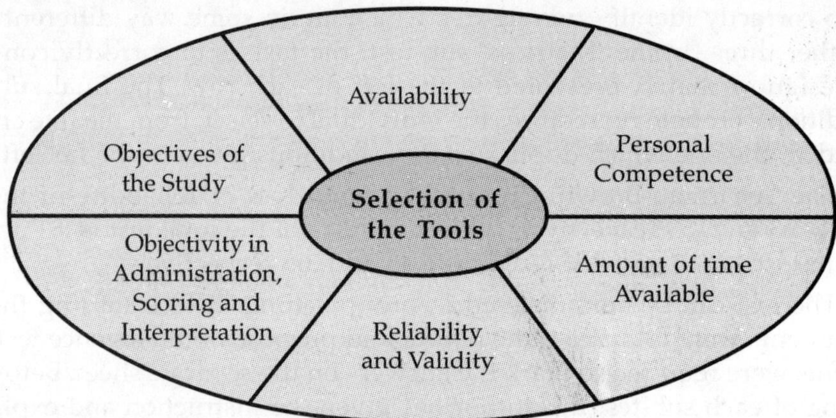


**Fig. 3.1: Criteria for Selection of a Tool**

Taking these factors into consideration, following tools were selected by the author –

1. Culture Fair Intelligence Test.
2. Test of Emotional Intelligence.
3. Test of Formal Reasoning.
4. Academic Motivation Inventory.
5. Causal Attribution Scale.
6. Learning Environment Inventory.
7. English Language Achievement Test.

**Culture Fair Intelligence Test**

Culture Fair Intelligence Test (Scale 3, Form B) developed by R. B. Cattell and A. K .S. Cattell (1973) has been used to measure intelligence of students. It contains 50 multiple choice non-verbal items related to intelligence of students. It has four sub-tests. Detailed description of the test is shown in Table. 3.2.

**Table 3.2: Items and time allotted to each sub-test of culture fair intelligence test, scale 3, form B**

| Sub-tests | No. of Items | Time Allotted |
|---|---|---|
| Test 1 Series | 13 | 3 minute |
| Test 2 Classifications | 14 | 4 minute |
| Test 3 Matrices | 13 | 3 minute |
| Test 4 Conditions (Topology) | 10 | 2½ minute |
| **Total** | **50 items** | **12½ minute** |

In the first sub-test, the individual is presented with an incomplete, progressive series. His task is to select, from the choices provided, the answer which best continues the series. In the 'Classification', sub-test, the individual has to correctly identify two figures which are in some way different from the other three. In the 'Matrices' sub-test, the task is to correctly complete the design or matrix presented at the left of each row. The final sub-test, 'Conditions' (Topology) requires the individual to select, from the five choices provided, the one which duplicates the conditions given in the far left box.

The Spearman-Brown, Cronbach's $\propto$ and K-R 21 reliability of the test are .64, .63 and .53 respectively. Direct validity of the total test is .81 and for the sub-test 1, 2, 3 and 4 it is .64, .48, .45 and .66 respectively.

The test can be administered in group setting. Before starting the test the students were told about the nature and purpose of intelligence test. The students were required to mark the answers on the separate sheet. Before the starting of each sub-test the author has given the instruction and explained the examples.

Scoring was done with the help of stencil. '1' mark was given for every correct response and '0' mark was given for each wrong response.

**Test of Emotional Intelligence (TEI)**

Test of Emotional Intelligence (Student Form) developed by K. S. Misra has been used for measuring students emotional intelligence. TEI (SF) contains 41 multiple choice items related to emotional intelligence. There is no time-limit for giving responses. Students have to respond to each item by choosing one of the four alternative responses.

Test-retest reliability of TEI (Student Form) has been found to be .6957 (N=64). Reliability has also been calculated by using Kudar-Richardson method by the author and it has been found to be .70 (N=100). Validity has been established against the ratings of teachers. The value of the validity co-efficient has been found to be .377 (N=100). Percentile norms for the test are available.

TET (SF) can be administered in group setting. Before administering the test, the respondents were told about the nature and purpose of measurement of emotional intelligence. They were instructed to write the serial number of correct answers against the relevant question number on the separate answer sheet. They were assured that their answers will be kept confidential.

Scoring was done with the help of stencil. '1' mark was given for correct response and '0' score was given for wrong response.

**Test of Formal Reasoning (TFR)**

Test of Formal Reasoning developed by L. K. Oad and K. S. Misra has been used for measuring formal reasoning ability of students. Test of Formal Reasoning contains 2 items related to formal reasoning ability of students.

Test-retest reliability of the TFR is .76. Predictive validity of the TFR was found by calculating co-efficient of correlation between the test scores and scores on the achievement of VIII class female students. The value of validity co-efficient is .46. Construct validity of the test was found by correlating scores on TFR with scores on the test of eight cognitive abilities namely – Classification, Verbal Facility, Mathematical Reasoning, Figural Evaluation, Similarity Exploration, and Inquisitiveness. The values of correlation were .54, .46, .48, .51, .45, .52, .59 and .54 respectively. Stanine score norms for boys and girls are available.

The Test of Formal Reasoning can be administered in group setting. Before administering the test, the respondents were given instruction regarding the test. Time limit for the test is five minutes.

Scoring was done manually. '1' marks was given for every correct response and '0' marks was given for every wrong response.

**Academic Motivation Inventory (AMI)**

Academic Motivation Inventory developed by J. P. Srivastava has been used for measuring academic motivation of students. It measures three dimensions of academic motivation *viz.,* academic aspiration, study habits and attitude towards school. AMI contains 58 items out of which 29 items were positive and 29 were negative. Each item is expected to be checked by the respondent in terms of the degree of agreement or disagreement on a five-point scale.

A score of 5, 4, 3, 2 and 1 for 'totally agree, agree, undecided disagree and totally disagree' responses is given for positive items respectively while a score of 1, 2, 3, 4 and 5 is given for 'totally agree, agree, undecided, disagree and totally disagree' responses respectively for negative items.

Test-retest reliability of the AMI was found to be .89 and .83 at the interval of one and three months respectively. AMI has content validity. Validity of AMI was established against the criterion of Aberdeen Academic Motivation Inventory. The co-efficient of correlation was found to be .49.

**Causal Attribution Scale (CAS)**

Causal Attribution Scale prepared by the author was used to measure causal attribution of students. It contains 14 items (11 positive and 3 negative items) related to attribution of success and failure in English. It is a five-point scale. It measures six causal attributions of success and failure namely – *(i)* task difficulty, *(ii)* ability, *(iii)* effort, *(iv)* luck, *(v)* spiritual and *(vi)* support.

Test-retest reliability has been found to be .61, .56, .58, .46, .55 and .43 for task difficulty, ability, effort, luck, spiritual and support respectively (N=100). Face validity has been established.

CAS can be administered in group setting. Responses are given by putting a tick marks (√) on only one of the five options given against each statement. A score of 5, 4, 3, 2 and 1 for 'very much, much, average, less and very less' responses is given for positive items respectively while a score of 1, 2, 3, 4 and 5 is given for 'very much, much, average, less and very less responses' respectively for the negative statements.

**Learning Environment Inventory (LEI)**

The Learning Environment Inventory prepared by K. S. Misra (2001) was used to measure the classroom environment as perceived by the students. It measures 18 dimensions of learning environment of classroom. They are cohesiveness, diversity, formality, speed, facilitation, friction, goal direction, favouritism, difficulty, apathy, democratic orientation, cliqueness, disorganization, competition, creative stimulation, encouragement, involvement and conformity. The Learning Environment Inventory consists of 126 statements. There are seven statements for each dimension. It has been shown in the Table 3.3.

**Table 3.3: Serial no. of items belonging to different dimensions of learning environment**

| Sl. No. | Dimensions of Learning Environment | Item No. | | | | | | |
|---|---|---|---|---|---|---|---|---|
| 1. | Cohesiveness | 1 | 19 | 37 | 55 | 73 | 91 | 109 |
| 2. | Diversity | 2 | 20 | 38 | 56 | 74 | 92 | 110 |
| 3. | Formality | 3 | 21 | 39 | 57 | 75 | 93 | 111 |
| 4. | Speed | 4 | 22 | 40 | 58 | 76 | 94 | 112 |
| 5. | Facilitation | 5 | 23 | 41 | 59 | 77 | 95 | 113 |
| 6. | Friction | 6 | 24 | 42 | 60 | 78 | 96 | 114 |
| 7. | Goal Direction | 7 | 25 | 43 | 61 | 79 | 97 | 115 |
| 8. | Favouritism | 8 | 26 | 44 | 62 | 80 | 98 | 116 |
| 9. | Difficulty | 9 | 27 | 45 | 63 | 81 | 99 | 117 |
| 10. | Apathy | 10 | 28 | 46 | 64 | 82 | 100 | 118 |
| 11. | Democratic Orientation | 11 | 29 | 47 | 65 | 83 | 101 | 119 |
| 12. | Cliqueness | 12 | 30 | 48 | 66 | 84 | 102 | 120 |
| 13. | Disorganization | 13 | 31 | 49 | 67 | 85 | 103 | 121 |
| 14. | Competition | 14 | 32 | 50 | 68 | 86 | 104 | 122 |
| 15. | Creative Stimulation | 15 | 33 | 51 | 69 | 87 | 105 | 123 |
| 16. | Encouragement | 16 | 34 | 52 | 70 | 88 | 106 | 124 |
| 17. | Involvement | 17 | 35 | 53 | 71 | 89 | 107 | 125 |
| 18. | Conformity | 18 | 36 | 54 | 72 | 90 | 108 | 126 |

Test-retest reliability of the LEI was found by correlating scores obtained by students on two different occasions with an interval of eleven days. The co-efficient of correlation ranged from 0.69 - 0.84 (N=87). Face validity of LEI was found by finding out whether the seven items belonging to each dimension of learning environment measure the concerned dimension of the learning environment as defined operationally. Factorial validity of the test was found by performing factor analysis. It resulted in extraction of four factors *viz.*, *(i)* Academic Thrust, *(ii)* Inhibition, *(iii)* Support and *(iv)* Diversity.

Mean and standard deviations for the eighteen dimensions of learning environment and the cut scores for high and low groups on each dimension for boys and girls are available.

The respondents were asked to express the degree of his or her agreement with the statement by selecting one of the five alternate responses namely – *(i)* strongly disagree, *(ii)* disagree, *(iii)* undecided, *(iv)* agree and *(v)* strongly agree. A score of 1, 2, 3, 4 and 5 is given for these responses respectively. It provides eighteen scores for eighteen dimensions of learning environment in the classroom.

**English Language Achievement Test (ELAT)**

English Language Achievement Test prepared by the investigator has been used to measure students' achievement in English. ELAT contains 56 objective type items related to English language of High School level.

Split-half and Kudar-Richardson reliability of ELAT has been found to be .85 and .84 respectively. Face validity and concurrent validity has been established (r = .50).

ELAT can be administered in group setting. Time limit of ELAT is 30 minutes. Responses were given in the booklet itself. A score of '1' mark was given for every correct response and '0' mark was given for wrong response.

**CONSTRUCTION OF CAUSAL ATTRIBUTION SCALE (CAS)**

For measuring the causal attribution of students, Causal Attribution Scale developed by the author was used. This section embodies the description of the procedure for the construction of CAS.

**Construction of the Tryout Form**

As a result of the review of the present status of knowledge regarding causal categories and methods of assessing attribution, it was clear that a number of different causal categories were used by different researches. The methods of measuring attribution also differed. On the basis of the review of literature, ability, effort, luck and task difficulty, the four causes of Wieners model, were retained. Two new additional causal factors namely – *(i)* spiritual and *(ii)* support, were included. Items were prepared on each of the six dimensions *i.e.*, task difficulty, effort, ability, luck, spiritual and support. A five-point scale with 11 positive and 3 negative statements was prepared.. The items were subjected to evaluation by the author and 12 experts.

**Item Analysis**

For tryout, the tool was administered on 130 students (60 male and 65 female) studying in class XI of D. P. Girls Inter College and Bharat Scouts and Guide Inter College.

Causal Attribution Scale (CAS) was administered in group setting. Students were told about the nature and purpose of measurement of causal attributions. They were instructed to give responses with reference to their success and failure in English subject at the High School examination. They were told to put a tick mark (√) on only one of the five response given against each statement and were assured that their responses will be kept confidential.

Scoring was done by awarding a score of 5, 4, 3, 2 and 1 for 'very much, much, average, less and very less' responses respectively for positive statements. A score of 1, 2, 3, 4 and 5 was given for 'very much, much, average, less and very less' responses respectively for negative statements.

Items analysis was done using chi-square. Items were selected on the basis of significance of values of chi-square which had been calculated to see whether the proportions of responses to various response categories are equally distributed.

The values of chi-square have been presented in the Table 3.4. All the 14 items have been selected because the values of chi-square for each item were found significant at .05 level. Thus, all the 14 items were included in the final form of CAS. Out of the fourteen items, 11 were positive and 3 were negative. It takes approximately 10 minutes to give responses to the final form of CAS.

**Table 3.4: Results of item analysis of CAS**

| Item No. | Response / Attribution | Very Much | Much | Average | Less | Very Less | $X^2$ |
|---|---|---|---|---|---|---|---|
| 1. | Luck | 18 | 17 | 55 | 19 | 21 | 40.78* |
| 2. | Task | 14 | 27 | 54 | 14 | 21 | 42.23* |
| 3. | Ability | 23 | 50 | 36 | 14 | 7 | 45.78* |
| 4. | Luck | 5 | 16 | 17 | 44 | 48 | 55.01* |
| 5. | Ability | 10 | 23 | 29 | 35 | 33 | 15.56* |
| 6. | Effort | 11 | 16 | 32 | 28 | 43 | 25.16* |
| 7. | Spiritual | 48 | 32 | 30 | 12 | 8 | 40.63* |
| 8. | Ability | 7 | 12 | 25 | 38 | 48 | 45.63* |
| 9. | Support | 26 | 28 | 17 | 18 | 36 | 9.58** |
| 10. | Support | 31 | 28 | 17 | 18 | 36 | 10.54* |
| 11. | Support | 2 | 25 | 26 | 25 | 52 | 48.29* |
| 12. | Support | 72 | 32 | 13 | 5 | 8 | 118.7* |
| 13. | Spiritual | 83 | 27 | 16 | 3 | 1 | 173.29* |
| 14. | Effort | 19 | 16 | 56 | 20 | 19 | 43.64* |

*/** Significant at .05/.01 level.

**Reliability and Validity of the Tool**

Test-retest reliability co-efficient has been found to be .61, .56, .58, .46, .55 and .43 for task difficulty, ability, effort, luck, spiritual and support respectively (N=100). Face validity has been found by asking 12 experts related to the field of Education, Psychology and English, to indicate the extent to which the items of the CAS measure attribution for success or failure in English.

## CONSTRUCTION OF ENGLISH LANGUAGE ACHIEVEMENT TEST (ELAT)

For measuring the achievement of students in English an objective type English Language Achievement Test developed by the author was used. This section describes the procedure of constructing and standardising ELAT. As a result of the review of the present status of knowledge, it has been found that most of the achievement tests of English language were made for the students of states other than U. P. The present study is limited to the sample of students studying in schools associated with U. P. Board. So, it becomes necessary for the author to construct an Achievement Test of English Language based on the course prescribed by the U. P. Board for X class.

**Construction of the Tryout Form**

The author has gone through the English language text books of high school level and consulted the teachers of English of schools associated with U. P. Board for deciding the content, objectives and type of questions to be included in the test.

In order to have maximum coverage of the syllabus 14 sub-areas were included and equal weightage was given to each area after consulting the teachers. This has been represented in Table 3.5.

**Table 3.5: Weightage given to various content areas**

| | Areas/Contents | Weightage (%) |
|---|---|---|
| 1. | Pronoun | 7 |
| 2. | Adjective | 7 |
| 3. | Noun | 7 |
| 4. | Verb | 7 |
| 5. | Adverb | 7 |
| 6. | Preposition | 7 |
| 7. | Spelling | 7 |
| 8. | Tenses | 7 |
| 9. | Sentence | 7 |
| 10. | Article | 7 |
| 11. | Translation | 7 |
| 12. | Word-formation | 7 |
| 13. | Active/Passive | 7 |
| 14. | Direct/Indirect | 7 |

As there were 14 areas so in order to have equal weightage 7 per cent was allotted for each areas.

After consulting the English teachers, it was decided that items will be made for knowledge, understanding and application level objectives. It was decided to give equal weightage to questions pertaining to application and knowledge/understanding objectives.

After consulting the teachers teaching English it was decided that three types of items will be prepared i.e. underline (identify), fill in the blanks and multiple choice. 45 per cent weightage was given to fill in the blanks and multiple-choice items and 10 per cent weightage was given to underline type questions.

Keeping in mind the above considerations items were prepared. These items were subjected to evaluation by the author and experts.

**Item Analysis**

For tryout the tool was administered on 130 students (male + female) studying in class XI of D. P. Girl's Inter College and Bharat Scouts and Guide Inter College of Allahabad city.

Achievement Test of English Language (ELAT) was administered in group setting. Responses were given in the booklet itself. Scoring was done by awarding '1' mark for each correct response and '0' for wrong response. After scoring, the tests were arranged in an ascending order of scores on English Language Achievement Test.

27 per cent students (N=130) with their achievement score > 83 were classified as high group while 27 per cent students with achievement scores < 50 were classified as low group. Numbers of correct responses to each item in high and low group were calculated. Difficulty value (D. V.), and discrimination index (D. I.), for each item were calculated by using the following formulae –

$$\text{Difficulty Value} = 100\left(\frac{R_H + R_L}{2n}\right) \text{ where,}$$

$R_H$ – No. of right responses in the high group.
$R_L$ – No. of right responses in the low group.
n – No. of cases in each group.

$$\text{Discrimination Index} = \frac{R_H - R_L}{n} \text{ where,}$$

$R_H$ – No. of right responses in the high group.
$R_L$ – No. of right responses in the low group.
n – No. of cases in each group.

D. V. and D. I. of all the items has been presented in Table 3.6. Items with difficulty value in the range 20 per cent – 80 per cent and discrimination index ranging from .3 to .8 were selected for inclusion in the final form of the ELAT. Table 3.6 shows the D. V. and D. I. of various items –

**Table 3.6: Item analysis of english language achievement test**

| Q. No. | Difficulty Value | Discrimination Index | Item No. in Final Form |
|---|---|---|---|
| 1 | 2 | 3 | 4 |
| 1.1 | 70 | .49 | 51 |
| 1.2 | 57.14 | .51 | 53 |
| 2.1 | 82.86 | .34 | |
| 2.2 | 52.86 | .27 | |
| 2.3 | 17.14 | .06 | |
| 3.1 | 67.14 | .65 | 52 |
| 3.2 | 87.14 | .25 | |
| 3.3 | 81.43 | .37 | |
| 4.1 | 10.71 | .07 | |
| 4.2 | 39.43 | .5 | 56 |
| 5.1 | 31.43 | .28 | |
| 5.2 | 4.28 | –.08 | |
| 5.3 | 60 | .68 | 11 |
| 6.1 | 21.42 | .08 | |
| 6.2 | 14.29 | –.17 | |
| 6.3 | 51.42 | .08 | 54 |
| 6.4 | 44.28 | .31 | 55 |
| 7.1 | 18.15 | .06 | |
| 7.2 | 5.71 | .11 | |
| 7.3 | 2.85 | .05 | |
| 7.4 | 40 | .72 | 42 |
| 7.5 | 53.57 | .64 | 33 |
| 7.6 | 46.43 | .79 | 38 |
| 8.1 | 18.57 | .25 | |
| 8.2 | 37.14 | .62 | 44 |
| 8.3 | 38.57 | .31 | 43 |
| 8.4 | 8.57 | .11 | |

*Contd...*

| 1 | 2 | 3 | 4 |
|---|---|---|---|
| 9.1 | 37.14 | .74 | 45 |
| 9.2 | 21.43 | .38 | 47 |
| 9.3' | 30 | .6 | 50 |
| 9.4 | 0 | 0 | |
| 10.1 | 17.86 | .07 | |
| 10.2 | 53.57 | .73 | 32 |
| 11.1 | 28.57 | .4 | 29 |
| 11.2 | 71.43 | .31 | 26 |
| 11.3 | 62.85 | .68 | 30 |
| 11.4 | 55.71 | .42 | 49 |
| 12.1 | 70 | .02 | |
| 12.2 | 68.57 | .57 | 27 |
| 13.1 | 18.57 | .37 | |
| 13.2 | 42.86 | .43 | 40 |
| 14.1 | 44.29 | .65 | 39 |
| 14.2 | 40 | .74 | 41 |
| 15.1 | 7.14 | .14 | |
| 15.2 | 4.28 | .08 | |
| 15.3 | 17.14 | .17 | |
| 15.4 | 52.85 | .54 | 34 |
| 16.1 | 14.28 | .22 | |
| 16.2 | 17.14 | .28 | |
| 16.3 | 18.57 | .09 | |
| 16.4 | 18.57 | .31 | |
| 17.1 | 61.42 | .54 | 48 |
| 17.2 | 18.57 | .37 | |
| 17.3 | 17.14 | .22 | |
| 17.4 | 51.42 | .62 | 31 |
| 18.1 | 32.14 | .5 | 46 |
| 18.2 | 10.71 | .21 | |
| 19.1 | 4.4 | .23 | |
| 19.2 | 18.57 | .2 | |
| 20.1 | 48.57 | .68 | 37 |

*Contd...*

| 1 | 2 | 3 | 4 |
|---|---|---|---|
| 20.2 | 17.14 | .34 | |
| 20.3 | 11.42 | .22 | |
| 21.1 | 40 | .84 | |
| 21.2 | 54.28 | .91 | |
| 22.1 | 89.29 | .21 | |
| 22.2 | 64.29 | .43 | 28 |
| 22.3 | 75 | .21 | |
| 23.1 | 62.85 | .51 | 8 |
| 23.2 | 34.29 | .23 | |
| 24.1 | 68.57 | .17 | |
| 24.2 | 68.57 | .4 | 5 |
| 25.1 | 75 | .35 | 2 |
| 25.2 | 32.14 | .64 | 23 |
| 26.1 | 47.17 | .25 | |
| 26.2 | 72.85 | .25 | |
| 26.3 | 52.85 | .37 | 14 |
| 26.4 | 71.42 | .22 | |
| 27.1 | 72.85 | .37 | 3 |
| 27.2 | 80 | .34 | 1 |
| 27.3 | 42.85 | -.11 | |
| 27.4 | 41.42 | .14 | |
| 27.5 | 60 | .62 | 9 |
| 28.1 | 31.42 | .17 | |
| 28.2 | 48.57 | .57 | 16 |
| 28.3 | 31.42 | .17 | |
| 29.1 | 64.28 | .42 | 7 |
| 29.2 | 21.42 | .2 | |
| 30.1 | 24.28 | .31 | 25 |
| 30.2 | 55.71 | .48 | 12 |
| 30.3 | 40 | .05 | |
| 30.4 | 30 | .08 | |
| 31.1 | 48.57 | .51 | 17 |
| 31.2 | 41.42 | .31 | 18 |

*Contd...*

| | | | |
|---|---|---|---|
| 31.3 | 67.86 | .5 | 6 |
| 32.1 | 50 | .42 | 15 |
| 32.2 | 40 | .34 | 19 |
| 32.3 | 27.14 | .2 | |
| 32.4 | 38.57 | .2 | |
| 33.1 | 25.71 | 0 | |
| 33.2 | 60 | .68 | 4 |
| 33.3 | 71.42 | .4 | 10 |
| 33.4 | 32.85 | -.02 | |
| 33.5 | 53.57 | .5 | 13 |
| 34.1 | 32.14 | .36 | 22 |
| 34.2 | 18.57 | .2 | |
| 35.1 | 25.71 | .28 | |
| 35.2 | 34.28 | .11 | |
| 36 | 31.42 | 17 | |
| 37 | 20 | 17 | |
| 38.1 | 37.14 | .4 | 21 |
| 38.2 | 31.14 | .57 | 24 |
| 39 | 40 | .45 | 20 |
| 40.1 | 50 | .57 | 36 |
| 40.2 | 44.23 | .82 | |
| 41.1 | 4.28 | .08 | |
| 41.2 | 64.28 | .54 | 35 |
| 42 | 31.42 | .17 | |
| 43 | 20 | .17 | |

Only 56 items have been included in the final form of the achievement test. The test is divided into three sections – A, B and C on the basis of type of items. In each section items were arranged on the basis of descending order of difficulty value *i.e.,* from easy to difficult. Blue print for the ELAT has been given in Table 3.7. It takes approximately 20 minutes to complete the test.

**Reliability and Validity**

Split half reliability and Kuder-Richardson reliability co-efficient of the test have been found to be .85 and .84 respectively (N=100).

Face validity has been found by asking experts belonging to the field of Education and English. Concurrent validity has been found by correlating English Language Achievement Test scores and English marks in U. P. Board High School Examination of the students. It was found to be .50.

**Table 3.7: Consolidated blue print of the english language achievement test**

| Content | | Knowledge + Understanding 50% | | | Application 50% | | |
|---|---|---|---|---|---|---|---|
| | | Under Line 10% | Fill in the Blanks 20% | Multiple Choice 20% | Fill in the Blanks 25% | Multiple Choice 25% | |
| Pronoun | 7% | 2 | | | 2 | | 4 |
| Adjective | 7% | | 2 | | 1 | 1 | 4 |
| Noun | 7% | | 2 | | 1 | 1 | 4 |
| Verb | 7% | 1 | 1 | | 2 | | 4 |
| Adverb | 7% | 1 | | 1 | 1 | 1 | 4 |
| Preposition | 7% | | 1 | 1 | 1 | 1 | 4 |
| Spelling | 7% | 2 | | | 1 | 1 | 4 |
| Tenses | 7% | | 1 | 1 | 1 | 1 | 4 |
| Sentence | 7% | | | 2 | | 2 | 4 |
| Article | 7% | | 2 | | 2 | | 4 |
| Translation | 7% | | | 2 | 1 | 1 | 4 |
| Word formation | 7% | | | 2 | 1 | 1 | 4 |
| Active/Passive | 7% | | 1 | 1 | | 2 | 4 |
| Direct/Indirect | 7% | | 1 | 1 | | 2 | 4 |
| | | 6 | 11 | 11 | 14 | 14 | 56 |

## STATISTICS USED

For the processing of data Stata Graphic software has been used. Step-wise multiple regression analysis has been used to find out the extent to which intelligence, emotional intelligence, formal reasoning, academic motivation, causal attribution and classroom environment can contribute to prediction of variance in achievement in English language among students.

Product moment co-efficients of correlation have been computed to find out the relationship between achievement in English on one hand and intelligence, emotional intelligence, formal reasoning, academic motivation, each factor of causal attribution and each of the 18 dimensions of classroom environment on the other hand. One way ANOVA followed by Multiple Range test has been used for finding out:

1. Whether students with low, moderate or high level of intelligence differ from one another on achievement in English.
2. Whether students with low, moderate or high emotional intelligence differ from one another on achievement in English.
3. Whether students with low, moderate or high level of formal reasoning differ from one another on achievement in English.

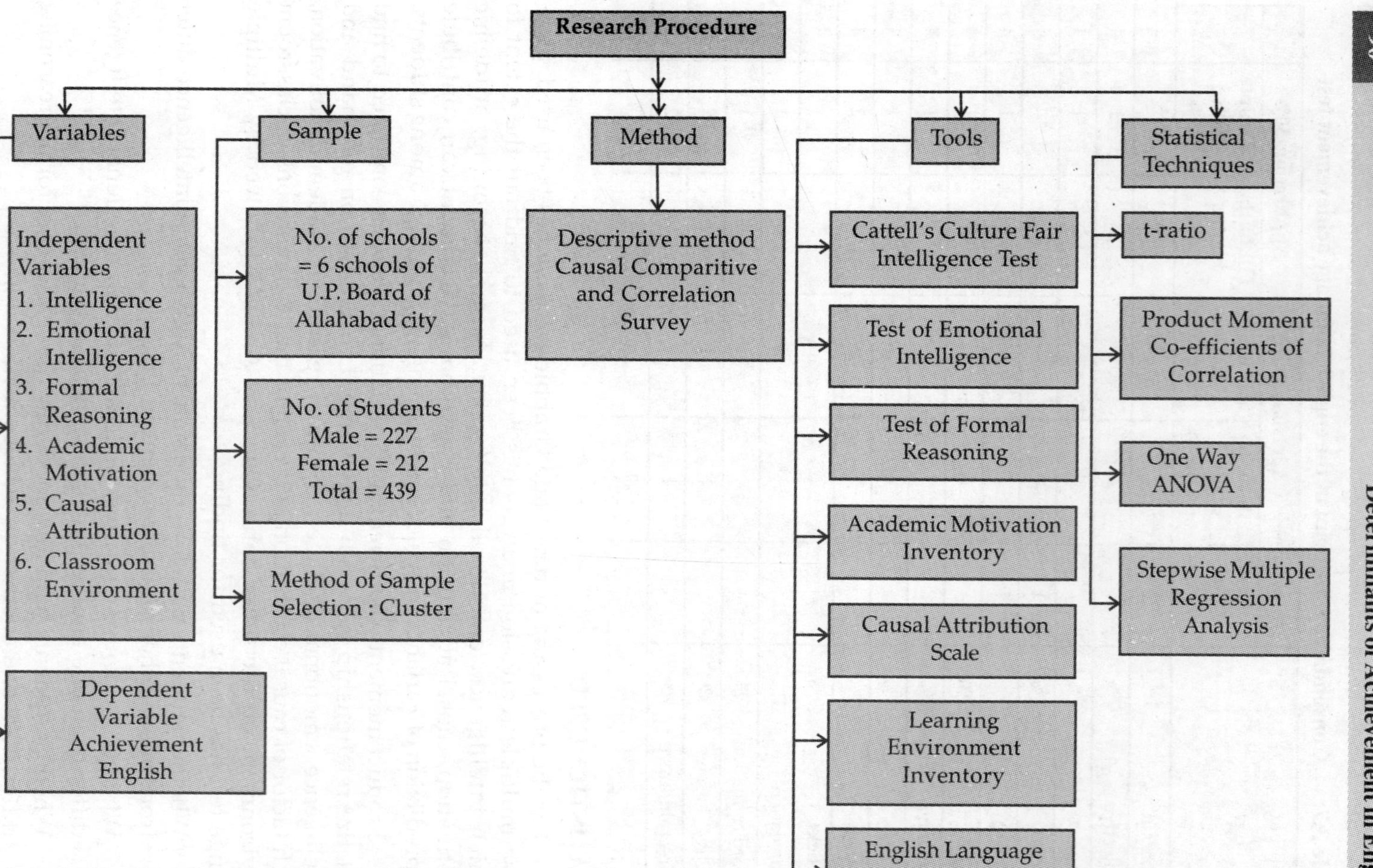


**Fig. 3.2: Research Design for the study**

4. Whether students with low, moderate or high level of academic motivation differ from one another on achievement in English.
5. Whether students with low moderate or high level of causal attribution differ from one another on achievement in English.
6. Whether students perceiving low, moderate or high level of stimulation in classroom environment differ from one another on achievement in English.

t-ratio has been used to find out difference between male and female students on intelligence, emotional intelligence, formal reasoning, academic motivation, causal attribution, classroom environment and achievement in English.

Significance of F-ratio, t-ratio and r was tested at .05 level. Whenever the values of F-ratio, t-ratio and r were found significant at .05 level, the author tried to test their significance at .01 level too.

The design of the present study can be summarised in the Fig. 3.2

CHAPTER

4

# RESULTS AND DISCUSSION

THE PRESENT STUDY was undertaken to compare male and female students on intelligence, emotional intelligence, formal reasoning, academic motivation, causal attribution, perception of classroom learning environment and achievement in English; to study the relationship between achievement in English and intelligence; to study the relationship between achievement in English and emotional intelligence; to study the relationship between achievement in English and formal reasoning; to study the relationship between achievement in English and academic motivation; to study the relationship between achievement in English and causal attributions; to study the relationship between achievement in English and classroom environment; to study achievement in English among students differing with respect to intelligence; to study achievement in English among students differing with respect to emotional intelligence; to study achievement in English among students differing with respect to formal reasoning; to study achievement in English among students differing with respect to academic motivation; to study achievement in English among students differing with respect to causal attribution; to study achievement in English among students perceiving different amount of stimulation in classroom environment; and to find out the extent to which intelligence, emotional intelligence, formal reasoning, academic motivation, causal attribution and classroom environment can predict achievement in English. Sample for the study consisted of 439 students of class XI. T-ratio, product moment co-efficients of correlation, ANOVA and step-wise multiple regression were used to analyse the data. The present chapter deals with the results and discussion part of the research problem.

## RESULTS

### Study of Intelligence, Emotional Intelligence, Formal Reasoning, Academic Motivation, Causal Attributions, Classroom Environment and Achievement in English among Male and Female Students

It was hypothesised that there is no significant difference between male and female students on intelligence, emotional intelligence, formal reasoning, academic motivation, causal attributions, perception of classroom environment and achievement in English.

**Table 4.1: Comparison between male and female students on different variables**

| S. No. | Variables | Male (N=227) | | Female (N=212) | | T-ratio |
|---|---|---|---|---|---|---|
| | | Mean | S.D. | Mean | S.D. | |
| 1 | 2 | 3 | | 4 | | 5 |
| 1. | Intelligence | 16.98 | 5.17 | 15.74 | 5.49 | 2.43* |
| 2. | Emotional intelligence | 20.92 | 5.76 | 19.75 | 5.15 | 2.23* |
| 3. | Formal reasoning | 18.59 | 6.04 | 19.46 | 6.56 | 1.44 |
| 4. | Academic motivation | 213.87 | 25.11 | 214.27 | 20.48 | 0.18 |
| 5. | Ability attribution | 9.56 | 1.74 | 9.74 | 1.82 | 1.05 |
| 6. | Effort attribution | 7.58 | 1.69 | 7.44 | 1.59 | 0.89 |
| 7. | Task difficulty attribution | 3.02 | 1.07 | 3.02 | 1.05 | 0.00 |
| 8. | Luck attribution | 6.84 | 1.65 | 6.39 | 1.63 | 2.87** |
| 9. | Support attribution | 13.22 | 3.44 | 12.40 | 3.65 | 2.42* |
| 10. | Spiritual attribution | 7.51 | 1.96 | 7.82 | 1.85 | 1.70 |
| 11. | Cohesiveness | 27.53 | 4.37 | 27.83 | 3.78 | 0.76 |
| 12. | Diversity | 25.53 | 3.61 | 26.31 | 2.93 | 2.47* |
| 13. | Formality | 27.35 | 4.02 | 27.42 | 4.06 | 0.18 |
| 14. | Speed | 20.70 | 4.38 | 22.38 | 4.02 | 4.17** |
| 15. | Facilitation | 24.92 | 5.04 | 24.35 | 4.92 | 1.19 |
| 16. | Friction | 20.43 | 5.51 | 19.95 | 4.66 | 0.98 |
| 17. | Goal direction | 26.33 | 3.70 | 26.70 | 3.13 | 1.12 |
| 18. | Favouritism | 21.56 | 5.61 | 22.29 | 5.38 | 1.38 |
| 19. | Difficulty | 19.47 | 4.69 | 20.11 | 4.25 | 1.49 |
| 20. | Apathy | 17.84 | 4.80 | 17.30 | 4.09 | 1.26 |
| 21. | Democratic orientation | 24.72 | 4.98 | 25.43 | 4.32 | 1.59 |
| 22. | Cliqueness | 22.32 | 4.53 | 23.32 | 4.57 | 2.30* |
| 23. | Disorganization | 19.29 | 5.13 | 20.16 | 4.86 | 1.82 |

*Contd...*

| 1 . | 2 | 3 | | 4 | | 5 |
|---|---|---|---|---|---|---|
| 24. | Competition | 28.77 | 3.80 | 29.16 | 3.63 | 1.09 |
| 25. | Creative stimulation | 27.52 | 4.19 | 27.18 | 3.94 | 0.87 |
| 26. | Encouragement | 28.61 | 3.97 | 27.87 | 4.11 | 1.91 |
| 27. | Involvement | 28.24 | 4.55 | 27.94 | 4.23 | 0.71 |
| 28. | Conformity | 27.34 | 3.77 | 27.29 | 3.90 | 0.13 |
| 29. | Achievement in English | 28.57 | 10.99 | 27.05 | 12.17 | 1.37 |

*/** Significant at .05/.01 level

From the perusal of the Table 4.1 it is evident that the values of t-ratio are significant for intelligence, emotional intelligence, support attribution and perceived diversity and cliqueness in the classroom ($p<.05$). T-ratios for luck attribution and perceived speed in classroom environment are significant at .01 level. So, it can be inferred that as compared to female students, male students have more intelligence, emotional intelligence, luck attribution and support attribution, and as compared to male students, female students have higher perception of diversity, speed and cliqueness in classroom environment. For the remaining variables *viz.*, achievement in English, formal reasoning, academic motivation, task difficulty, ability, effort and spiritual attributions, and perceived cohesiveness, formality, facilitation, friction, goal direction, favouritism, difficulty, apathy, democratic orientation, disorganization, competition, creative stimulation, encouragement, involvement and conformity in classroom environment, t-ratios are not significant at .05 level. It means that male and female students do not differ from one another on the above mentioned variables.

**Study of Relationship between Achievement in English and Intelligence**

It was hypothesised that there is no significant relationship between achievement in English and intelligence. Product moment co-efficients of correlation have been computed to test this hypothesis. Results have been depicted in Table 4.2.

**Table 4.2: Correlation between achievement in english and intelligence for male and female students**

| S. No. | Groups | N | Values of Correlation |
|---|---|---|---|
| 1. | Male students | 227 | .42** |
| 2. | Female students | 212 | .57** |

** Significant at .01 level

Observation of the Table 4.2 shows that the values of correlation between achievement in English and intelligence for male and female students of class

XI are .42 and .57 respectively and both are significant at .01 level. So, the null hypothesis can be rejected. This means that intelligence is positively related to achievement in English among male and female students.

**Study of Relationship between Achievement in English and Emotional Intelligence**

It was hypothesised that there is no significant relationship between achievement in English and emotional intelligence. Product moment co-efficients of correlation have been computed to test this hypothesis. Results have been depicted in Table 4.3.

**Table 4.3: Correlation between achievement in english and emotional intelligence for male and female students**

| S. No. | Groups | N | Values of Correlation |
|---|---|---|---|
| 1. | Male students | 227 | .22** |
| 2. | Female students | 212 | .09 |

** Significant at .01 level

Observation of the Table 4.3 shows that the values of correlation between achievement in English and emotional intelligence for male and female students of class XI are .22 and .09 respectively. The former is significant at .01 level while the latter is not significant at .05 level. So, it can be inferred that emotional intelligence is positively related to achievement in English among male students, while for the female students emotional intelligence is not related to achievement in English.

**Study of Relationship between Achievement in English and Formal Reasoning**

It was hypothesised that there is no significant relationship between achievement in English and formal reasoning. Product moment co-efficients of correlation have been computed to test this hypothesis. Results have been depicted in Table 4.4.

**Table 4.4: Correlation between achievement in english and formal reasoning for male and female students**

| S. No. | Groups | N | Values of Correlation |
|---|---|---|---|
| 1. | Male students | 227 | .42** |
| 2. | Female students | 212 | .57** |

** Significant at .01 level

Observation of the Table 4.4 shows that the values of correlation between achievement in English and formal reasoning for male and female students of class XI are .42 and .57 respectively and both are significant at .01 level. So, the null hypothesis can be rejected. This means that formal reasoning is positively related to achievement in English among male as well as female students.

**Study of Relationship between Achievement in English and Academic Motivation**

It was hypothesised that there is no significant relationship between achievement in English and academic motivation. Product moment co-efficients of correlation have been computed to test this hypothesis. Results have been depicted in Table 4.5.

**Table 4.5: Correlation between achievement in english and academic motivation for male and female students**

| S. No. | Groups | N | Values of Correlation |
|---|---|---|---|
| 1. | Male students | 227 | .22** |
| 2. | Female students | 212 | .49** |

** Significant at .01 level

From the Table 4.5 it is evident that the values of correlation between achievement in English and academic motivation for male and female students of class XI are .22 and .49 respectively and both are significant at .01 level. So, the null hypothesis can be rejected. This means that academic motivation is positively related to achievement in English among male as well as female students.

**Study of Relationship between Achievement in English and Causal Attributions**

It was hypothesised that there is no significant relationship between achievement in English and causal attributions. This hypothesis has been tested with reference to six dimensions of causal attributions *viz., (i)* task difficulty, *(ii)* ability, *(iii)* effort, *(iv)* luck, *(v)* spiritual and *(vi)* support separately for male and female students. Product moment co-efficients of correlation have been computed to test this hypothesis. Results have been depicted in Table 4.6 to 4.11.

***Study of Relationship between Achievement in English and Task Difficulty Attribution***

It was hypothesised that there is no significant relationship between achievement in English and task difficulty attribution. Product moment co-efficients of correlation have been computed to test this hypothesis. Results have been depicted in Table 4.6.

**Table 4.6: Correlation between achievement in english and task difficulty attribution for male and female students**

| S. No. | Groups | N | Values of Correlation |
|---|---|---|---|
| 1. | Male students | 227 | .05 |
| 2. | Female students | 212 | -.04 |

Observation of the Table 4.6 shows that the values of correlation between achievement in English and task difficulty attribution for male and female students of class XI are .05 and -.04 respectively and both are not significant at .05 level. So, the null hypothesis can be accepted. This means that task attribution is not related to achievement in English among male as well as female students.

***Study of Relationship between Achievement in English and Ability Attribution***

It was hypothesised that there is no significant relationship between achievement in English and ability attribution. Product moment co-efficients of correlation have been computed to test this hypothesis. Results have been depicted in Table 4.7.

**Table 4.7: Correlation between achievement in english and ability attribution for male and female students**

| S. No. | Groups | N | Values of Correlation |
|---|---|---|---|
| 1. | Male students | 227 | -.01 |
| 2. | Female students | 212 | -.08 |

Perusal of the Table 4.7 reveals that the values of correlation between achievement in English and ability attribution for male and female students of class XI are -.01 and -.08 respectively and both are not significant at .05 level. So, the null hypothesis can be accepted. This means that ability attribution is not related to achievement in English among male as well as female students.

***Study of Relationship between Achievement in English and Effort Attribution***

It was hypothesised that there is no significant relationship between achievement in English and effort attribution. Product moment co-efficients of correlation have been computed to test this hypothesis. Results have been depicted in Table 4.8.

**Table 4.8: Correlation between achievement in english and effort attribution for male and female students**

| S. No. | Groups | N | Values of Correlation |
|---|---|---|---|
| 1. | Male students | 227 | .13 |
| 2. | Female students | 212 | .05 |

Observation of Table 4.8 shows that the values of correlation between achievement in English and effort attribution for male and female students of class XI are .13 and .05 respectively and both are not significant at .05 level. So, the null hypothesis can be accepted. This means that effort attribution is not related to achievement in English among male as well as female students.

***Study of Relationship between Achievement in English and Luck Attribution***

It was hypothesised that there is no significant relationship between achievement in English and luck attribution. Product moment co-efficients of correlation have been computed to test this hypothesis. Results have been depicted in Table 4.9.

**Table 4.9: Correlation between achievement in english and luck attribution for male and female students**

| S. No. | Groups | N | Values of Correlation |
|---|---|---|---|
| 1. | Male students | 227 | -.02 |
| 2. | Female students | 212 | -.22** |

** Significant at .01 level

Perusal of the Table 4.9 reveals that the values of correlation between achievement in English and luck attribution for male and female students of class XI are -.02 and -.22 respectively. The former is not significant at .05 level while the latter is significant at .01 level. So, it can be inferred that luck attribution is not related to achievement in English among male students. While for female students luck attribution is negatively related to achievement in English.

***Study of Relationship between Achievement in English and Spiritual Attribution***

It was hypothesised that there is no significant relationship between achievement in English and spiritual attribution. Product moment co-efficients of correlation have been computed to test this hypothesis. Results have been depicted in Table 4.10.

**Table 4.10: Correlation between achievement in english and spiritual attribution for male and female students**

| S. No. | Groups | N | Values of Correlation |
|---|---|---|---|
| 1. | Male students | 227 | -.02 |
| 2. | Female students | 212 | -.07 |

Observation of the Table 4.10 shows that the values of correlation between achievement in English and spiritual attribution for male and female students of class XI are -.02 and -.07 respectively and both are not significant at .05 level. So, the null hypothesis can be accepted. This means that spiritual attribution is not related to achievement in English among male as well as female students.

***Study of Relationship between Achievement in English and Support Attribution***

It was hypothesised that there is no significant relationship between achievement in English and support attribution. Product moment co-efficients of correlation have been computed to test this hypothesis. Results have been depicted in Table 4.11.

**Table 4.11: Correlation between achievement in english and support attribution for male and female students**

| S. No. | Groups | N | Values of Correlation |
|---|---|---|---|
| 1. | Male students | 227 | .03 |
| 2. | Female students | 212 | .03 |

Observation of the Table 4.11 shows that the values of correlation between achievement in English and support attribution for male and female students of class XI are .03 and .03 respectively and both are not significant at .05 level. So, the null hypothesis can be accepted. This means that support attribution is not related to achievement in English among male as well as female students.

To sum up, it can be said that achievement in English is not related to five dimensions of causal attributions *viz.*, *(i)* task difficulty, *(ii)* ability, *(iii)* effort, *(iv)* spiritual and *(v)* support among male as well as female students. Luck is negatively related to achievement in English among female students but it is not related to boys' achievement in English.

**Study of Relationship between Achievement in English and Classroom Environment**

It was hypothesised that there is no significant relationship between achievement in English and classroom environment. This hypothesis has been tested with reference to eighteen dimensions of learning environment in classroom for male and female students separately. Product moment co-efficients of correlation have been computed to test this hypothesis. Results have been shown from Table 4.12 to 4.30.

***Study of Relationship between Achievement in English and Perceived Cohesiveness in Classroom Environment***

It was hypothesised that there is no significant relationship between achievement in English and perceived cohesiveness in classroom environment. Product moment co-efficients of correlation have been computed to test this hypothesis. Results have been depicted in Table 4.12.

**Table 4.12: Correlation between achievement in english and cohesiveness in classroom environment for male and female students**

| S. No. | Groups | N | Values of Correlation |
|---|---|---|---|
| 1. | Male students | 227 | -.06 |
| 2. | Female students | 212 | .10 |

Observation of the Table 4.12 shows that the values of correlation between achievement in English and cohesiveness for male and female students of class XI are -.06 and .10 respectively and both are not significant at .05 level. So, the null hypothesis can be accepted. This means that perceived cohesiveness in classroom environment is not related to achievement in English among male as well as female students.

***Study of Relationship between Achievement in English and Perceived Diversity in Classroom Environment***

It was hypothesised that there is no significant relationship between achievement in English and perceived diversity in classroom environment. Product moment co-efficients of correlation have been computed to test this hypothesis. Results have been depicted in Table 4.13.

**Table 4.13: Correlation between achievement in english and diversity in classroom environment for male and female students**

| S. No. | Groups | N | Values of Correlation |
|---|---|---|---|
| 1. | Male students | 227 | -.04 |
| 2. | Female students | 212 | .25** |

** Significant at .01 level

Observation of the Table 4.13 shows that the values of correlation between achievement in English and diversity for male and female students of class XI are -.04 and .25 respectively. The former is not significant at .05 level while the latter is significant at .01 level. So, it can be inferred that diversity in classroom environment is positively related to achievement in English among female students, while for the male students diversity is not related to achievement in English.

***Study of Relationship between Achievement in English and Perceived Formality in Classroom Environment***

It was hypothesised that there is no significant relationship between achievement in English and perceived formality in classroom environment. Product moment co-efficients of correlation have been computed to test this hypothesis. Results have been depicted in Table 4.14.

**Table 4.14: Correlation between achievement in english and formality in classroom environment for male and female students**

| S. No. | Groups | N | Values of Correlation |
|---|---|---|---|
| 1. | Male students | 227 | .03 |
| 2. | Female students | 212 | .06 |

Observation of the Table 4.14 shows that the values of correlation between achievement in English and formality for male and female students of class XI are .03 and .06 respectively and both are not significant at .05 level. So, the null hypothesis can be accepted. This means that formality in classroom environment is not related to achievement in English among male as well as female students.

***Study of Relationship between Achievement in English and Perceived Speed in Classroom Environment***

It was hypothesised that there is no significant relationship between achievement in English and perceived speed in classroom environment. Product moment co-efficients of correlation have been computed to test this hypothesis. Results have been depicted in Table 4.15.

**Table 4.15: Correlation between achievement in english and speed in classroom environment for male and female students**

| S. No. | Groups | N | Values of Correlation |
|---|---|---|---|
| 1. | Male students | 227 | -.18* |
| 2. | Female students | 212 | -.15* |

* Significant at .05 level

Observation of the Table 4.15 shows that the values of correlation between achievement in English and speed for male and female students of class XI are -.08 and -.15 respectively and both are significant at .05 level. So, the null hypothesis can be rejected. This means that speed in classroom environment is negatively related to achievement in English among male as well as female students.

***Study of Relationship between Achievement in English and Perceived Facilitation in Classroom Environment***

It was hypothesised that there is no significant relationship between achievement in English and perceived facilitation in classroom environment Product moment co-efficients of correlation have been computed to test this hypothesis. Results have been depicted in Table 4.16.

**Table 4.16: Correlation between achievement in english and facilitation in classroom environment for male and female students**

| S. No. | Groups | N | Values of Correlation |
|---|---|---|---|
| 1. | Male students | 227 | -.06 |
| 2. | Female students | 212 | -.02 |

Observation of the Table 4.16 shows that the values of correlation between achievement in English and facilitation for male and female students of class XI are -.06 and -.02 respectively and both are not significant at .05 level. So, the null hypothesis can be accepted. This means that facilitation in classroom environment is not related to achievement in English among male as well as female students.

***Study of Relationship between Achievement in English and Perceived Friction in Classroom Environment***

It was hypothesised that there is no significant relationship between achievement in English and perceived friction in classroom environment. Product moment co-efficients of correlation have been computed to test this hypothesis. Results have been depicted in Table 4.17.

**Table 4.17: Correlation between achievement in english and friction in classroom environment for male and female students**

| S. No. | Groups | N | Values of Correlation |
|---|---|---|---|
| 1. | Male students | 227 | -.14* |
| 2. | Female students | 212 | .05 |

* Significant at .05 level

Observation of the Table 4.17 shows that the values of correlation between achievement in English and friction for male and female students of class XI are -.14 and .05 respectively. The former is significant at .05 level, while the latter is not significant at .05 level. So, it can be inferred that friction in classroom environment is negatively related to achievement in English among male students, while for female students friction is not related to achievement in English.

***Study of Relationship between Achievement in English and Perceived Goal Direction in Classroom Environment***

It was hypothesised that there is no significant relationship between achievement in English and perceived goal direction in classroom environment Product moment co-efficients of correlation have been computed to test this hypothesis. Results have been depicted in Table 4.18.

**Table 4.18: Correlation between achievement in english and goal direction in classroom environment for male and female students**

| S. No. | Groups | N | Values of Correlation |
|---|---|---|---|
| 1. | Male students | 227 | .11 |
| 2. | Female students | 212 | .20** |

** Significant at .01 level

Observation of the Table 4.18 shows that the values of correlation between achievement in English and goal direction for male and female students of class XI are .11 and .20 respectively. The former is not significant at .05 level, while the latter is significant at .01 level. This means that goal direction in classroom environment is positively related to achievement in English among female students, while for male students it is not related to achievement in English.

***Study of Relationship between Achievement in English and Perceived Favouritism in Classroom Environment***

It was hypothesised that there is no significant relationship between achievement in English and perceived favouritism in classroom environment. Product moment co-efficients of correlation have been computed to test this hypothesis. Results have been depicted in Table 4.19.

**Table 4.19: Correlation between achievement in english and favouritism in classroom environment for male and female students**

| S. No. | Groups | N | Values of Correlation |
|---|---|---|---|
| 1. | Male students | 227 | -.05 |
| 2. | Female students | 212 | -.23** |

** Significant at .01 level

Observation of the Table 4.19 shows that the values of correlation between achievement in English and favouritism for male and female students of class XI are -.05 and -.23 respectively. The former is not significant at .05 level, while the latter is significant at .01 level. So, it can be inferred that favouritism in classroom environment is negatively related to achievement in English among female students, while for male students it is not related to achievement in English.

***Study of Relationship between Achievement in English and Perceived Difficulty in Classroom Environment***

It was hypothesised that there is no significant relationship between achievement in English and perceived difficulty in classroom environment. Product moment co-efficients of correlation have been computed to test this hypothesis. Results have been depicted in Table 4.20.

**Table 4.20: Correlation between achievement in english and difficulty in classroom environment for male and female students**

| S. No. | Groups | N | Values of Correlation |
|---|---|---|---|
| 1. | Male students | 227 | -.20** |
| 2. | Female students | 212 | -.23** |

** Significant at .01 level

Observation of the Table 4.20 shows that the values of correlation between achievement in English and difficulty for male and female students of class XI are -.20 and -.23 respectively and both are significant at .01 level. So, the null hypothesis can be rejected. This means that difficulty in classroom environment is negatively related to achievement in English among male as well as female students.

### *Study of Relationship between Achievement in English and Perceived Apathy in Classroom Environment*

It was hypothesised that there is no significant relationship between achievement in English and perceived apathy in classroom environment. Product moment co-efficients of correlation have been computed to test this hypothesis. Results have been depicted in Table 4.21.

**Table 4.21: Correlation between achievement in english and apathy in classroom environment for male and female students**

| S. No. | Groups | N | Values of Correlation |
|---|---|---|---|
| 1. | Male students | 227 | -.16* |
| 2. | Female students | 212 | -.24** |

*/** Significant at .05/.01 level

Observation of the Table 4.21 shows that the values of correlation between achievement in English and apathy for male and female students of class XI are -.16 and .24 respectively. The former is significant at .05 level, while the latter is significant at .01 level. So, the null hypothesis can be rejected. This means that apathy in classroom environment is negatively related to achievement in English among male as well as female students.

### *Study of Relationship between Achievement in English and Perceived Democratic Orientation in Classroom Environment*

It was hypothesised that there is no significant relationship between achievement in English and perceived democratic orientation in classroom environment. Product moment co-efficients of correlation have been computed to test this hypothesis. Results have been depicted in Table 4.22.

**Table 4.22: Correlation between achievement in english and democratic orientation in classroom environment for male and female students**

| S. No. | Groups | N | Values of Correlation |
|---|---|---|---|
| 1. | Male students | 227 | -.07 |
| 2. | Female students | 212 | .10 |

Observation of the Table 4.22 shows that the values of correlation between achievement in English and democratic orientation for male and female students of class XI are -.07 and .10 respectively and both are not significant at .05 level. So, the null hypothesis can be accepted. This means that democratic orientation in classroom environment is not related to achievement in English among male as well as female students.

***Study of Relationship between Achievement in English and Perceived Cliqueness in Classroom Environment***

It was hypothesised that there is no significant relationship between achievement in English and perceived cliqueness in classroom environment Product moment co-efficients of correlation have been computed to test this hypothesis. Results have been depicted in Table 4.23.

**Table 4.23: Correlation between achievement in english and cliqueness in classroom environment for male and female students**

| S. No. | Groups | N | Values of Correlation |
|---|---|---|---|
| 1. | Male students | 227 | -.16* |
| 2. | Female students | 212 | .10 |

* Significant at .05 level

Observation of the Table 4.23 shows that the values of correlation between achievement in English and cliqueness for male and female students of class XI are -.16 and .10 respectively. The former is significant at .05 level, while the latter is not significant at .05 level. So, it can be inferred that cliqueness in classroom environment is negatively related to achievement in English among male students, while for the female students it is not related to achievement in English.

***Study of Relationship between Achievement in English and Perceived Disorganization in Classroom Environment***

It was hypothesised that there is no significant relationship between achievement in English and perceived disorganization in classroom environment. Product moment co-efficients of correlation have been computed to test this hypothesis. Results have been depicted in Table 4.24.

**Table 4.24: Correlation between achievement in english and disorganization in classroom environment for male and female students**

| S. No. | Groups | N | Values of Correlation |
|---|---|---|---|
| 1. | Male students | 227 | -.16* |
| 2. | Female students | 212 | -.12 |

* Significant at .05 level

Observation of the Table 4.24 shows that the values of correlation between achievement in English and disorganization for male and female students of class XI are -.16 and -.12 respectively. The former is significant at .05 level, while the latter is not significant at .05 level. So, it can be inferred that disorganization in classroom environment is negatively related to achievement in English among male students, while for the female students it is not related to achievement in English.

***Study of Relationship between Achievement in English and Perceived Competition in Classroom Environment***

It was hypothesised that there is no significant relationship between achievement in English and perceived competition in classroom environment Product moment co-efficients of correlation have been computed to test this hypothesis. Results have been depicted in Table 4.25.

**Table 4.25: Correlation between achievement in english and competition in classroom environment for male and female students**

| S. No. | Groups | N | Values of Correlation |
|---|---|---|---|
| 1. | Male students | 227 | .12 |
| 2. | Female students | 212 | .11 |

Observation of the Table 4.24 shows that the values of correlation between achievement in English and competition for male and female students of class XI are .12 and .11 respectively and both are not significant at .05 level. So, the null hypothesis can be accepted. This means that competition in classroom environment is not related to achievement in English among male as well as female students.

***Study of Relationship between Achievement in English and Perceived Creative Stimulation in Classroom Environment***

It was hypothesised that there is no significant relationship between achievement in English and perceived creative stimulation in classroom environment. Product moment co-efficients of correlation have been computed to test this hypothesis. Results have been depicted in Table 4.26.

**Table 4.26: Correlation between achievement in english and creative stimulation in classroom environment for male and female students**

| S. No. | Groups | N | Values of Correlation |
|---|---|---|---|
| 1. | Male students | 227 | 0.03 |
| 2. | Female students | 212 | 0.03 |

Observation of the Table 4.26 shows that the values of correlation between achievement in English and creative stimulation for male and female students of class XI are .03 and .03 respectively and both are not significant at .05 level. So, the null hypothesis can be accepted. This means that perceived creative stimulation in the classroom environment is not related to achievement in English among male as well as female students.

***Study of Relationship between Achievement in English and Perceived Encouragement in Classroom Environment***

It was hypothesised that there is no significant relationship between achievement in English and encouragement. Product moment co-efficients of correlation have been computed to test this hypothesis. Results have been depicted in Table 4.27.

**Table 4.27: Correlation between achievement in english and encouragement in classroom environment for male and female students**

| S. No. | Groups | N | Values of Correlation |
|---|---|---|---|
| 1. | Male students | 227 | .12 |
| 2. | Female students | 212 | .17* |

* Significant at .05 level

Observation of the Table 4.27 shows that the values of correlation between achievement in English and encouragement for male and female students of class XI are .12 and .17 respectively. The former is not significant at .05 level while the latter is significant at .05 level. So, it can be inferred that, encouragement in classroom environment is positively related to achievement in English among female students while for male students it is not related to achievement in English.

***Study of Relationship between Achievement in English and Perceived Involvement in Classroom Environment***

It was hypothesised that there is no significant relationship between achievement in English and perceived involvement in classroom environment. Product moment co-efficients of correlation have been computed to test this hypothesis. Results have been depicted in Table 4.28.

**Table 4.28: Correlation between achievement in english and involvement in classroom environment for male and female students**

| S. No. | Groups | N | Values of Correlation |
|---|---|---|---|
| 1. | Male students | 227 | .02 |
| 2. | Female students | 212 | .01 |

Observation of the Table 4.28 shows that the values of correlation between achievement in English and involvement for male and female students of class XI are .02 and .01 respectively and both are not significant at .05 level. So, the null hypothesis can be accepted. This means that involvement in the classroom environment is not related to achievement in English among male as well as female students.

***Study of Relationship between Achievement in English and Perceived Conformity in Classroom Environment***

It was hypothesised that there is no significant relationship between achievement in English and perceived conformity in classroom environment. Product moment co-efficients of correlation have been computed to test this hypothesis. Results have been depicted in Table 4.29.

**Table 4.29: Correlation between achievement in english and conformity for male and female students**

| S. No. | Groups | N | Values of Correlation |
|---|---|---|---|
| 1. | Male students | 227 | -.07 |
| 2. | Female students | 212 | -.09 |

Observation of the Table 4.29 shows that the values of correlation between achievement in English and conformity for male and female students of class XI are -.07 and -.09 respectively and both are not significant at .05 level. So, the null hypothesis can be accepted. This means that conformity in classroom environment is not related to achievement in English among male as well as female students.

To sum up it can be said that among male students achievement in English is negatively related to six dimensions of classroom environment *viz., (i)* speed, *(ii)* friction, *(iii)* difficulty, *(iv)* apathy, *(v)* cliqueness and *(vi)* disorganization, while it is not related to cohesiveness, diversity, facilitation, formality, goal direction, favouritism, democratic orientation, creative stimulation, encouragement, involvement, competition and conformity. For female students achievement in English is positively related to diversity, goal direction and encouragement dimensions of classroom environment while it is negatively related to four dimensions of classroom environment *viz., (i)* speed, *(ii)* favouritism, *(iii)* difficulty and *(iv)* apathy. Achievement in English is not related to cohesiveness, formality, facilitation, friction, democratic orientation, cliqueness, competition, creative stimulation, involvement, conformity and disorganization dimensions of classroom environment.

**Study of Achievement in English among Students with Different Levels of Intelligence**

It was hypothesised that students with high, moderate and low intelligence do not differ from one another in their achievement in English. This hypothesis was tested for male and female students separately. Male students were classified into three groups *viz.*, high, moderate and low intelligence groups on the basis of Mean ± 1 S.D. (Mean = 16.98 and S.D. = [illegible] Male students with intelligence scores ≤ 12 were classified as low intelligence group while those with intelligence scores ≥ 22 were classified as high intelligence group. Male students with intelligence score greater than 12 but less than 22 were included in the group of students with moderate intelligence. ANOVA was used for comparing achievement in English among male students belonging to these three groups. Results have been shown in the Table 4.30.

**Table 4.30: Summary of results of ANOVA showing difference in achievement in english among male students with high, moderate and low level of intelligence**

| Source | df | Sum of Squares | Mean Squares | F-ratio |
|---|---|---|---|---|
| Between group | 2 | 3641.02 | 1820.51 | 17.21** |
| Within group | 224 | 23694.5 | 105.779 | |

** Significant at .01 level

Table 4.30 shows that the value of F-ratio (= 17.21) is significant at .01 level. So, the null hypothesis stands rejected It means that male students with high, moderate and low level of intelligence differ from one another on achievement in English. Further analysis was done by using multiple range test.

**Table 4.31: Results of multiple range test showing difference in achievement in english among male students with high, moderate and low level of intelligence**

| Group No. | Level | Mean | Groups Compared | Difference between Means |
|---|---|---|---|---|
| 1. | Low | 21.12 | 1 and 2 | 7.93** |
| 2. | Moderate | 29.05 | 1 and 3 | 12.61** |
| 3. | High | 33.73 | 2 and 3 | 4.68** |

** Significant at .01 level

Table 4.31 shows that the mean score on achievement in English for male students with low, moderate and high level of intelligence are 21.12, 29.05 and 33.73 respectively. Significant paired comparisons found by using multiple range test show that as compared to male students with low intelligence, male students with moderate and high intelligence have high achievement in English. As compared to male students with moderate intelligence, male students with high intelligence have high achievement in English.

In the case of female students too, three groups were formed on the basis of Mean ± 1 S.D. (Mean = 15.74 and S.D. = 5.49). Female students with intelligence scores ≤ 10 were classified as low intelligence group while those with intelligence scores $\geq 21$ were grouped as high intelligence group. Female students with intelligence score greater than 10 but less than 21 were included in the group of female students with moderate level of intelligence. ANOVA was used for comparing achievement in English among female students belonging to these groups. Results have been shown in the Table 4.32.

**Table 4.32: Summary of results of ANOVA showing difference in achievement in english among female students with high, moderate and low level of intelligence**

| Source | df | Sum of Squares | Mean Squares | F-ratio |
|---|---|---|---|---|
| Between group | 2 | 7454.7 | 3727.35 | 32.67** |
| Within group | 209 | 23846.8 | 114.1 | |

** Significant at .01 level

Observation of the Table 4.32 shows that the value of F-ratio (= 32.67) is significant at .01 level. So, the null hypothesis stands rejected It means that female students with high, moderate and low level of intelligence differ from one another on achievement in English. Further analysis was done by using multiple range test.

**Table 4.33: Results of multiple range test showing difference in achievement in english among female students with high, moderate and low level of intelligence**

| Group No. | Level | Mean | Groups Compared | Difference between Means |
|---|---|---|---|---|
| 1. | Low | 17.6 | 1 and 2 | 9.17** |
| 2. | Moderate | 26.77 | 1 and 3 | 18.33** |
| 3. | High | 36.43 | 2 and 3 | 9.66** |

** Significant at .01 level

Table 4.33 shows that the mean score on achievement in English for female students with low, moderate and high level of intelligence are 17.6, 26.77 and 36.43 respectively. Significant paired comparisons found by using multiple range test show that as compared to female students with low level of intelligence, female students with moderate and high level of intelligence have high achievement in English. As compared to female students with moderate intelligence, female students with high intelligence have high achievement in English.

To sum up, it can be said that as compared to students with low intelligence, students with moderate and high intelligence have high achievement in English and students with high intelligence have high achievement in English than those with moderate intelligence.

**Study of Achievement in English among Students with Different Levels of Emotional Intelligence**

It was hypothesised that students with high, moderate and low emotional intelligence do not differ from one another in their achievement in English. This hypothesis was tested for male and female students separately. Male students were classified into three groups *viz.*, *(i)* high, *(ii)* moderate and *(iii)* low emotional intelligence groups on the basis of Mean ± 1 S.D. (Mean= 20.92 and S.D.= 5.76). Male students with emotional intelligence scores ≤ 15 were classified as those with low emotional intelligence while those with emotional intelligence scores ≥ 27 were classified as male students with high emotional intelligence. Male students with emotional intelligence score greater than 15 but less than 27 were included in the group of male students with moderate emotional intelligence. ANOVA was used for comparing achievement in English among male students belonging to these three groups. Results have been shown in the Table 4.34.

**Table 4.34: Summary of results of ANOVA showing difference in achievement in english among male students with high, moderate and low level of emotion-' intelligence**

| Source | df | Sum of Squares | Mean Squares | F-ratio |
|---|---|---|---|---|
| Between group | 2 | 889.22 | 444.61 | 3.77* |
| Within group | 224 | 26446.3 | 118.06 | |

* Significant at .05 level

Table 4.34 shows that the value of F-ratio (= 3.77) is significant at .05 level. So, the null hypothesis stands rejected. It means that male students with high, moderate and low level of emotional intelligence differ from one another on achievement in English. Further analysis was done by using multiple range test.

**Table 4.35: Results of multiple range test showing difference in achievement in english among male students with high, moderate and low level of emotional intelligence**

| Group No. | Level | Mean | Groups Compared | Difference between Means |
|---|---|---|---|---|
| 1. | Low | 26.46 | 1 and 2 | 1.62 |
| 2. | Moderate | 28.09 | 1 and 3 | 6.46* |
| 3. | High | 32.92 | 2 and 3 | 4.83* |

* Significant at .05 level

Table 4.35 shows that the mean score on achievement in English for male students with low, moderate and high level of emotional intelligence are 26.46, 28.09 and 32.92 respectively. Significant paired comparisons show that as compared to male students with low or moderate emotional intelligence, male students with high emotional intelligence have high achievement in English and male students with low and moderate emotional intelligence do not differ from one another on achievement in English.

In case of female students too, three groups were formed on the basis of Mean ± 1 S.D. (Mean = 19.75 and S.D. = 5.15). Female students with emotional intelligence scores ≤ 15 were included in the low emotional intelligence group while those with emotional intelligence scores ≥ 25 were included in the high emotional intelligence group. Female students with emotional intelligence score greater than 15 but less than 25 were included in the group of female students with moderate level of emotional intelligence. ANOVA was used for comparing achievement in English among female students belonging to these three groups. Results have been shown in the Table 4.36.

**Table 4.36: Summary of results of ANOVA showing difference in achievement in english among female students with high, moderate and low level of emotional intelligence**

| Source | df | Sum of Squares | Mean Squares | F-ratio |
|---|---|---|---|---|
| Between group | 2 | 191.19 | 95.60 | 0.64 |
| Within group | 209 | 31110.3 | 148.85 | |

Mean achievement in English scores of female students with low, moderate and high emotional intelligence were 26.90, 26.48 and 28.93 respectively. Table 4.36 shows that the value of F-ratio (= .64) is not significant at .05 level. So, the null hypothesis can be accepted. It means that female students with high, moderate and low level of emotional intelligence have equal achievement in English.

**Study of Achievement in English among Students with Different Levels of Formal Reasoning**

It was hypothesised that students with high, moderate and low formal reasoning do not differ from one another in their achievement in English. This hypothesis was tested for male and female students separately. Male students were classified into three groups *viz.*, high, moderate and low formal reasoning groups on the basis of Mean ± 1 S.D. (Mean= 18.59 and S.D.= 6.04). Male students with formal reasoning scores ≤ 13 were included in the low formal reasoning group while those with formal reasoning scores ≥ 25 were included in the high formal reasoning group. Male students with formal reasoning score greater than 13 but less than 25 were included in the group of male students with moderate formal reasoning. ANOVA was used for comparing achievement in English among male students belonging to these three groups. Results have been shown in the Table 4.37.

**Table 4.37: Summary of results of ANOVA showing difference in achievement in english among male students with high, moderate and low level of formal reasoning**

| Source | df | Sum of Squares | Mean Squares | F-ratio |
|---|---|---|---|---|
| Between group | 2 | 3795.03 | 1897.51 | 18.06** |
| Within group | 224 | 23540.5 | 105.09 | |

** Significant at .01 level

Table 4.37 shows that the value of F-ratio (= 18.06) is significant at .01 level. So, the null hypothesis stands rejected It means that male students with high, moderate and low level of formal reasoning differ from one another on achievement in English. Further analysis was done by using multiple range test.

**Table 4.38: Results of multiple range test showing difference in achievement in english among male students with high, moderate and low level of formal reasoning**

| Group No. | Level | Mean | Groups Compared | Difference between Means |
|---|---|---|---|---|
| 1. | Low | 20.43 | 1 and 2 | 9.33** |
| 2. | Moderate | 29.76 | 1 and 3 | 13.06** |
| 3. | High | 33.49 | 2 and 3 | 3.73 |

** Significant at .01 level

Table 4.38 shows that the mean score on achievement in English for male students with low, moderate and high level of formal reasoning are 20.43, 29.76 and 33.49 respectively. Significant paired comparisons show that as compared to male students with low level of formal reasoning, male students with moderate or high level of formal reasoning have high achievement in English. Male students with moderate and high level of formal reasoning have equal achievement in English.

In case of female students too, three groups were formed on the basis of Mean ± 1 S.D. (Mean = 19.46 and S. D. = 6.56). Female students with formal reasoning scores ≤ 13 were included in the low formal reasoning group while those with formal reasoning scores ≥ 26 were included in the high formal reasoning group. Female students with formal reasoning score greater than 13 but less than 26 were included in the group of female students with moderate formal reasoning. ANOVA was used for comparing achievement in English among female students belonging to these three groups. Results have been shown in the Table 4.39.

**Table 4.39: Summary of results of ANOVA showing difference in achievement in english among female students with high, moderate and low level of formal reasoning**

| Source | df | Sum of Squares | Mean Squares | F-ratio |
|---|---|---|---|---|
| Between group | 2 | 7805.33 | 3902.66 | 34.71** |
| Within group | 209 | 23496.2 | 112.42 | |

* *Significant at .01 level

Observation of the Table 4.39 shows that the value of F-ratio (= 34.71) is significant at .01 level. So, the null hypothesis can be rejected. It means that female students with high, moderate and low level of formal reasoning differ from one another on achievement in English. Further analysis was done by using multiple range test.

**Table 4.40: Results of multiple range test showing difference in achievement in english among female students with high, moderate and low level of formal reasoning**

| Group No. | Level | Mean | Groups Compared | Difference between Means |
|---|---|---|---|---|
| 1. | Low | 16.23 | 1 and 2 | 12.22** |
| 2. | Moderate | 28.45 | 1 and 3 | 19.09** |
| 3. | High | 35.31 | 2 and 3 | 6.86** |

** Significant at .01 level

· Table 4.40 shows that the mean scores on achievement in English for female students with low, moderate and high level of formal reasoning are 16.23, 28.45 and 35.31 respectively. Significant paired comparisons show that as compared to female students with low formal reasoning, female students with moderate or high formal reasoning have high achievement in English. As compared to female students with moderate formal reasoning, female students with high level of formal reasoning have high achievement in English.

**Study of Achievement in English among Students with Different Levels of Academic Motivation**

It was hypothesised that students with high, moderate and low academic motivation do not differ from one another in their achievement in English. This hypothesis was tested for male and female students separately. Male students were classified into three groups *viz.*, high, moderate and low academic motivation groups on the basis of Mean ± 1 S.D. (Mean = 213.87 and S.D. = 25.11). Male students with academic motivation scores ≤ 189 were classified as low academic motivation male students while those with academic motivation scores ≥ 239 were classified as high academic motivation male students. Male students with academic motivation score greater than 189 but less than 239 were included in the group of male students with moderate academic motivation. ANOVA was used for comparing achievement in English among male students belonging to these three groups. Results have been shown in the Table 4.41.

**Table 4.41: Summary of results of ANOVA showing difference in achievement in english among male students with high, moderate and low level of academic motivation**

| Source | df | Sum of Squares | Mean Squares | F-ratio |
|---|---|---|---|---|
| Between group | 2 | 564.24 | 282.12 | 2.36 |
| Within group | 224 | 26771.3 | 119.52 | |

Mean English achievement scores for male students with low, moderate or high academic motivation were 26.51, 28.41 and 31.58 respectively. Observation of the Table 4.41 shows that the value of F-ratio (= 2.36) is not significant at .05 level. So, the null hypothesis stands accepted. It means that male students with high, moderate and low level of academic motivation have equal achievement in English.

In case of female students too, three groups were formed on the basis of Mean ± 1 S.D. (Mean = 214.27 and S.D. = 20.48). Female students with academic motivation scores ≤ 194 were included in the low academic motivation group while those with academic motivation scores ≥ 235 were grouped as high academic motivation female students. Female students with academic motivation score greater than 194 but less than 235 were included in the group of female students with moderate academic motivation. ANOVA was used for comparing achievement in English among female students belonging to these three groups. Results have been shown in the Table 4.42.

**Table 4.42: Summary of results of ANOVA showing difference in achievement in english among female students with high, moderate and low level of academic motivation**

| Source | df | Sum of Squares | Mean Squares | F-ratio |
|---|---|---|---|---|
| Between group | 2 | 5760.64 | 2880.32 | 23.57** |
| Within group | 209 | 25540.9 | 122.21 | |

** Significant at .01 level

Observation of the Table 4.42 shows that the value of F-ratio (= 23.57) is significant at .01 level. So, the null hypothesis can be rejected. It means that female students with high, moderate and low level of academic motivation differ from one another on achievement in English. Further analysis was done by using multiple range test.

**Table 4.43: Results of multiple range test showing difference in achievement in english among female students with high, moderate and low level of academic motivation**

| Group No. | Level | Mean | Groups Compared | Difference between Means |
|---|---|---|---|---|
| 1. | Low | 17.23 | 1 and 2 | 10.86** |
| 2. | Moderate | 28.09 | 1 and 3 | 16.80** |
| 3. | High | 34.03 | 2 and 3 | 5.94** |

** Significant at .01 level

Table 4.43 shows that the mean scores on achievement in English for female students with low, moderate and high level of academic motivation are 17.23, 28.09 and 34.03 respectively. Significant paired comparisons show that as compared to female students with low academic motivation, female students with moderate or high academic motivation have high achievement in English. As compared to female students with moderate academic motivation, female students with high academic motivation have high achievement in English.

To sum up, it can be said that male students with low, moderate or high academic motivation have equal achievement in English while female students with high academic motivation excel those with low/moderate academic motivation in their achievement in English.

**Study of Achievement in English among Students Differing with Respect to Causal Attributions**

It was hypothesised that students differing with respect to causal attributions do not differ from one another in their achievement in English. This hypothesis has been tested separately for male and female students with reference to six dimensions of causal attribution *viz., (i)* task difficulty, *(ii)* ability, *(iii)* effort, *(iv)* luck, *(v)* spiritual and *(vi)* support. Results have been reported from Table 4.44 to 4.55. For testing this hypothesis with reference to each dimensions of causal attribution, students were classified into three groups *viz.,* low, moderate and high on the basis of Mean ± 1 S.D. on the concerned dimension of causal attribution. ANOVA was used for comparing achievement in English among students belonging to these three groups. Subsequent analysis was done with the help of multiple range test.

***Study of Achievement in English among Students with Different Levels of Task Difficulty Attribution***

It was hypothesised that students with high, moderate and low task difficulty attribution do not differ from one another in their achievement in English. This hypothesis was tested for male and female students separately. Male students were classified into three groups *viz.,* high, moderate and low task difficulty attribution groups on the basis of Mean ± 1 S.D. (Mean = 3.02 and S.D. = 1.07). Male students with task difficulty attribution scores ≤ 2 were classified as low task difficulty attribution students while those with task difficulty attribution scores ≥ 4 were classified as high task difficulty attribution students. Male students with task difficulty attribution score 3 were included in the group of students with moderate level of task difficulty attribution. ANOVA was used for comparing achievement in English among male students belonging to these groups. Results have been shown in the Table 4.44.

**Table 4.44: Summary of results of ANOVA showing difference in achievement in english among male students with high, moderate and low level of task difficulty attribution**

| Source | df | Sum of Squares | Mean Squares | F-ratio |
|---|---|---|---|---|
| Between group | 2 | 23.25 | 11.63 | .10 |
| Within group | 224 | 27312.3 | 121.93 | |

Mean English achievement scores of male students of low, moderate and high groups on task difficulty attribution are 28.11, 28.76 and 28.83 respectively. Table 4.44 shows that the value of F-ratio (= .10) is not significant at .05 level. So, the null hypothesis can be accepted. It means that male students with high, moderate and low level of task difficulty attribution have equal achievement in English.

In case of female students too, three groups were formed on the basis of Mean ± 1 S.D. (Mean = 3.02 and S.D.= 1.05). Female students with task difficulty attribution scores ≤ 2 were included in the low task difficulty attribution group while those with task difficulty attribution scores ≥ 4 were grouped as high task difficulty attribution female students. Female students with task difficulty attribution score of 3 were included in the moderate task difficulty attribution group. ANOVA was used for comparing achievement in English among female students belonging to these three groups. Results have been shown in the Table 4.45.

**Table 4.45: Summary of results of ANOVA showing difference in achievement in english among female students with high, moderate and low level of task difficulty attribution**

| Source | df | Sum of Squares | Mean Squares | F-ratio |
|---|---|---|---|---|
| Between group | 2 | 230.55 | 115.27 | .78 |
| Within group | 209 | 310.71 | 148.67 | |

Mean English achievement scores of female students of low, moderate and high groups on task difficulty attribution are 25.89, 26.81 and 28.38

respectively. Perusal of the Table 4.45 shows that the value of F-ratio (= .78) is not significant at .05 level. So, the null hypothesis stands accepted. It means that female students with high, moderate and low level of task difficulty attribution do not differ from one another on achievement in English.

***Study of Achievement in English among Students with Different Levels of Ability Attribution***

It was hypothesised that students with high, moderate and low ability attribution do not differ from one another in their achievement in English. This hypothesis was tested for male and female students separately. Male students were classified into three groups *viz.*, high, moderate and low ability attribution groups on the basis of Mean ± 1 S.D. (Mean = 9.56 and S.D. = 1.74). Male students with ability attribution scores ≤ 8 were classified as low ability attribution male students while those with ability attribution scores ≥ 11 were classified as high ability attribution male students. Male students with ability attribution score greater than 8 but less than 11 were included in the group of male students with moderate ability attribution. ANOVA was used for comparing achievement in English among male students belonging to these groups. Results have been shown in the Table 4.46.

**Table 4.46: Summary of results of ANOVA showing differences in achievement in english among male students with high, moderate and low level of ability attribution**

| Source | df | Sum of Squares | Mean Squares | F-ratio |
|---|---|---|---|---|
| Between group | 2 | 60 | 30 | .25 |
| Within group | 224 | 27275.6 | 121.77 | |

Mean English achievement scores of male students of low, moderate and high groups on ability attribution are 28.6, 28.97 and 27.71 respectively. Table 4.46 shows that the value of F-ratio (= .25) is not significant at .05 level. So, the null hypothesis can be accepted. It means that male students with high, moderate and low level of ability attribution do not differ from one another on achievement in English.

In case of female students too, three groups were formed on the basis of Mean ± 1 S.D. (Mean = 9.74 and S.D. = 1.82). Female students with ability attribution scores ≤ 8 were included in the low ability attribution group while those with ability attribution scores ≥ 12 were grouped as high ability attribution female students. Female students with ability attribution score greater than 8 but less than 12 were included in the group of female students with moderate level of ability attribution. ANOVA was used for comparing achievement in English among female students belonging to these three groups. Results have been shown in the Table 4.47.

**Table 4.47: Summary of results of ANOVA showing difference in achievement in english among female students with high, moderate and low level of ability attribution**

| Source | df | Sum of Squares | Mean Squares | F-ratio |
|---|---|---|---|---|
| Between group | 2 | 202.12 | 101.06 | .68 |
| Within group | 209 | 31099.4 | 148.80 | |

Mean English achievement scores of female students of low, moderate and high group are 27.70, 27.35 and 24.62 respectively. Table 4.47 shows that the value of F-ratio (= .68) is not significant at .05 level. So, the null hypothesis can be accepted. It means that female students with high, moderate and low level of ability attribution do not differ from one another on achievement in English.

***Study of Achievement in English among Students with Different Levels of Effort Attribution***

It was hypothesised that students with high, moderate and low effort attribution do not differ from one another in their achievement in English. This hypothesis was tested for male and female students separately. Male students were classified into three groups *viz.,* high, moderate and low effort attribution groups on the basis of Mean ± 1 S.D. (Mean = 7.58 and S.D. = 1.69). Male students with effort attribution scores ≤ 6 were classified as low effort attribution male students while those with effort attribution scores ≥ 9 were classified as high effort attribution male students. Male students with effort attribution score greater than 6 but less than 9 were included in the group of male students with moderate effort attribution. ANOVA was used for comparing achievement in English among male students belonging to these three groups. Results have been shown in the Table 4.48.

**Table 4.48: Summary of results of ANOVA showing difference in achievement in english among male students with high, moderate and low level of effort attribution**

| Source | df | Sum of Squares | Mean Squares | F-ratio |
|---|---|---|---|---|
| Between group | 2 | 690.16 | 345.08 | 2.90 |
| Within group | 224 | 26645.4 | 118.95 | |

Mean English achievement scores for low, moderate and high groups of male students are 26.97, 27.73 and 31.14 respectively. Table 4.48 shows that the value of F-ratio (= 2.90) is not significant at .05 level. So, the null hypothesis can be accepted. It means that male students with high, moderate and low level of effort attribution do not differ from one another on achievement in English.

In case of female students too, three groups were formed on the basis of Mean ± 1 S.D. (Mean = 7.44 and S.D. = 1.59). Female students with effort attribution scores ≤ 6 were included in the low effort attribution group while those with effort attribution scores ≥ 9 were included in the as high effort attribution group. Female students with effort attribution score greater than 6 but less than 9 were included in the group of students with moderate effort attribution. ANOVA was used for comparing achievement in English among female students belonging to these groups. Results have been shown in the Table 4.49.

**Table 4.49: Summary of results of ANOVA showing difference in achievement in english among female students with high, moderate and low level of effort attribution**

| Source | df | Sum of Squares | Mean Squares | F-ratio |
|---|---|---|---|---|
| Between group | 2 | 41.71 | 20.85 | .14 |
| Within group | 209 | 31259.8 | 149.57 | |

Mean English achievement scores for low, moderate and high effort attribution are 26.5, 27.01 and 27.67 respectively. Perusal of the Table 4.49 shows that the value of F-ratio (= .14) is not significant at .05 level. So, the null hypothesis stands accepted. It means that female students with high, moderate and low level of effort attribution do not differ from one another on achievement in English.

***Study of Achievement in English among Students with Different Levels of Luck Attribution***

It was hypothesised that students with high, moderate and low luck attribution do not differ from one another in their achievement in English. This hypothesis was tested for male and female students separately. Male students were classified into three groups *viz.,* high, moderate and low luck attribution groups on the basis of Mean ± 1 S.D. (Mean = 6.84 and S.D. = 1.65). Male students with luck attribution scores ≤ 5 were included in the low luck attribution group while those with luck attribution scores ≥ 8 were included in the high luck attribution group. Male students with luck attribution scores ranging between 5 - 8 were included in the group of students with moderate luck attribution. ANOVA was used for comparing achievement in English among male students belonging to these groups. Results have been shown in the Table 4.50. (*See table on next page*)

Mean English achievement scores of male students with low, moderate and high group were 27.52, 29.62 and 27.76 respectively. Observation of the Table 4.50 shows that the value of F-ratio (= .89) is not significant at .05 level. So, the null hypothesis stands accepted. It means that male students with high, moderate and low level of luck attribution have equal achievement in English.

**Table 4.50: Summary of results of ANOVA showing difference in achievement in english among male students with high, moderate and low level of luck attribution**

| Source | df | Sum of Squares | Mean Squares | F-ratio |
|---|---|---|---|---|
| Between group | 2 | 215.44 | 107.72 | .89 |
| Within group | 224 | 27120.1 | 121.07 | |

In case of female students too, three groups were formed on the basis of Mean ± 1 S.D. (Mean = 6.39 and S.D. = 1.63 ). Female students with luck attribution scores ≤ 5 were included in the low group while those with luck attribution scores ≥ 8 were included in the high group. Female students with. luck attribution scores ranging between 5 - 8 were included in the group of students with moderate luck attribution ANOVA was used for comparing achievement in English among female students belonging to these groups. Results have been shown in the Table 4.51.

**Table 4.51: Summary of results of ANOVA showing difference in achievement in english among female students with high, moderate and low level of luck attribution**

| Source | df | Sum of Squares | Mean Squares | F-ratio |
|---|---|---|---|---|
| Between group | 2 | 1686.63 | 843.32 | 5.95** |
| Within group | 209 | 29614.9 | 141.70 | |

**Significant at .01 level

Table 4.51 shows that the value of F-ratio (= 5.95) is significant at .01 level. So, the null hypothesis can be rejected. It means that female students with high, moderate and low level of luck attribution differ from one another on achievement in English. Further analysis was done by using multiple range test.

**Table 4.52: Results of multiple range test showing difference in achievement in english among female students with high, moderate and low level of luck attribution**

| Group No. | Level | Mean | Groups Compared | Difference between Means |
|---|---|---|---|---|
| 1. | Low | 30.57 | 1 and 2 | 3.11 |
| 2. | Moderate | 27.46 | 1 and 3 | 7.62** |
| 3. | High | 22.95 | 2 and 3 | 4.51* |

*/** Significant at .05/.01 level

Table 4.52 shows that the mean English achievement scores for female students with low, moderate and high level of luck attribution are 30.57,

27.46 and 22.95 respectively. Significant paired comparisons show that as compared to female students with high level of luck attribution, female students with low or moderate level of luck attribution have high achievement in English, while female students with low or moderate luck attribution have equal achievement in English.

***Study of Achievement in English among Students with Different Levels of Spiritual Attribution***

It was hypothesised that students with high, moderate and low spiritual attribution do not differ from one another in their achievement in English. This hypothesis was tested for male and female students separately. Male students were classified into three groups *viz.*, high, moderate and low spiritual attribution groups on the basis of Mean ± 1 S.D. (Mean = 7.51 and S.D. = 1.96). Male students with spiritual attribution scores ≤ 6 were classified as low spiritual attribution male students while those with spiritual attribution scores ≥ 9 were classified as high spiritual attribution male students. Male students with spiritual attribution score greater than 6 but less than 9 were included in the group of students with moderate spiritual attribution. ANOVA was used for comparing achievement in English among male students belonging to these groups. Results have been shown in the Table 4.53.

**Table 4.53: Summary of results of ANOVA showing difference in achievement in english among male students with high, moderate and low level of spiritual attribution**

| Source | df | Sum of Squares | Mean Squares | F-ratio |
|---|---|---|---|---|
| Between group | 2 | 50.46 | 25.22 | .21 |
| Within group | 224 | 27285.1 | 121.81 | |

Mean English achievement scores of male students with low, moderate and high spiritual attribution were 28.94, 27.95 and 28.92 respectively. Observation of the Table 4.53 shows that the value of F-ratio (= .21) is not significant at .05 level. So, the null hypothesis can be accepted. It means that male students with high, moderate and low level of spiritual attribution have equal achievement in English.

In case of female students too, three groups were formed on the basis of Mean ± 1 S.D. (Mean = 7.82 and S.D. = 1.85). Female students with spiritual attribution scores ≤ 6 were included in the low spiritual attribution group while those with spiritual attribution scores ≥ 10 were included in the high spiritual attribution female group. Female students with spiritual attribution score greater than 6 but less than 10 were included in the group of female students with moderate spiritual attribution. ANOVA was used for comparing achievement in English among female students belonging to these three groups. Results have been shown in the Table 4.54.

**Table 4.54: Summary of results of ANOVA showing difference in achievement in english among female students with high, moderate and low level of spiritual attribution**

| Source | df | Sum of Squares | Mean Squares | F-ratio |
|---|---|---|---|---|
| Between group | 2 | 18.46 | 9.23 | .06 |
| Within group | 209 | 31283.1 | 149.68 | |

Mean English achievement scores of female students with low, moderate and high spiritual attribution were 26.89, 26.86 and 27.55 respectively. Perusal of the Table 4.54 shows that the value of F-ratio (= .06) is not significant at .05 level. So, the null hypothesis can be accepted. It means that female students with high, moderate and low level of spiritual attribution do not differ from one another on achievement in English.

***Study of Achievement in English among Students with Different Levels of Support Attribution***

It was hypothesised that students with high, moderate and low support attribution do not differ from one another in their achievement in English. This hypothesis was tested for male and female students separately. Male students were classified into three groups *viz.*, high, moderate and low support attribution groups on the basis of Mean ± 1 S.D. (Mean = 13.22 and S.D. = 3.44). Male students with support attribution scores ≤ 10 were included in the low support attribution group while those with support attribution scores ≥ 17 were included in the high support attribution group. Male students with support attribution score greater than 10 but less than 17 were included in the group of students with moderate support attribution group. ANOVA was used for comparing achievement in English among male students belonging to these groups. Results have been shown in the Table 4.55.

**Table 4.55: Summary of results of ANOVA showing difference in achievement in english among male students with high, moderate and low level of support attribution**

| Source | df | Sum of Squares | Mean Squares | F-ratio |
|---|---|---|---|---|
| Between group | 2 | 461.17 | 230.57 | 1.92 |
| Within group | 224 | 26874.4 | 119.58 | |

Mean English achievement scores of male students with low, moderate and high support attribution were 29.60, 27.42 and 30.90 respectively. Table 4.55 shows that the value of F-ratio (= 1.92) is not significant at .05 level. So, the null hypothesis can be accepted. It means that male students with high, moderate and low level of support attribution do not differ from one another on achievement in English.

In case of female students too, three groups were formed on the basis of Mean ± 1 S.D. (Mean = 12.40 and S.D. = 3.65). Female students with support attribution scores ≤ 9 were included in the low support attribution female group while those with support attribution scores ≥ 16 were included in the high support attribution group. Female students with support attribution score greater than 9 but less than 16 were included in the group of female students with moderate support attribution. ANOVA was used for comparing achievement in English among female students belonging to these three groups. Results have been shown in the Table 4.56.

**Table 4.56: Summary of results of ANOVA showing difference in achievement in english among female students with high, moderate and low level of support attribution**

| Source | df | Sum of Squares | Mean Squares | F-ratio |
|---|---|---|---|---|
| Between group | 2 | 209.03 | 104.51 | .70 |
| Within group | 209 | 31092.5 | 148.77 | |

Mean English achievement scores of female students with low, moderate and high support attribution were 26.75, 26.44 and 28.89 respectively. From the observation of the Table 4.56 it is evident that the value of F-ratio (= .70) is not significant at .05 level. So, the null hypothesis can be accepted. It means that female students with high, moderate and low level of support attribution do not differ from one another on achievement in English.

To sum up, it can be said that male and female students with low, moderate or high task difficulty, ability, effort, spiritual and support attribution do not differ from one another on achievement in English. Female students with high luck attribution have low achievement in English in comparison to the female students with low or moderate luck attribution. Male students who attribute their success in English achievement test to their luck in different degrees do not differ from one another on achievement English.

**Study of Achievement in English among Students Perceiving Different Levels of Stimulation in Classroom Environment**

It was hypothesised that students perceiving different amount of stimulation in classroom environment do not differ from one another in their achievement in English. This hypothesis has been tested separately for male and female students with reference to eighteen dimensions of classroom environment *viz.*, *(i)* cohesiveness, *(ii)* diversity, *(iii)* formality, *(iv)* speed, *(v)* facilitation, *(vi)* friction, *(vii)* goal direction, *(viii)* favouritism, *(ix)* difficulty, *(x)* apathy, *(xi)* democratic orientation, *(xii)* cliqueness, *(xiii)* disorganization, *(xiv)* competition, *(xv)* creative stimulation, *(xvi)* encouragement, *(xvii)* involvement and *(xviii)* conformity. Results have been reported in Table 4.57 to 4.102. For testing this hypothesis with reference to each dimension of classroom environment students were classified into three groups *viz.*, low, moderate and high on the basis of Mean ± 1 S.D. of scores on each dimension of classroom environment. ANOVA was used for comparing achievement in English among students belonging to these three groups. Subsequent analysis was done with the help of multiple range test.

***Study of Achievement in English among Students Perceiving Different Levels of Cohesiveness in Classroom Environment***

It was hypothesised that students perceiving high, moderate and low cohesiveness in classroom environment do not differ from one another in their achievement in English. This hypothesis was tested for male and female students separately. Male students were classified into three groups *viz.*, high, moderate and low cohesiveness groups on the basis of Mean ± 1 S.D. (Mean = 27.53 and S.D. = 4.37). Male students with cohesiveness scores ≤ 23 were included in the low cohesiveness group while those with cohesiveness scores ≥ 32 were included in the high cohesiveness group. Male students with cohesiveness score greater than 23 but less than 32 were included in the group of students with moderate cohesiveness. ANOVA was used for comparing achievem :nt in English among male students belonging to these groups. Results have been shown in the Table 4.57.

**Table 4.57: Summary of results of ANOVA showing difference in achievement in english among male students perceiving high, moderate and low level of cohesiveness in classroom environment**

| Source | df | Sum of Squares | Mean Squares | F-ratio |
|---|---|---|---|---|
| Between group | 2 | 1177.96 | 588.98 | 5.04** |
| Within group | 224 | 26157.6 | 116.78 | |

** Significant at .01 level

Table 4.57 shows that the value of F-ratio (= 5.04) is significant at .01 level. So, the null hypothesis stands rejected. It means that male students perceiving high, moderate and low level of cohesiveness in classroom environment differ from one another on achievement in English.

**Table 4.58: Results of multiple range test showing difference in achievement in english among male students perceiving high, moderate and low level of cohesiveness in classroom environment**

| Group No. | Level | Mean | Groups Compared | Difference between Means |
|---|---|---|---|---|
| 1. | Low | 33.55 | 1 and 2 | 6.30* |
| 2. | Moderate | 27.24 | 1 and 3 | 3.06 |
| 3. | High | 30.49 | 2 and 3 | 3.25 |

* Significant at .05 level

Table 4.58 shows that the mean score on achievement in English for male students perceiving low, moderate and high level of cohesiveness in classroom environment are 33.55, 27.24 and 30.49 respectively. Significant paired comparisons show that as compared to male students perceiving moderate cohesiveness in classroom environment, male students perceiving low cohesiveness in classroom environment have high achievement in English. Male students perceiving high cohesiveness in classroom environment do not differ from those perceiving low or moderate cohesiveness on achievement in English.

In case of female students too, three groups were formed on the basis of Mean ± 1 S.D. (Mean = 27.83 and S.D. = 3.78). Female students with cohesiveness scores ≤ 24 were included in the low cohesiveness group while those with cohesiveness scores ≥ 32 were included in the high cohesiveness group. Female students with cohesiveness score greater than 24 but less than 32 were included in the group of female students perceiving moderate cohesiveness in classroom environment. ANOVA was used for comparing achievement in English among female students belonging to these groups. Results have been shown in the Table 4.59.

**Table 4.59: Summary of results of ANOVA showing difference in achievement in english among female students perceiving high, moderate and low level of cohesiveness in classroom environment**

| Source | df | Sum of Squares | Mean Squares | F-ratio |
|---|---|---|---|---|
| Between group | 2 | 227.47 | 75.82 | .51 |
| Within group | 209 | 31074.1 | 149.40 | |

Mean English achievement score of female students of low, moderate and high group are 25.46, 26.99 and 28.94 respectively. Observation of the Table 4.59 shows that the value of F-ratio (= .51) is not significant at .05 level. So, the null hypothesis can be accepted. It means that female students perceiving high, moderate and low cohesiveness in classroom environment do not differ from one another on achievement in English.

***Study of Achievement in English among Students Perceiving Different Levels of Diversity in Classroom Environment***

It was hypothesised that students perceiving high, moderate and low diversity in classroom environment do not differ from one another in their achievement in English. This hypothesis was tested for male and female students separately. Male students were classified into three groups *viz.*, high, moderate and low on the basis of Mean ± 1 S.D. (Mean = 25.53 and S.D. = 3.61). Male students with diversity scores ≤ 22 were included in the low group while those with diversity scores ≥ 29 were included in the high group. Male students with diversity score greater than 22 but less than 29 were included in the group of students perceiving moderate diversity in classroom environment. ANOVA was used for comparing achievement in English among male students belonging to these three groups. Results have been shown in the Table 4.60.

**Table 4.60: Summary of results of ANOVA showing differences in achievement in english among male students perceiving high, moderate and low level of diversity in classroom environment**

| Source | df | Sum of Squares | Mean Squares | F-ratio |
|---|---|---|---|---|
| Between group | 2 | 12.08 | 6.04 | .05 |
| Within group | 224 | 27323.5 | 121.98 | |

Mean English achievement score of male students of low, moderate and high group are 28.71, 28.67 and 28.08 respectively. Table 4.60 shows that the value of F-ratio (= .05) is not significant at .05 level. So, the null hypothesis stands accepted. It means that male students perceiving high, moderate and low level of diversity in classroom environment do not differ from one another on achievement in English.

In case of female students too, three groups were formed on the basis of Mean ± 1 S.D. (Mean = 26.31 and S.D. = 2.93). Female students with diversity scores ≤ 23 were included in the low group while those with diversity scores ≥ 29 were included in the high group. Female students with diversity scores ranging in between 23 and 29 were included in the group of students perceiving moderate level of diversity in classroom environment. ANOVA was used for comparing achievement in English among female students belonging to these three groups. Results have been shown in the Table 4.61.

**Table 4.61: Summary of results of ANOVA showing difference in achievement in english among female students perceiving high, moderate and low level of diversity in classroom environment**

| Source | df | Sum of Squares | Mean Squares | F-ratio |
|---|---|---|---|---|
| Between group | 2 | 1463.02 | 731.51 | 5.12** |
| Within group | 209 | 29838.5 | 142.77 | |

** Significant at .01 level

Table 4.61 shows that the value of F-ratio (= 5.12) is significant at .01 level. So, the null hypothesis stands rejected. It means that female students perceiving high, moderate and low level of diversity in classroom environment differ from one another on achievement in English.

Table 4.62 shows that the mean score on achievement in English for female students perceiving low, moderate and high diversity in classroom environment are 20.45, 28.08 and 28.14 respectively. Significant paired

**Table 4.62: Results of multiple range test showing difference in achievement in english among female students perceiving high, moderate and low level of diversity in classroom environment**

| Group No. | Level | Mean | Groups Compared | Difference between Means |
|---|---|---|---|---|
| 1. | Low | 20.45 | 1 and 2 | 7.63** |
| 2. | Moderate | 28.08 | 1 and 3 | 7.69** |
| 3. | High | 28.14 | 2 and 3 | 0.05 |

** Significant at .01 level

comparisons show that as compared to female students perceiving low diversity in classroom environment, female students perceiving moderate or high level of diversity in classroom environment have high achievement in English. Female students perceiving moderate or high diversity in classroom environment have equal achievement in English.

***Study of Achievement in English among Students Perceiving Different Levels of Formality in Classroom Environment***

It was hypothesised that students perceiving high, moderate and low formality in classroom environment do not differ from one another in their achievement in English. This hypothesis was tested for male and female students separately. Male students were classified into three groups *viz.*, high, moderate and low on the basis of Mean ± 1 S.D. (Mean = 27.35 and S.D. = 4.02). Male students with formality scores ≤ 23 were included in the low group while those with formality scores ≥ 31 were included in the high group. Male students with formality scores ranging between 23 and 31 were included in the group of male students perceiving moderate formality. ANOVA was used for comparing achievement in English among male students belonging to these three groups. Results have been shown in the Table 4.63.

**Table 4.63: Summary of results of ANOVA showing difference in achievement in english among male students perceiving high, moderate and low level of formality in classroom environment**

| Source | df | Sum of Squares | Mean Squares | F-ratio |
|---|---|---|---|---|
| Between group | 2 | 243.95 | 121.97 | 1.01 |
| Within group | 224 | 27091.6 | 120.95 | |

Mean English achievement scores for male students perceiving low, moderate and high formality are 30.17, 28.83 and 29.86 respectively. Table 4.63 shows that the value of F-ratio (= 1.01) is not significant at .05 level. So, the null hypothesis can be accepted. It means that male students perceiving high, moderate and low level of formality in classroom environment do not differ from one another on achievement in English.

In case of female students too, three groups were formed on the basis of Mean ± 1 S.D. (Mean = 27.42 and S.D. = 4.06). Female students with formality scores ≤ 23 were classified as low formality group while those with formality scores ≥ 31 were included in the high formality group. Female students with formality scores ranging from 23 to 31 were included in the group of students perceiving moderate formality in classroom environment. ANOVA was used for comparing achievement in English among female students belonging to these groups. Results have been shown in the Table 4.64.

**Table 4.64: Summary of results of ANOVA showing difference in achievement in english among female students perceiving high, moderate and low level of formality in classroom environment**

| Source | df | Sum of Squares | Mean Squares | F-ratio |
|---|---|---|---|---|
| Between group | 2 | 482.41 | 241.20 | 1.64 |
| Within group | 209 | 30819.1 | 147.46 | |

Mean English achievement score of female students perceiving low, moderate or high formality in classroom environment were 28.5, 25.95 and 29.42 respectively. From the Table 4.64 it is evident that the value of F-ratio (= 1.64) is not significant at .05 level. So, the null hypothesis can be accepted. It means that female students perceiving high, moderate and low formality in classroom environment do not differ from one another on achievement in English.

***Study of Achievement in English among Students Perceiving Different Levels of Speed in Classroom Environment***

It was hypothesised that students perceiving high, moderate and low speed in classroom environment do not differ from one another in their achievement in English. This hypothesis was tested for male and female students separately. Male students were classified into three groups *viz.,* high, moderate and low groups on the basis of Mean ± 1 S.D. (Mean = 20.70 and S.D. = 4.38). Male students with speed scores ≤ 16 were included in the low group while those with speed scores ≥ 25 were included in the high group. Male students with speed scores ranging from 16 to 25 were included in the group of students perceiving moderate speed in classroom environment. ANOVA was used for comparing achievement in English among male students belonging to these three groups. Results have been shown in the Table 4.65. (*See table on next page*)

Table 4.65 shows that the value of F-ratio (= 3.63) is significant at .05 level. So, the null hypothesis can be rejected. It means that male students perceiving high, moderate and low speed in classroom environment differ from one another on achievement in English. Further analysis was done by using multiple range test.

**Table 4.65: Summary of results of ANOVA showing difference in achievement in english among male students perceiving high, moderate and low level of speed in classroom environment**

| Source | df | Sum of Squares | Mean Squares | F-ratio |
|---|---|---|---|---|
| Between group | 2 | 857.75 | 428.88 | 3.63* |
| Within group | 224 | 26477.8 | 118.20 | |

* Significant at .05 level

**Table 4.66: Results of multiple range test showing difference in achievement in english among male students perceiving high, moderate and low level of speed in classroom environment**

| Group No. | Level | Mean | Groups Compared | Difference between Means |
|---|---|---|---|---|
| 1. | Low | 32.78 | 1 and 2 | 5.12* |
| 2. | Moderate | 27.65 | 1 and 3 | 5.03* |
| 3. | High | 27.74 | 2 and 3 | 0.09 |

* Significant at .05 level

Table 4.66 shows that the mean score on achievement in English for male students perceiving low, moderate and high speed in classroom environment are 32.78, 27.65 and 27.74 respectively. Significant paired comparisons show that as compared to male students perceiving low speed in classroom environment, male students perceiving moderate or high speed in classroom environment have low achievement in English. Male students perceiving moderate or high speed in classroom environment have equal achievement in English.

In case of female students too, three groups were formed on the basis of Mean ± 1 S.D. (Mean = 22.38 and S.D. = 4.02). Female students with speed scores ≤ 18 were included in the low group while those with speed scores ≥ 27 were included in the high group. Female students with speed scores ranging from 18 to 27 were included in the group of students perceiving moderate level of speed in classroom environment. ANOVA was used for comparing achievement in English among female students belonging to these groups. Results have been shown in the Table 4.67.

**Table 4.67: Summary of results of ANOVA showing difference in achievement in english among female students perceiving high, moderate and low level of speed in classroom environment**

| Source | df | Sum of Squares | Mean Squares | F-ratio |
|---|---|---|---|---|
| Between group | 2 | 665.66 | 332.83 | 2.27 |
| Within group | 209 | 30635.9 | 146.58 | |

Mean English achievement scores of female students with low, moderate or high perception of speed in classroom environment were 30.75, 26.03 and 27.45 respectively. Observation of the Table 4.67 shows that the value of F-ratio (= 2.27) is not significant at .05 level. So, the null hypothesis can be accepted. It means that female students perceiving high, moderate and low speed in classroom environment do not differ from one another on achievement in English.

***Study of Achievement in English among Students Perceiving Different Levels of Facilitation in Classroom Environment***

It was hypothesised that students perceiving high, moderate and low facilitation in classroom environment do not differ from one another in their achievement in English. This hypothesis was tested for male and female students separately. Male students were classified into three groups *viz,* high, moderate and low perceived facilitation groups on the basis of Mean ± 1 S.D. (Mean = 24.92 and S.D. = 5.04). Male students with perceived facilitation scores ≤ 20 were included in the low group while those with perceived facilitation scores ≥ 30 were classified as high group. Male students with perceived facilitation score greater than 20 but less than 30 were included in the group of students perceiving moderate facilitation in classroom environment. ANOVA was used for comparing achievement in English among male students belonging to these three groups. Results have been shown in the Table 4.68.

**Table 4.68: Summary of results of ANOVA showing difference in achievement in english among male students perceiving high, moderate and low level of facilitation in classroom environment**

| Source | df | Sum of Squares | Mean Squares | F-ratio |
|---|---|---|---|---|
| Between group | 2 | 114.10 | 57.05 | 0.47 |
| Within group | 224 | 27221.4 | 121.52 | |

Mean English achievement scores for male students perceiving low, moderate and high facilitation in classroom environment were 29.67, 29.03 and 29.24 respectively. Table 4.68 shows that the value of F-ratio (= .47) is not significant at .05 level. So, the null hypothesis can be accepted. It means that male students perceiving high, moderate and low facilitation in classroom environment do not differ from one another on achievement in English.

In case of female students too, three groups were formed on the basis of Mean ± 1 S.D. (Mean = 24.35 and S.D. = 4.92). Female students with facilitation scores ≤ 19 were included in the low group while those with facilitation scores ≥ 29 were included in the high group. Female students with facilitation scores ranging between 19 and 29 were included in the group of female students perceiving moderate facilitation in classroom environment. ANOVA was used for comparing achievement in English among female students belonging to these groups. Results have been shown in the Table 4.69.

**Table 4.69: Summary of results of ANOVA showing difference in achievement in english among female students perceiving high, moderate and low level of facilitation in classroom environment**

| Source | df | Sum of Squares | Mean Squares | F-ratio |
|---|---|---|---|---|
| Between group | 2 | 813.49 | 406.75 | 2.79 |
| Within group | 209 | 30488 | 145.88 | |

Mean English achievement scores of female students perceiving low, moderate or high facilitation in classroom environment were 29.68, 25.64 and 29.85 respectively. Perusal of the Table 4.69 shows that the value of F-ratio (= 2.79) is not significant at .05 level. So, the null hypothesis can be accepted. It means that female students perceiving high, moderate and low level of facilitation in classroom environment do not differ from one another on achievement in English.

***Study of Achievement in English among Students Perceiving Different Levels of Friction in Classroom Environment***

It was hypothesised that students perceiving high, moderate and low friction in classroom environment do not differ from one another in their achievement in English. This hypothesis was tested for male and female students separately. Male students were classified into three groups *viz.*, high, moderate and low groups on the basis of Mean ± 1 S.D. (Mean = 20.43 and S.D. = 5.51). Male students with friction scores $\leq 15$ were included in the low group while those with friction scores $\geq 25$ were included in the high group. Male students with friction score greater than 15 but less than 25 were included in the group of students perceiving moderate friction in classroom environment. ANOVA was used for comparing achievement in English among male students belonging to these three groups. Results have been shown in the Table 4.70.

**Table 4.70: Summary of results of ANOVA showing difference in achievement in english among male students perceiving high, moderate and low level of friction in classroom environment**

| Source | df | Sum of Squares | Mean Squares | F-ratio |
|---|---|---|---|---|
| Between group | 2 | 492.59 | 246.29 | 2.06 |
| Within group | 224 | 26843 | 119.84 | |

Mean English achievement scores of male students perceiving low, moderate or high friction in classroom environment are 31.94, 28.05 and 27.65 respectively. From the Table 4.70 it is evident that the value of F-ratio

(= 2.06) is not significant at .05 level. So, the null hypothesis stands accepted. It means that male students perceiving high, moderate and low friction do not differ from one another on achievement in English.

In case of female students too, three groups were formed on the basis of Mean ± 1 S.D. (Mean = 19.95 and S.D. = 4.66). Female students with friction scores ≤ 15 were included in the low group while those with friction scores ≥ 25 were included in the high group. Female students with friction score greater than 15 but less than 25 were included in the group of female students perceiving moderate level of friction in classroom environment. ANOVA was used for comparing achievement in English among female students belonging to these three groups. Results have been shown in the Table 4.71.

**Table 4.71: Summary of results of ANOVA showing difference in achievement in english among female students perceiving high, moderate and low level of friction in classroom environment**

| Source | df | Sum of Squares | Mean Squares | F-ratio |
|---|---|---|---|---|
| Between group | 2 | 164.96 | 82.48 | 0.55 |
| Within group | 209 | 31136.6 | 148.98 | |

Mean English achievement scores of female students perceiving low, moderate or high friction in classroom environment are 25.10, 27.58 and 26.62 respectively. Observation of the Table 4.71 shows that the value of F-ratio (= .55) is not significant at .05 level. So, the null hypothesis can be accepted. It means that female students perceiving high, moderate and low level of friction in classroom environment do not differ from one another on achievement in English.

***Study of Achievement in English among Students Perceiving Different Levels of Goal Direction in Classroom Environment***

It was hypothesised that students perceiving high, moderate and low goal direction in classroom environment do not differ from one another in their achievement in English. This hypothesis was tested for male and female students separately. Male students were classified into three groups *viz.*, high, moderate and low goal direction groups on the basis of Mean ± 1 S.D. (Mean = 26.63 and S.D. = 3.70). Male students with goal direction scores ≤ 23 were included in the low group while those with goal direction scores ≥ 30 were included in the high group. Male students with goal direction score greater than 23 but less than 30 were included in the group of male students perceiving moderate goal direction. ANOVA was used for comparing achievement in English among male students belonging to these three groups. Results have been shown in the Table 4.72.

**Table 4.72: Summary of results of ANOVA showing difference in achievement in english among male students perceiving high, moderate and low level of goal direction in classroom environment**

| Source | df | Sum of Squares | Mean Squares | F-ratio |
|---|---|---|---|---|
| Between group | 2 | 831.63 | 415.81 | 3.51* |
| Within group | 224 | 26503.9 | 118.32 | |

* Significant at .05 level

Table 4.72 shows that the value of F-ratio (= 3.51) is significant at .05 level. So, the null hypothesis stands rejected. It means that male students perceiving high, moderate and low level of goal direction in classroom environment differ from one another on achievement in English.

**Table 4.73: Results of multiple range test showing difference in achievement in english among male students perceiving high, moderate and low level of goal direction in classroom environment**

| Group No. | Level | Mean | Groups Compared | Difference between Means |
|---|---|---|---|---|
| 1. | Low | 30.36 | 1 and 2 | 3.19 |
| 2. | Moderate | 27.17 | 1 and 3 | 1.48 |
| 3. | High | 31.84 | 2 and 3 | 4.67* |

* Significant at .05 level

Table 4.73 shows that the mean score on achievement in English for male students perceiving low, moderate and high goal direction are 30.36, 27.17 and 31.84 respectively. Significant paired comparisons show that as compared to male students perceiving moderate goal direction in classroom environment, male students perceiving high goal direction in classroom environment have high achievement in English. Male students with moderate or high perceived goal direction do not differ from their counterparts perceiving low goal direction on achievement in English.

In case of female students too, three groups were formed on the basis of Mean ± 1 S.D. (Mean = 26.70 and S.D. = 3.13). Female students with goal direction scores ≤ 24 were included in the low group while those with goal direction scores ≥ 30 were included in the high group. Female students with goal direction score greater than 24 but less than 30 were included in the group of students perceiving moderate goal direction in classroom environment. ANOVA was used for comparing achievement in English among female students belonging to these groups. Results have been shown in the Table 4.74.

**Table 4.74: Summary of results of ANOVA showing difference in achievement in english among female students perceiving high, moderate and low level of goal direction in classroom environment**

| Source | df | Sum of Squares | Mean Squares | F-ratio |
|---|---|---|---|---|
| Between group | 2 | 1340.37 | 670.19 | 4.68* |
| Within group | 209 | 29961.2 | 143.36 | |

* Significant at .05 level

Table 4.74 shows that the value of F-ratio (= 4.68) is significant at .05 level. So, the null hypothesis can be rejected. It means that female students perceiving high, moderate and low level of goal direction in classroom environment differ from one another on achievement in English.

**Table 4.75: Results of multiple range test showing difference in achievement in english among female students perceiving high, moderate and low level of goal direction in classroom environment**

| Group No. | Level | Mean | Groups Compared | Difference between Means |
|---|---|---|---|---|
| 1. | Low | 23.77 | 1 and 2 | 3.35 |
| 2. | Moderate | 27.12 | 1 and 3 | 7.97** |
| 3. | High | 31.74 | 2 and 3 | 4.62* |

**/* Significant at .01/.05 level

Table 4.75 shows that the mean score on achievement in English for female students perceiving low, moderate and high level of goal direction in classroom environment are 23.77, 27.12 and 31.74 respectively. Significant paired comparisons show that as compared to female students perceiving low or moderate goal direction in classroom environment, female students perceiving high goal direction in classroom environment have high achievement in English. Male students perceiving low or moderate goal direction in classroom environment do not differ from one another on achievement in English.

***Study of Achievement in English among Students Perceiving Different Levels of Favouritism in Classroom Environment***

It was hypothesised that students perceiving high, moderate and low favouritism in classroom environment do not differ from one another in their achievement in English. This hypothesis was tested for male and female students separately. Male students were classified into three groups *viz.*, high, moderate and low favouritism groups on the basis of Mean ± 1 S.D. (Mean = 21.56 and S.D. = 5.61). Male students with favouritism scores $\leq 16$ were included in the low group while those with favouritism scores $\geq 27$ were included in the high group. Male students with favouritism score greater than 16 but less than 27 were included in the group of male students perceiving moderate favouritism in classroom environment. ANOVA was used for comparing achievement in English among male students belonging to these three groups. Results have been shown in the Table 4.76.

**Table 4.76: Summary of results of ANOVA showing difference in achievement in english among male students perceiving high, moderate and low favouritism in classroom environment**

| Source | df | Sum of Squares | Mean Squares | F-ratio |
|---|---|---|---|---|
| Between group | 2 | 33.17 | 16.89 | 0.14 |
| Within group | 224 | 27302.4 | 121.89 | |

Mean English achievement scores of male students with low, moderate or high perception of favouritism in classroom environment are 29.04, 28.27 and 29.07 respectively. Perusal of the Table 4.76 shows that the value of F-ratio (= .14) is not significant at .05 level. So, the null hypothesis can be accepted. It means that male students perceiving high, moderate and low level of favouritism in classroom environment do not differ from one another on achievement in English.

In case of female students too, three groups were formed on the basis of Mean ± 1 S.D. (Mean = 22.29 and S.D. = 5.38). Female students with favouritism scores ≤ 17 were included in the low group while those with favouritism scores ≥ 28 were included in the high group. Female students with favouritism score greater than 17 but less than 28 were included in the group of students perceiving moderate favouritism in classroom environment. ANOVA was used for comparing achievement in English among female students belonging to these three groups. Results have been shown in the Table 4.77.

**Table 4.77: Summary of results of ANOVA showing difference in achievement in english among female students perceiving high, moderate and low favouritism in classroom environment**

| Source | df | Sum of Squares | Mean Squares | F-ratio |
|---|---|---|---|---|
| Between group | 2 | 1914.77 | 957.39 | 6.81** |
| Within group | 209 | 29386.8 | 140.61 | |

** Significant at .01 level

Observation of the Table 4.77 shows that the value of F-ratio (= 6.81) is significant at .01 level. So, the null hypothesis stands rejected. It means that female students perceiving high, moderate and low level of favouritism in classroom environment differ from one another on achievement in English.

**Table 4.78: Results of multiple range test showing difference in achievement in english among female students perceiving high, moderate and low favouritism in classroom environment**

| Group No. | Level | Mean | Groups Compared | Difference between Means |
|---|---|---|---|---|
| 1. | Low | 32.95 | 1 and 2 | 6.85** |
| 2. | Moderate | 26.10 | 1 and 3 | 9.09** |
| 3. | High | 23.86 | 2 and 3 | 2.24 |

* *Significant at .01 level

Table 4.78 shows that the mean score on achievement in English for female students perceiving low, moderate and high favouritism in classroom environment are 32.95, 26.10 and 23.86 respectively. Significant paired comparisons show that as compared to female students perceiving low favouritism in classroom environment, female students perceiving moderate or high favouritism in classroom environment have less achievement in English. Female students with moderate or high perception of favouritism in classroom environment do not differ from one another on achievement in English.

***Study of Achievement in English among Students Perceiving Different Levels of Difficulty in Classroom Environment***

It was hypothesised that students perceiving high, moderate and low difficulty in classroom environment do not differ from one another in their achievement in English. This hypothesis was tested for male and female students separately. Male students were classified into three groups *viz.*, high, moderate and low difficulty groups on the basis of Mean ± 1 S.D. (Mean = 19.47 and S.D. = 4.69). Male students with difficulty scores ≤ 15 were included in the low group while those with difficulty scores ≥ 24 were included in the high group. Male students with difficulty score greater than 15 but less than 24 were included in the group of male students perceiving moderate difficulty in classroom environment. ANOVA was used for comparing achievement in English among male students belonging to these three groups. Results have been shown in the Table 4.79.

**Table 4.79: Summary of results of ANOVA showing difference in achievement in english among male students perceiving high, moderate and low difficulty in classroom environment**

| Source | df | Sum of Squares | Mean Squares | F-ratio |
|---|---|---|---|---|
| Between group | 2 | 1379.08 | 689.54 | 5.95** |
| Within group | 224 | 25956.5 | 115.88 | |

** Significant at .01 level

Table 4.79 shows that the value of F-ratio (=5.95) is significant at .01 level. So, the null hypothesis stands rejected. It means that male students perceiving high, moderate and low level of difficulty in classroom environment differ from one another on achievement in English.

**Table 4.80: Results of multiple range test showing difference in achievement in english among male students perceiving high, moderate and low difficulty in classroom environment**

| Group No. | Level | Mean | Groups Compared | Difference between Means |
|---|---|---|---|---|
| 1. | Low | 33.18 | 1 and 2 | 5.72** |
| 2. | Moderate | 27.47 | 1 and 3 | 6.43** |
| 3. | High | 26.75 | 2 and 3 | 0.72 |

** Significant at .01 level

Perusal of the Table 4.80 shows that the mean score on achievement in English for male students perceiving low, moderate and high level of difficulty in classroom environment are 33.18, 27.47 and 26.75 respectively. Significant paired comparisons show that as compared to male students perceiving low difficulty in classroom environment, male students perceiving moderate or high difficulty in classroom environment have less achievement in English. Male students perceiving moderate or high level of difficulty in classroom environment do not differ from one another on achievement in English.

In case of female students too, three groups were formed on the basis of Mean ± 1 S.D. (Mean = 20.11 and S.D. = 4.25). Female students with difficulty scores ≤16 were included in the low group while those with difficulty scores ≥ 24 were included in the high group. Female students with difficulty scores ranging between 16 and 24 were included in the group of students perceiving moderate difficulty in classroom environment. ANOVA was used for comparing achievement in English among female students belonging to these groups. Results have been shown in the Table 4.81.

**Table 4.81: Summary of results of ANOVA showing difference in achievement in english among female students perceiving high, moderate and low difficulty in classroom environment**

| Source | df | Sum of Squares | Mean Squares | F-ratio |
|---|---|---|---|---|
| Between group | 2 | 1389.25 | 694.63 | 4.85** |
| Within group | 209 | 29912.3 | 143.12 | |

** Significant at .01 level

Table 4.81 shows that the value of F-ratio (= 4.85) is significant at .01 level. So, the null hypothesis stands rejected. It means that female students perceiving high, moderate and low level of difficulty in classroom environment differ from one another on achievement in English.

**Table 4.82: Results of multiple range test showing difference in achievement in english among female students perceiving high, moderate and low difficulty in classroom environment**

| Group No. | Level | Mean | Groups Compared | Difference between Means |
|---|---|---|---|---|
| 1. | Low | 31.36 | 1 and 2 | 4.42* |
| 2. | Moderate | 26.94 | 1 and 3 | 7.94** |
| 3. | High | 23.41 | 2 and 3 | 3.52 |

**/* Significant at .01/.05 level

Table 4.82 shows that the mean score on achievement in English for female students perceiving low, moderate and high level of difficulty in classroom environment are 31.36, 26.94 and 23.41 respectively. Significant paired comparisons found by using multiple range test show that as compared to female students perceiving low difficulty in classroom environment, female students perceiving moderate or high difficulty in classroom environment have less achievement in English. Female students perceiving moderate or high difficulty in classroom environment have equal achievement in English.

***Study of Achievement in English among Students Perceiving Different Levels of Apathy in Classroom Environment***

It was hypothesised that students perceiving high, moderate and low apathy in classroom environment do not differ from one another in their achievement in English. This hypothesis was tested for male and female students separately. Male students were classified into three groups on the basis of Mean ± 1 S.D. (Mean = 17.84 and S.D. = 4.80). Male students with perceived apathy scores ≤ 13 were included in the low group while those with scores ≥ 23 were included in the high group. Male students with apathy scores ranging between 13 and 23 were included in the group of male students perceiving moderate apathy in classroom environment. ANOVA was used for comparing achievement in English among male students belonging to these three groups. Results have been shown in the Table 4.83.

**Table 4.83: Summary of results of ANOVA showing difference in achievement in english among male students perceiving high, moderate and low apathy in classroom environment**

| Source | df | Sum of Squares | Mean Squares | F-ratio |
|---|---|---|---|---|
| Between group | 2 | 470.81 | 235.40 | 1.96 |
| Within group | 224 | 26864.7 | 119.93 | |

Mean English achievement scores of male students perceiving low, moderate or high apathy in classroom environment were 31.34, 28.21 and 26.95 respectively. From the Table 4.83 it is evident that the value of F-ratio (= 1.96) is not significant at .05 level. So, the null hypothesis can be accepted. It means that male students perceiving high, moderate and low apathy in classroom environment do not differ from one another on achievement in English.

In case of female students too, three groups were formed on the basis of Mean ± 1 S.D. (Mean = 17.30 and S.D. = 4.09). Female students with apathy scores ≤ 13 were included in the low group while those with apathy scores ≥ 21 were included in the high group. Female students with apathy score greater than 13 but less than 21 were included in the group of female students perceiving moderate apathy in classroom environment. ANOVA was used for comparing achievement in English among female students belonging to these groups. Results have been shown in the Table 4.84.

**Table 4.84: Summary of results of ANOVA showing difference in achievement in english among female students perceiving high, moderate and low level of apathy in classroom environment**

| Source | df | Sum of Squares | Mean Squares | F-ratio |
|---|---|---|---|---|
| Between group | 2 | 1518.67 | 759.34 | 5.33** |
| Within group | 209 | 29782.9 | 142.50 | |

** Significant at .01 level

Table 4.84 shows that the value of F-ratio (= 5.33) is significant at .01 level. So, the null hypothesis can be rejected. It means that female students perceiving high, moderate and low apathy in classroom environment differ from one another on achievement in English.

**Table 4.85: Results of multiple range test showing difference in achievement in english among female students perceiving high, moderate and low level of apathy in classroom environment**

| Group No. | Level | Mean | Groups Compared | Difference between Means |
|---|---|---|---|---|
| 1. | Low | 32.30 | 1 and 2 | 6.34** |
| 2. | Moderate | 25.97 | 1 and 3 | 7.26** |
| 3. | High | 25.04 | 2 and 3 | 0.92 |

** Significant at .01 level

Perusal of the Table 4.85 reveals that the mean score on achievement in English for female students perceiving low, moderate and high apathy in classroom environment are 32.30, 25.97 and 25.04 respectively. Significant paired comparisons show that as compared to female students perceiving low apathy in classroom environment, female students perceiving moderate or high apathy in classroom environment have low achievement in English. Female students perceiving moderate or high apathy in classroom environment have equal achievement in English.

***Study of Achievement in English among Students Perceiving Different Levels of Democratic Orientation in Classroom Environment***

It was hypothesised that students perceiving high, moderate and low democratic orientation in classroom environment do not differ from one another in their achievement in English. This hypothesis was tested for male and female students separately. Male students were classified into high, moderate and low democratically oriented groups on the basis of Mean ± 1 S.D. (Mean = 24.72 and S.D. = 4.98). Male students with scores ≤ 20 were included in the low group while those with scores ≥ 30 were included in the high group. Male students with scores ranging between 20 and 30 were included in the group of female students perceiving moderate democratic orientation in the classroom environment. ANOVA was used for comparing achievement in English among male students belonging to these three groups. Results have been shown in the Table 4.86.

**Table 4.86: Summary of results of ANOVA showing difference in achievement in english among male students perceiving high, moderate and low democratic orientation in classroom environment**

| Source | df | Sum of Squares | Mean Squares | F-ratio |
|---|---|---|---|---|
| Between group | 2 | 501.12 | 250.56 | 2.09 |
| Within group | 224 | 26834.4 | 119.80 | |

Mean English achievement scores of male students perceiving low, moderate or high democratic orientation in classroom environment were 31.44, 27.61 and 29.41 respectively. Table 4.86 shows that the value of F-ratio (= 2.09) is not significant at .05 level. So, the null hypothesis can be accepted. It means that male students perceiving high, moderate and low level of democratic orientation in classroom environment do not differ from one another on achievement in English.

In case of female students too, three groups were formed on the basis of Mean ± 1 S.D. (Mean = 25.43 and S.D. = 4.32). Female students with scores ≤ 21 were included in the low group while those with scores ≥ 30 were included in the high group. Female students with scores greater than 21 but less than 30 were included in the group of female students perceiving moderate level of democratic orientation in classroom environment. ANOVA was used for comparing achievement in English among female students belonging to these three groups. Results have been shown in the Table 4.87.

**Table 4.87: Summary of results of ANOVA showing difference in achievement in english among female students perceiving high, moderate and low level of democratic orientation in classroom environment**

| Source | df | Sum of Squares | Mean Squares | F-ratio |
|---|---|---|---|---|
| Between group | 2 | 794.63 | 397.31 | 2.72 |
| Within group | 209 | 30506.9 | 145.97 | |

Mean English achievement scores of female students perceiving low, moderate or high democratic orientation in classroom environment were 25.91, 26.29 and 31.55 respectively. Table 4.87 shows that the value of F-ratio (= 2.72) is not significant at .05 level. So, the null hypothesis stands accepted. It means that female students perceiving high, moderate and low democratic orientation in classroom environment do not differ from one another on achievement in English.

***Study of Achievement in English among Students Perceiving Different Levels of Cliqueness in Classroom Environment***

It was hypothesised that students perceiving high, moderate and low cliqueness in classroom environment do not differ from one another in their achievement in English. This hypothesis was tested for male and female students separately. Male students were classified into three groups *viz.*, high, moderate and low cliqueness groups on the basis of Mean ± 1 S.D. (Mean = 22.32 and S.D. = 4.53). Male students with cliqueness scores ≤ 18 were included in the low group while those with cliqueness scores ≥ 27 were included in the high group. Male students with cliqueness score greater than 18 but less than 27 were included in the group of male students perceiving moderate cliqueness in classroom environment. ANOVA was used for comparing achievement in English among male students belonging to these three groups. Results have been shown in the Table 4.88.

**Table 4.88: Summary of results of ANOVA showing difference in achievement in english among male students perceiving high, moderate and low cliqueness in classroom environment**

| Source | df | Sum of Squares | Mean Squares | F-ratio |
|---|---|---|---|---|
| Between group | 2 | 615.06 | 307.53 | 2.58 |
| Within group | 224 | 26720.5 | 119.29 | |

Mean English achievement scores of male students perceiving low, moderate or high cliqueness in classroom environment were 32.07, 27.85 and 27.61 respectively. Observation of the Table 4.88 shows that the value of F-ratio (= 2.58) is not significant at .05 level. So, the null hypothesis stands accepted. It means that male students perceiving high, moderate and low cliqueness in classroom environment do not differ from one another on achievement in English.

In case of female students too, three groups were formed on the basis of Mean ± 1 S.D. (Mean = 23.32 and S.D. = 4.57). Female students with cliqueness scores ≤ 19 were included in the low group while those with cliqueness scores ≥ 28 were included in the high group. Female students with cliqueness score greater than 19 but less than 28 were included in the group of students perceiving moderate cliqueness in classroom environment. ANOVA was used for comparing achievement in English among female students belonging to these groups. Results have been shown in the Table 4.89.

**Table 4.89: Summary of results of ANOVA showing difference in achievement in english among female students perceiving high, moderate and low cliqueness in classroom environment**

| Source | df | Sum of Squares | Mean Squares | F-ratio |
|---|---|---|---|---|
| Between group | 2 | 516.24 | 258.12 | 1.75 |
| Within group | 209 | 30785.3 | 147.30 | |

Mean English achievement scores of female students perceiving low, moderate or high cliqueness in classroom environment were 26.86, 26.15 and 30.28 respectively. Perusal of the Table 4.89 shows that the value of F-ratio (= 1.75) is not significant at .05 level. So, the null hypothesis can be accepted. It means that female students perceiving high, moderate and low level of cliqueness in classroom environment do not differ from one another on achievement in English.

***Study of Achievement in English among Students Perceiving Different Levels of Disorganization in Classroom Environment***

It was hypothesised that students perceiving high, moderate and low disorganization in classroom environment do not differ from one another in their achievement in English. This hypothesis was tested for male and female students separately. Male students were classified into three groups *viz.*, high, moderate and low disorganization groups on the basis of Mean ± 1 S.D. (Mean = 19.29 and S.D. = 5.13). Male students with disorganization scores ≤ 14 were included in the low group while those with disorganization scores ≥ 24 were included in the high group. Male students with disorganization score greater than 14 but less than 24 were included in the group of students perceiving moderate cliqueness in classroom environment. ANOVA was used for comparing achievement in English among male students belonging to these three groups. Results have been shown in the Table 4.90.

**Table 4.90: Summary of results of ANOVA showing difference in achievement in english among male students perceiving high, moderate and low disorganization in classroom environment**

| Source | df | Sum of Squares | Mean Squares | F-ratio |
|---|---|---|---|---|
| Between group | 2 | 500.50 | 250.25 | 2.09 |
| Within group | 224 | 26835 | 119.80 | |

Mean English achievement scores of male students perceiving low, moderate or high disorganization in classroom environment are 31.76, 27.96 and 27.7 respectively. From the observation of the Table 4.90 it is evident that the value of F-ratio (= 2.09) is not significant at .05 level. So, the null hypothesis can be accepted. It means that male students perceiving high, moderate and low level of disorganization in classroom environment do not differ from one another on achievement in English.

In case of female students too, three groups were formed on the basis of Mean ± 1 S.D. (Mean = 20.16 and S.D. = 4.86). Female students with disorganization scores ≤ 15 were included in the low group while those with disorganization scores ≥ 25 were included in the high group. Female students with disorganization score greater than 15 but less than 25 were included in the group of students perceiving moderate disorganization in classroom environment. ANOVA was used for comparing achievement in English among female students belonging to these three groups. Results have been shown in the Table 4.91.

**Table 4.91: Summary of results of ANOVA showing difference in achievement in english among female students perceiving high, moderate and low level of disorganization in classroom environment**

| Source | df | Sum of Squares | Mean Squares | F-ratio |
|---|---|---|---|---|
| Between group | 2 | 391.37 | 195.68 | 1.32 |
| Within group | 209 | 30910.2 | 147.90 | |

Mean English achievement scores of female students perceiving low, moderate or high disorganization in classroom environment are 30.27, 26.74 and 25.79 respectively Table 4.91 shows that the value of F-ratio (= 1.32) is not significant at .05 level. So, the null hypothesis can be accepted. It means that female students perceiving high, moderate and low disorganization in classroom environment do not differ from one another on achievement in English.

***Study of Achievement in English among Students Perceiving Different Levels of Competition in Classroom Environment***

It was hypothesised that students perceiving high, moderate and low competition in classroom environment do not differ from one another in their achievement in English. This hypothesis was tested for male and female students separately. Male students were classified into three groups on the basis of Mean ± 1 S.D. (Mean = 28.77 and S.D. = 3.80). Male students with competition scores ≤ 25 were included in the low group while those with competition scores ≥ 33 were included in the high group. Male students with competition score greater than 25 but less than 33 were included in the group of students perceiving moderate competition in classroom environment. ANOVA was used for comparing achievement in English among male students belonging to these groups. Results have been shown in the Table 4.92.

**Table 4.92: Summary of results of ANOVA showing differences in achievement in english among male students perceiving high, moderate and low level of competition in classroom environment**

| Source | df | Sum of Squares | Mean Squares | F-ratio |
|---|---|---|---|---|
| Between group | 2 | 535.92 | 267.96 | 2.24 |
| Within group | 224 | 26799.6 | 119.64 | |

Mean English achievement scores of male students perceiving low, moderate or high competition in classroom environment were 27.24, 27.98 and 31.66 respectively. Observation of the Table 4.92 shows that the value of F-ratio (= 2.24) is not significant at .05 level. So, the null hypothesis stands accepted. It means that male students perceiving high, moderate and low competition in classroom environment do not differ from one another on achievement in English.

In case of female students too, three groups were formed on the basis of Mean ± 1 S.D. (Mean = 29.16 and S.D. = 3.63). Female students with competition scores ≤ 25 were included in the low group while those with competition scores ≥ 33 were included in the high group. Female students with competition score greater than 25 but less than 33 were included in the group of students perceiving moderate competition in classroom environment. ANOVA was used for comparing achievement in English among female students belonging to these groups. Results have been shown in the Table 4.93.

**Table 4.93: Summary of results of ANOVA showing difference in achievement in english among female students perceiving high, moderate and low level of competition in classroom environment**

| Source | df | Sum of Squares | Mean Squares | F-ratio |
|---|---|---|---|---|
| Between group | 2 | 877.79 | 438.89 | 3.02 |
| Within group | 209 | 30423.7 | 145.57 | |

Mean English achievement scores of female students perceiving low, moderate or high competition in classroom environment were 22.71, 27.89

and 28.39 respectively. Table 4.93 shows that the value of F-ratio (= 3.02) is not significant at .05 level. So, the null hypothesis can be accepted. It means that female students perceiving high, moderate and low level of competition in classroom environment do not differ from one another on achievement in English.

***Study of Achievement in English among Students Perceiving Different Levels of Creative Stimulation in Classroom Environment***

It was hypothesised that students perceiving high, moderate and low creative stimulation in classroom environment do not differ from one another in their achievement in English. This hypothesis was tested for male and female students separately. Male students were classified into three groups on the basis of Mean ± 1 S.D. (Mean = 27.52 and S.D. = 4.19). Male students with creative stimulation scores ≤ 23 were included in the low group while those with creative stimulation scores ≥ 32 were included in the high group. Male students with creative stimulation score greater than 23 but less than 32 were included in the group of students perceiving moderate creative stimulation in classroom environment. ANOVA was used for comparing achievement in English among male students belonging to these groups. Results have been shown in the Table 4.94.

**Table 4.94: Summary of results of ANOVA showing difference in achievement in english among male students perceiving high, moderate and low level of creative stimulation in classroom environment**

| Source | df | Sum of Squares | Mean Squares | F-ratio |
|---|---|---|---|---|
| Between group | 2 | 788.82 | 394.41 | 3.33* |
| Within group | 224 | 26546.7 | 118.51 | |

* Significant at .05 level

Perusal of the Table 4.94 shows that the value of F-ratio (= 3.23) is significant at .05 level. So, the null hypothesis stands rejected. It means that male students perceiving high, moderate and low creative stimulation in classroom environment differ from one another on achievement in English. Further analysis was done by using multiple range test.

**Table 4.95: Results of multiple range test showing difference in achievement in english among male students perceiving high, moderate and low level of creative stimulation in classroom environment**

| Group No. | Level | Mean | Groups Compared | Difference between Means |
|---|---|---|---|---|
| 1. | Low | 29.25 | 1 and 2 | 1.81 |
| 2. | Moderate | 27.44 | 1 and 3 | 3.07 |
| 3. | High | 32.32 | 2 and 3 | 4.88** |

** Significant at .05 level

Table 4.95 shows that the mean scores on achievement in English for male students with low, moderate and high level of creative stimulation are 29.25, 27.44 and 32.32 respectively. Significant paired comparisons show that as compared to male students perceiving moderate level of creative stimulation in classroom environment, male students perceiving high level of the same have high achievement in English. Male students perceiving low creative stimulation in classroom environment do not differ from those perceiving moderate or high creative stimulation in classroom environment on achievement in English.

In case of female students too, three groups were formed on the basis of Mean ± 1 S.D. (Mean = 27.18 and S.D. = 3.94). Female students with scores ≤ 23 were included in the low group while those with scores ≥ 31 were included in the high group. Female students with creative stimulation score greater than 23 but less than 31 were included in the group of female students perceiving moderate level of creative stimulation in classroom environment. ANOVA was used for comparing achievement in English among female students belonging to these groups. Results have been shown in the Table 4.96.

**Table 4.96: Summary of results of ANOVA showing difference in achievement in english among female students perceiving high, moderate and low level of creative stimulation in classroom environment**

| Source | df | Sum of Squares | Mean Squares | F-ratio |
|---|---|---|---|---|
| Between group | 2 | 172.28 | 86.14 | .58 |
| Within group | 209 | 31129.2 | 148.94 | |

Mean English achievement scores of female students perceiving low, moderate or high creative stimulation in classroom environment were 27.88, 26.36 and 28.4 respectively. Observation of the Table 4.96 shows that the value of F-ratio (= .58) is not significant at .05 level. So, the null hypothesis can be accepted. It means that female students perceiving high, moderate and low creative stimulation in classroom environment do not differ from one another on achievement in English.

***Study of Achievement in English among Students Perceiving Different Levels of Encouragement in Classroom Environment***

It was hypothesised that students perceiving high, moderate and low encouragement in classroom environment do not differ from one another in their achievement in English. This hypothesis was tested for male and female students separately. Male students were classified into three groups on the basis of Mean ± 1 S.D. (Mean = 28.61 and S.D. = 3.97). Male students with encouragement scores ≤ 25 were included in the low group while those with encouragement scores ≥ 33 were included in the high group. Male students with encouragement score greater than 25 but less than 33 were included in the group of students perceiving moderate creative stimulation in classroom environment. ANOVA was used for comparing achievement in English among male students belonging to these three groups. Results have been shown in the Table 4.97.

**Table 4.97: Summary of results of ANOVA showing difference in achievement in english among male students perceiving high, moderate and low level of encouragement in classroom environment**

| Source | df | Sum of Squares | Mean Squares | F-ratio |
|---|---|---|---|---|
| Between group | 2 | 366.64 | 183.32 | 1.52 |
| Within group | 224 | 26968.9 | 120.40 | |

Mean English achievement scores of female students perceiving low, moderate or high encouragement in classroom environment were 27.08, 28.40 and 31.02 respectively. From the Table 4.97 it is evident that the value of F-ratio (= 1.52) is not significant at .05 level. So, the null hypothesis can be accepted. It means that male students perceiving high, moderate and low level of encouragement in classroom environment have equal achievement in English.

In case of female students too, three groups were formed on the basis of Mean ± 1 S.D. (Mean = 27.87 and S.D. = 4.11). Female students with encouragement scores ≤ 24 were included in the low group while those with scores ≥ 32 were included in the high group. Female students with encouragement score greater than 24 but less than 32 were included in the group of students perceiving moderate level of encouragement in classroom environment. ANOVA was used for comparing achievement in English among female students belonging to these groups. Results have been shown in the Table 4.98.

**Table 4.98: Summary of results of ANOVA showing difference in achievement in english among female students perceiving high, moderate and low level of encouragement in classroom environment**

| Source | df | Sum of Squares | Mean Squares | F-ratio |
|---|---|---|---|---|
| Between group | 2 | 410.07 | 205.04 | 1.39 |
| Within group | 209 | 30891.5 | 147.81 | |

Mean English achievement scores of female students perceiving low, moderate or high encouragement in classroom environment are 24.44, 27.43 and 28.64 respectively. Perusal of the Table 4.98 shows that the value of F-ratio (= 1.39) is not significant at .05 level. So, the null hypothesis stands accepted. It means that female students perceiving high, moderate and low encouragement in classroom environment have equal achievement in English.

***Study of Achievement in English among Students Perceiving Different Levels of Involvement in Classroom Environment***

It was hypothesised that students perceiving high, moderate and low involvement in classroom environment do not differ from one another in their achievement in English. This hypothesis was tested for male and female students separately. Male students were classified into three groups on the basis of Mean ± 1 S.D. (Mean = 28.24 and S.D. = 4.55). Male students with involvement scores ≤ 24 were included in the low group while those with involvement scores ≥ 33 were included in the high group. Male students with involvement scores ranging between 24 and 33 were included in the group of students perceiving moderate involvement in classroom environment. ANOVA was used for comparing achievement in English among male students belonging to these three groups. Results have been shown in the Table 4.99.

**Table 4.99: Summary of results of ANOVA showing difference in achievement in english among male students perceiving high, moderate and low level of involvement in classroom environment**

| Source | df | Sum of Squares | Mean Squares | F-ratio |
|---|---|---|---|---|
| Between group | 2 | 258.61 | 129.31 | 1.07 |
| Within group | 224 | 27076.9 | 120.88 | |

Mean English achievement scores of male students perceiving low, moderate or high involvement in classroom environment were 27.93, 28.12 and 30.88 respectively. Observation of the Table 4.99 shows that the value of F-ratio (= 1.07) is not significant at .05 level. So, the null hypothesis can be accepted. It means that male students perceiving high, moderate and low level of involvement in classroom environment do not differ from one another on achievement in English.

In case of female students too, three groups were formed on the basis of Mean ± 1 S.D. (Mean = 27.94 and S.D. = 4.23). Female students with involvement scores ≤ 24 were included in the low group while those with scores ≥ 32 were included in the high group. Female students with scores greater than 24 but less than 32 were included in the group of female students perceiving moderate involvement in classroom environment. ANOVA was used for comparing achievement in English among female students belonging to these groups. Results have been shown in the Table 4.100. (*See table on next page*)

Mean English achievement scores of female students perceiving low, moderate or high involvement in classroom environment were 28, 26.17 and 29.02 respectively. Table 4.100 shows that the value of F-ratio (= 1.01) is not significant at .01 level. So, the null hypothesis can be accepted. It means that female students perceiving high, moderate and low level of involvement in classroom environment do not differ from one another on achievement in English.

**Table 4.100: Summary of results of ANOVA showing difference in achievement in english among female students perceiving high, moderate and low level of involvement in classroom environment**

| Source | df | Sum of Squares | Mean Squares | F-ratio |
|---|---|---|---|---|
| Between group | 2 | 298.19 | 149.10 | 1.01 |
| Within group | 209 | 31003.3 | 148.34 | |

***Study of Achievement in English among Students Perceiving Different Levels of Conformity in Classroom Environment***

It was hypothesised that students perceiving high, moderate and low level of conformity in classroom environment do not differ from one another in their achievement in English. This hypothesis was tested for male and female students separately. Male students were classified into three groups on the basis of Mean ± 1 S.D. (Mean = 27.34 and S.D. = 3.77). Male students with conformity scores ≤ 24 were included in the low group while those with scores ≥ 31 were included in the high group. Male students with conformity scores ranging between 24 and 31 were included in the group of students perceiving moderate level of conformity in classroom environment. ANOVA was used for comparing achievement in English among male students belonging to these groups. Results have been shown in the Table 4.101.

**Table 4.101: Summary of results of ANOVA showing difference in achievement in english among male students perceiving high, moderate and low level of conformity in classroom environment**

| Source | df | Sum of Squares | Mean Squares | F-ratio |
|---|---|---|---|---|
| Between group | 2 | 262.11 | 131.06 | 1.08 |
| Within group | 224 | 27073.4 | 120.86 | |

Mean English achievement scores of male students perceiving low, moderate or high conformity in classroom environment were 29.57, 28.92 and 26.53 respectively. From the Table 4.101 it is evident that the value of F-ratio (= 1.08) is not significant at .05 level. So, the null hypothesis can be accepted and it can be inferred that male students perceiving high, moderate and low level of conformity in classroom environment do not differ from one another on achievement in English.

In case of female students too, three groups were formed on the basis of Mean ± 1 S.D. (Mean = 27.29 and S.D. = 3.90). Female students with conformity scores ≤ 23 were included in the low group while those with scores ≥ 31 were included in the high group. Female students with conformity score greater than 23 but less than 31 were included in the group of female students perceiving moderate conformity in classroom environment. ANOVA was used for comparing achievement in English among female students belonging to these three groups. Results have been shown in the Table 4.102.

**Table 4.102: Summary of results of ANOVA showing difference in achievement in english among female students perceiving high, moderate and low level of conformity in classroom environment**

| Source | df | Sum of Squares | Mean Squares | F-ratio |
|---|---|---|---|---|
| Between group | 2 | 203.75 | 101.87 | .68 |
| Within group | 209 | 31097.8 | 148.79 | |

Mean English achievement scores of female students perceiving low, moderate or high conformity in classroom environment were 29.33, 26.93 and 25.85 respectively. Perusal of the Table 4.102 shows that the value of F-ratio (= .68) is not significant at .05 level. So, the null hypothesis stands accepted. It means that female students perceiving high, moderate and low conformity in classroom environment have equal achievement in English.

To sum up it can be said that, students (both male and female) perceiving low, moderate or high level of formality, facilitation, friction, democratic orientation, cliqueness, disorganization, competition, encouragement, involvement and conformity in classroom environment do not differ from one another on achievement in English. Male students perceiving low, moderate or high level of diversity, favouritism and apathy do not differ from one another on achievement in English. Female students perceiving low, moderate or high level of cohesiveness, speed and creative stimulation in classroom environment do not differ from one another on achievement in English. Students (both male and female) perceiving low, moderate or high level of goal direction and difficulty differ from one another on achievement in English. Male students perceiving different levels of cohesiveness, speed and creative stimulation in classroom environment and female students perceiving different levels of diversity, favouritism and apathy in classroom environment differ from one another on achievement in English.

**Study of Intelligence, Emotional Intelligence, Formal Reasoning, Academic Motivation, Causal Attribution and Classroom Environment as Predictors of Achievement in English**

It was hypothesised that intelligence, emotional intelligence, formal reasoning, academic motivation, causal attribution and classroom environment do not significantly contribute to prediction of achievement in English. This hypothesis was tested separately for male and female students. Step-wise multiple regression analysis was used for testing this hypothesis. To begin with intelligence, emotional intelligence, formal reasoning, academic motivation, six dimensions of causal attribution and eighteen dimensions of classroom environment were used as independent variables for predicting achievement in English. Simplified version has been found by discarding the independent variables on the basis of highest p-value. Results have been shown in Table 4.103 and 4.104.

**Table 4.103: Results of step-wise regression analysis for predicting achievement in english among male students**

| S. No. | Independent Variables | Estimates | |
|---|---|---|---|
| | | Initial Model | Simplified Model |
| 1. | Intelligence | .560 | .651 |
| 2. | Emotional intelligence | .294 | .366 |
| 3. | Formal reasoning | .516 | .503 |
| 4. | Academic motivation | .022 | |
| 5. | Task difficulty | .048 | |
| 6. | Ability | .036 | |
| 7. | Effort | -.218 | |
| 8. | Luck | -.402 | |
| 9. | Spiritual | -.084 | |
| 10. | Support | .008 | |
| 11. | Cohesiveness | -.175 | |
| 12. | Diversity | -.130 | |
| 13. | Formality | .012 | |
| 14. | Speed | -.214 | |
| 15. | Facilitation | -.156 | |
| 16. | Friction | -.347 | -.349 |
| 17. | Goal direction | .557 | .527 |
| 18. | Favouritism | .179 | |
| 19. | Difficulty | -.140 | |
| 20. | Apathy | -.034 | |
| 21. | Democratic orientation | -.284 | -.309 |
| 22. | Cliqueness | -.069 | |
| 23. | Disorganization | .093 | |
| 24. | Competition | .304 | |
| 25. | Creative stimulation | -.061 | |
| 26. | Encouragement | .133 | |
| 27. | Involvement | -.022 | |
| 28. | Conformity | -.496 | -.521 |
| | Constant | 20.497 | 15.689 |
| | F-ratio | 4.56 | 17.22 |
| | R-square | 39.198 | 35.499 |

Observation of the Table 4.103 shows that for male students, $R^2$ value is 39.198. It means that all independent variables taken together explain 39.198 per cent of the variance in achievement in English among male students. The value of F-ratio is 4.56 ($p<.01$) and the value of constant is 20.497. The regression equation at the initial stage can be written as:

Achievement in English = 20.497 +0.560 intelligence +0.294 emotional intelligence +0.516 formal reasoning +0.022 academic motivation +0.048 task difficulty attribution +0.036 ability attribution -0.218 effort attribution -0.402 luck attribution -0.084 spiritual attribution +0.008 support attribution -0.175 cohesiveness -0.130 diversity +0.012 formality -0.214 speed -0.156 facilitation -0.347 friction +0.557 goal direction +0.179 favouritism -0.140 difficulty -0.034 apathy -0.284 democratic orientation -0.069 cliqueness +0.093 disorganization +0.304 competition -0.061 creative stimulation +0.133 encouragement -0.022 involvement -0.496 conformity.

In the final simplified version, it was found that the value of constant is 15.689 and intelligence, emotional intelligence, formal reasoning, friction, goal direction, democratic orientation and conformity can contribute to prediction of achievement in English among male students of class XI. Regression equation for the final model can be written as follows:

Achievement in English = 15.689 + 0.651 intelligence + 0.366 emotional intelligence +0.503 formal reasoning -0.349 friction +0.527 goal direction -0.309 democratic orientation -0.521 conformity.

The value of $R^2$ is 35.499. It means that intelligence, emotional intelligence, formal reasoning, perceived friction, goal direction, democratic orientation, and conformity in classroom environment can explain 35.499 per cent of variance in achievement in English among male students of class XI (F-ratio = 17.22, $p<.01$).

Observation of the Table 4.104 shows that for female students, $R^2$ value is 58.220. It means that all independent variables can explain 58.22 per cent of the variance in achievement in English among female students. The value of F-ratio is 9.11 ($p<.01$) and the value of constant is -21.63. The regression equation at the initial stage can be written as: (*See table on next page*)

Achievement in English = -21.63 +0.717 intelligence +0.076 emotional intelligence +0.546 formal reasoning +0.122 academic motivation -0.780 task difficulty attribution -0.706 ability attribution -0.268 effort attribution -0.296 luck attribution -0.494 spiritual attribution +0.070 support attribution +0.051 cohesiveness +0.110 diversity +0.215 formality +0.180 speed -0.044 facilitation +0.381 friction +0.384 goal direction -0.261 favouritism -0.072 difficulty -0.151 apathy +0.093 democratic orientation +0.231 cliqueness -0.216 disorganization -0.188 competition -0.109 creative stimulation +0.198 encouragement -0.263 involvement -0.250 conformity.

**Table 4.104: Results of step-wise regression analysis for predicting achievement in english among female students**

| S. No. | Independent Variables | Estimates | |
|---|---|---|---|
| | | Initial Model | Simplified Model |
| 1. | Intelligence | 0.717 | 0.736 |
| 2. | Emotional intelligence | 0.076 | |
| 3. | Formal reasoning | 0.546 | 0.551 |
| 4. | Academic motivation | 0.122 | 0.155 |
| 5. | Task difficulty | -0.780 | |
| 6. | Ability | -0.706 | |
| 7. | Effort | -0.268 | |
| 8. | Luck | -0.296 | |
| 9. | Spiritual | 0.494 | |
| 10. | Support | 0.070 | |
| 11. | Cohesiveness | 0.051 | |
| 12. | Diversity | 0.110 | |
| 13. | Formality | 0.215 | |
| 14. | Speed | 0.180 | |
| 15. | Facilitation | -0.044 | |
| 16. | Friction | 0.381 | 0.527 |
| 17. | Goal direction | 0.384 | |
| 18. | Favouritism | -0.261 | -0.312 |
| 19. | Difficulty | -0.072 | |
| 20. | Apathy | -0.151 | |
| 21. | Democratic orientation | 0.093 | |
| 22. | Cliqueness | 0.231 | |
| 23. | Disorganization | -0.216 | |
| 24. | Competition | -0.188 | |
| 25. | Creative stimulation | -0.109 | |
| 26. | Encouragement | 0.198 | |
| 27. | Involvement | -0.263 | |
| 28. | Conformity | -0.250 | |
| | Constant | -21.630 | -32.108 |
| | F-ratio | 9.11 | 46.14 |
| | R-square | 58.220 | 52.829 |

In the final simplified version, it was found that the value of constant is -32.108 and intelligence, formal reasoning, academic motivation, friction, and favouritism emerged as the best predictors of achievement in English among female students of class XI. Regression equation for the final model can be written as:

Achievement in English = -32.108 + 0.736 intelligence +0.551 formal reasoning +0.155 academic motivation +0.527 friction -0.312 favouritism.

The value of $R^2$ is 52.829. It means that intelligence, formal reasoning, academic motivation and perceived friction and favouritism in classroom environment can explain 52.829 per cent of variance in achievement in English among female students of class XI (F-ratio = 46.14, p<.01).

## DISCUSSION

### Study of Intelligence, Emotional Intelligence, Formal Reasoning, Academic Motivation, Causal Attribution, Classroom Environment and Achievement in English among Male and Female Students

T-ratios related to differences among male and female students on intelligence, emotional intelligence, formal reasoning, academic motivation, causal attribution, classroom environment and achievement in English have shown that male and female students do not differ from one another on achievement in English, formal reasoning ability, academic motivation, task difficulty, ability, effort and spiritual attribution and perceived cohesiveness, formality, facilitation, friction, goal direction, favouritism, difficulty, apathy, democratic orientation, disorganization, competition, creative stimulation, encouragement, involvement and conformity in classroom environment. So, it can be inferred that male and female students are equal so far as their achievement in English, formal reasoning, academic motivation, task difficulty, ability, effort and spiritual attribution are concerned. Male and female students perceive equal amount of cohesiveness, formality, facilitation, friction, goal direction, favouritism, difficulty, apathy, democratic orientation, disorganization, competition, creative stimulation, encouragement, involvement and conformity in classroom environment. This may be due to the reason that formal reasoning ability develops in adolescent age after the concrete operational stage and both male and female students have passed the former stage and both have similar pattern of growth. Both male and female students have equal academic motivation *i.e.*, equal aspiration to achieve higher marks in English, equal favourable attitude towards learning English and similar study habits for learning English. Similar were the findings of Rani and Kaushik (2005), Varma (2003), Behera (2002), Upadhyaya (2000), Pillai and Salimkumar (1995) and Benno (1995. However, findings of Green Demers *et al.* (2008), Ellekkakumar and Elankathirselvan (2001), Mahapatra (1998), Meena Rani (1992), Ayishabi (1990), Gawande (1988), Mian (1988) and Chaudhary (1971) are contradictory to our finding. Both male and female students equally attribute their success in English to task difficulty, ability, effort and spiritual aspect. The finding that male and female students do not differ from one another on task difficulty, ability, effort and spiritual attribution is in contradiction with the findings of Jha (2008), Chan and Youlden (1995), Rosenfield and Stephan (1978), Stephan, Rosenfield and Stephan (1976), Levine *et al.* (1976) and Nicholls (1975). Jha reported significant difference between male and female students with respect to ability and effort attribution. Chan and Youlden found that girls attribute success more to effort than boys. Rosenfield and Stephan, Stephan, Rosenfield and Stephan, Levine *et al.*, and Nicholls found that as compared to females, males tend to attribute success more internally and failure more externally. Finding of Rusillo and Arias (2004) lend support to the above finding. They also reported that boys and girls equally attribute their success to internal factors such as effort and ability. Attributional studies have indicated that males tend to attribute their success to internal, stable causes while the females take personal responsibility for failures and external attribution for success (Smith, Sinclair and Chapman, 2002; Bar-Tal, 1978; and Weiner, 1974). The finding that male and female students have equal achievement in English is supported by the findings of Kumar and Ambedkar (2005), Srivastava (1995), Mazumdar (1992), Sankarappan (1992), Dey (1991), Singh (1989), Chakravorti (1988) and Patil (1985). They found that male and female students do not differ from one another on their achievement in English. According to Chandra (1988), achievement in English is not related to gender. Kakkar (1975) also found that sex does not make a difference in the achievement in English. Both male and female students have same interest, attitude, motivation and study habits towards learning English. However, contrary findings are of Tourani (2006), Deary, Strand, Smith and Fernandes (2007), Rusillo and Arias (2004), Kim (2001), Upadhyaya (2000), Bhatnagar (1999), Visvesvaran (1975), and Terman and Tyler (1954) who found that female students have higher achievement in English in comparison to their male counterparts. Bag (1990) and Khan (1989) found that achievement in English is higher among male students as compared to female students. Mehrotra and Nigam (2008), Singh (2008b), Dwivedi (2005), and Misra (2002) had also tried to study gender differences in perception of classroom climate. Mehrotra and Nigam reported that boys and girls perceive equal creative stimulation. According to Singh, male and female students perceived equal difficulty in their classroom climate. However, she also reported that as compared to female students, male students perceived more cohesiveness, friction, favouritism, apathy and disorganization. As compared to male students, female students perceived more formality, facilitation, goal direction, democratic orientation, competition, creative stimulation, encouragement, involvement and conformity. The study conducted by Dwivedi also revealed that male and female students of U.P. Board affiliated schools have equal perception of cohesiveness, formality, facilitation, friction, goal direction difficulty, apathy, democratic orientation disorganization, competition, creative stimulation, encouragement, involvement and conformity in their classroom. However, he found that as compared to girls, boys perceive less favouritism in their classroom. Misra also found boys and girls perceive equal amounts of cohesiveness, formality, facilitation, friction, goal direction, favouritism, democratic orientation, competition, encouragement, involvement and conformity. However, he found that as compared to girls, boys perceive more difficulty, apathy and disorganization, and less creative stimulation. Baek and Choi (2002) reported that girls have high perception of task orientation as compared to boys.

It was also found that male students have more emotional intelligence than female students. Higher emotional intelligence of male students may be due to the reason that men appear to have better self-regard, are more self-reliant, flexible and optimistic, solve problems better, cope better with stress than women. In other words it can be said that, as compared to boys, more emotionally immature behaviour such as immaturity, hyperactivity, self-monitoring deficit, social-skill deficit, learning difficulties, aggression, distorted thinking, extreme anxiety and abnormal mood swings can be seen in girls. The above finding draws support from the findings of Mishra and Ranjan (2008), Dipti and Sharma (2008), Upadhyaya and Upadhyaya (2004), Fatt and Howe (2003), Jerath (1979) and George (1969). They also found that males are more emotionally intelligent/stable than females. Contrary to this, Reddy and Venu (2010), Alam (2010), Hassan, Sulaiman and Ishak (2009), Dubey (2009a), Prieto, Ferrandiz, Ferrando, Sainz, Bermejo and Hernandez (2008), Austin *et al.* (2005), Van Rooy, Alonso and Viswesvaran (2005), Brackett, Warner and Bosco (2005), Priyadarshini (2005), Katyal and Awasthi (2005), Petrides, Furnhum and Martin (2004b), Pandey and Tripathi (2004), Alloway (2004), Brackett, Mayer and Warner (2004), Kafetsios (2004), Shanwal (2003), Chauhan and Bhatnagar (2003), Ciarrochi and Bajgar (2001), Ciarrochi, Chan and Caputi (2000), Mayer *et al.* (2000), Brenner and Salovey (1997) and Sarojini (1971) provided evidence to support the view that female students excel male on emotional intelligence. Findings of Olatoye, Akintunde and Yakasai (2010), Kaur and Meenakshi (2010), Srivastava (2009), Gupta (2009), Goswami (2009), Singh (2008b), Malviya (2008), Chauhan (2008), Malviya (2007), Abdullah (2007), Manhas and Gakhar (2006), Kumar and Bhatia (2005), Adeyemo (2004), Pant and Prakash (2004), Tiwari and Srivastava (2004), Paul and Croucher (2003), Sharma (2003), Click (2002), Roberts (2002), Pandey (2002), Kaur (2001), Reif, Halzes, Bramel and Gibbon (2001), Bar-On (2000), Petrides and Furnham (2000), and Koh (1999) have indicated that there is no gender difference with regard to emotional intelligence.

It was found that male students have more luck and support attribution in comparison to their female counterparts. This may be due to the reason that boys are more likely to seek help from coaching institutions, teachers, parents and peer groups. The present finding is in accordance with the findings of Rusillo and Arias (2004), Lightbody, Siann, Stocks and Walsch (1996) and Burgner and Hewstone (1993). They also found that boys rate luck more than girls in attributing to academic success. This finding is in contradiction with the findings of Rosenfield and Stephan (1978), Stephan, Rosenfield and Stephan (1976), Levine *et al.* (1976) and Nicholls (1975). They found that as compared to females, males tend to attribute success more to internal factors. The above finding is also contrary to the finding of Sianna *et al.* (1998) who found that students of both the sex rated parents and friends as more important in contributing to academic success.

The finding that male students have more intelligence in comparison to their female counterparts is contradictory to the established notion that intelligence is not influenced by gender. Sex differences in intelligence have been reported in number of studies (Varma, 2003). Evidence (Kaur and Bawa, 1995; Faroqui, 1974; Deshpande, 1971) suggests that boys are more intelligent than girls. In contrast, Dhall and Thukral (2010), Mian (1988), Hundal (1969) found girls to be more intelligent than boys. However, Behera (2002), Halpern and Lamay (2000), and Sutherland (1990) reported no sex difference in intelligence.

Further it was also found that as compared to male students, female students perceived more diversity, speed and cliqueness in classroom climate. Singh (2008b) found that female students perceived more diversity in classroom climate as compared to their male counterparts. But she found that male and female students have equal perception of cliqueness in classroom environment and as compared to female students, male students perceived more speed in classroom climate. The study conducted by Dwivedi (2005) revealed that as compared to boys, girls perceive more speed in their classroom. Both Dwivedi (2005) and Misra (2002) found that male and female students do not differ from one another on perceived diversity and cliquness in classroom environment. Perception of more speed in their classroom by female students may be due to the reason that the female students are less dependent on tuition classes, keeping this fact into consideration their teachers teach them with high speed so that they can revise what has been taught (Dwivedi, 2005).

**Study of Relationship between Achievement in English and Intelligence**

Achievement in English was found to be positively related with intelligence among both male and female students. Mitra (1985) also found that intelligence is a significant correlate of achievement irrespective of sex. This means that intelligent students may show better achievement in English. As intelligence of students increases their thinking, reasoning, analysing and memory power also increases which in turn can increase their achievement. The findings of Dubey (2010a), Kaur and Bawa (1995), Kaur

(1992), Chandy (1991), Singh (1989), Brahmabhatt (1983) support our finding. They also found that intelligence is positively related to achievement in English. Khare (1986) found that intelligence is an important factor of achievement in the areas of comprehension, composition, pronunciation, spelling, vocabulary and applied grammar in English. The findings of Joshi (1984) indicated that there exists significant relationship between intelligence and growth of various language abilities. Cattell and Butcher (1968) reported that intelligence is related to achievement in language. The present finding also draws support from the findings of Patel (1987) and Gaur (1982). The former found that intelligence is positively related to achievement in Oriya and the latter found that intelligence is related to speed of reading comprehension and vocabulary of students in Hindi. Studies by Palta Singh (2008), Chamundesweri and Vaidharani (2006), Panigrahi (2005), Verma (2003), Pradhan (1997), Mavi and Patel (1997), Venugopal (1994), Agarwal (1993), Kulshrestha (1993), Gupta, Mukerjee and Chatterjee (1993), Lynn, Hampson and Magee (1983), Kashiwagi, Azuma and Miyake (1982), Kanderian (1969), Flescher (1963), Derfingier (1943), Fael (1927) and Tupas (1926) have also indicated that intelligence is related to achievement. However, the finding of Anandmani (2006) that girls' achievement is not significantly related to general intelligence is contradictory to the present finding.

**Study of Relationship between Achievement in English and Emotional Intelligence**

Achievement in English was found to be positively related with emotional intelligence among male students. It means that emotionally intelligent male students may show better achievement in English. As emotional intelligence of male students increases, they are able to handle well their stress and anxiety about studies which helps them to remain balanced and focused for examination/test. In other words, it can be said that as emotional intelligence of male students increases their achievement in English also increases because they are better able to evaluate and handle their emotions that arises due to the study of a foreign language. Students generally feel stress because of the high expectations of parents for better performance. Emotional intelligence of students helps them to understand their own feelings and manage their stress effectively. All this leads to better academic performance. This finding corroborates the findings of Sucaromana (2004) who found that emotional intelligence has a direct effect on Thai student's achievement in English. Pandey (2008) also reported that emotional intelligence is positively related to achievement in English among boys. Dubey (2010a), Sabath (2010), Salami and Ogundokun (2009), Hassan, Sulaiman and Ishak (2009), Adeyemo (2007), Besharat *et al.* (2005), Manhas (2004), O'Connor and Little (2003), Shanwal (2003) reported that academic achievement has positive correlation with emotional intelligence. The finding is also consistent with the findings of Swart (1996) who found that the ability to manage one's emotions, to be able to validate one's feelings and to solve problems of a personal and interpersonal nature are important for being academically successful. Researches also indicated that emotional intelligence is related to academic achievement (Marquez, Martin and Brackett, 2006; Emeke, Adeoye and Torubeli, 2006; Petrides *et al.* 2004a; Drago, 2004; Parker *et al.* 2004; Bar-On, 2003; Barchard, 2003; Brackett and Mayer, 2003; Stewart, 1998). However, finding of Dubey (2008b) is contradictory. She found that emotional intelligence is not related to achievement in English.

Among female students, achievement in English was not found to be related to emotional intelligence. This means that emotionally intelligent female students may or may not achieve better in English. The finding draws support from the finding of Pandey (2008) who found that emotional intelligence is not related to achievement in English among Arts stream girls. The findings of Anandmani (2006), Szuberia (2006), Phillips (2005), Bastian, Burns and Nettelbeck (2005), Sibia, Mishra and Srivastava (2005), Lori (2003) and Chico (1999) lend support to the aforementioned finding. They also found that emotional intelligence is not related to academic achievement. However, Hassan, Sulaiman and Ishak (2009) reported that emotional intelligence is positively related to academic achievement among female students.

**Study of Relationship between Achievement in English and Formal Reasoning**

In the present study, achievement in English was found to be positively related with formal reasoning among both male and female students. This means that students with formal reasoning ability may show better achievement in English. As formal reasoning ability of students' increases, they become capable of analysing logically, arriving at conclusions which help them to apply and use the rules of grammar while dealing with English language. The present finding is in accordance with the finding of Misra (1999). He reported that formal reasoning is positively related to achievement among female students. This finding draws indirect support from the findings of Dubey (2007), Strahan (1988) and Lawson *et al.* (1975). Dubey reported that formal reasoning is positively related to achievement in Environmental Studies. Strahan found that performance on reasoning test is related to performance on achievement tests. Lawson *et al.* also found that formal reasoning ability is significantly related to achievement. However, the finding of Dubey (2010a, 2008a) is in contradiction with the present finding. She found that formal reasoning is not related to achievement among students.

**Study of Relationship between Achievement in English and Academic Motivation**

Achievement in English was found to be positively related with academic motivation among both male and female students. This means that academically motivated students may show better achievement in English. As academic motivation of students' increases, their aspiration to achieve higher in English and their attitude towards learning of English become more favourable and they develop better study habits for learning English. Motivation will also arouse and sustain students' interest in learning English. This will increase students' achievement in English. The finding draws direct support from the finding of Dubey (2010b). She also found that academic motivation is positively related to achievement in English. Tella (2007) also emphasised the importance of motivation for academic performance. This finding corroborates with that of John (1996) who reported that academic achievement is highly correlated with students' motivation. The finding draws support from the findings of Agarwal (1993), Singhal (1991), Veekarchavan and Bhattacharya (1989), Desai (1979), Srivastava (1974) and Rosen (1956) which indicate that academic motivation is positively related to academic achievement. The findings of Behera (2002), Rani (1992), Devanesan (1990), Ramasamy (1988), Tripathi (1986), Mitra (1985) and Abrol (1977)) indicated that achievement motivation is positively correlated with academic achievement. It also lends support to our findings. However, the results of the studies of Harikrishnan (1992) and Tripathi (1990) which indicate that achievement is not related to academic motivation are contradictory to the present finding. Findings of Varma (2003) and Kulshrestha (1993) are also contradictory. They found negative relationship between academic achievement and achievement motivation and academic motivation respectively.

**Study of Relationship between Achievement in English and Causal Attributions**

It was found that achievement in English was not related to task attribution, ability attribution, effort attribution, luck attribution, spiritual attribution and support attribution among both male and female students. The only exception is that achievement in English among female students was found to be negatively related to luck attribution. This means that female students' achievement in English increases as they attribute their success less to luck. This finding corroborates the finding of Kovenklioglu and Greenhause (1978) who found that among students who succeeded on the test, their expected actual performance were negatively related to attribution to good luck. This finding is also supported by the finding of Frieze *et al.* (1982) who said that women are unlikely to attribute their success to ability. However the findings of Dubey (2009b), Gupta (1994), Sahay (1991) and Crandal *et al.* (1965) are contradictory to our finding. Gupta found that attribution of achievement outcome is positively related to effort, ability and external factors. Findings in the literature support the notion that people are more likely to attribute successful performance to ability or skill when the successful individual is male; in addition, tasks are judged more difficult when they are successfully accomplished by males and less difficult when accomplished by females (Feather and Simon, 1975; Rosenfield and Stephan, 1978; Stephan, Rosenfield and Stephan, 1976). But the present finding is not in conformity with the said notion.

**Study of Relationship between Achievement in English and Classroom Environment**

The present study has revealed that eight dimensions of classroom climate namely: *(i)* cohesiveness, *(ii)* formality, *(iii)* facilitation, *(iv)* democratic orientation, *(v)* competition, *(vi)* creative stimulation, *(vii)* involvement and *(viii)* conformity are not related to achievement in English among both male and female students. It indicates that students' perception of class members tendency to remain friendly to each other; paying attention to rules, forms, expectations and conventions; existence of situations which make learning or doing things easy; class members' equal treatment to each other; competitive activities; conditions and opportunities for creative thinking; teachers' behaviour to structure and monitor students' learning, and students' action which are required to be in agreement with what is accepted or required by their teacher will neither increase nor decrease students' achievement in English. The finding draws support from the finding of Dubey (2010d) and Allen and Fraser (2007). They also found that cohesiveness dimension of learning environment is not related to achievement. The findings of Yadav (2006), Dwivedi (2005), Zareen (2001), Padhi (1991) and Upadhyaya (1984) lends indirect support to our finding. Yadav and Zareen found that achievement in Mathematics is not related to the perception of cohesiveness, formality, facilitation, democratic orientation, competition, creative stimulation, involvement and conformity dimensions of classroom environment. The study of Dwivedi revealed that perception of these dimensions of classroom environment are not related to different dimensions of environmental cognition among both male and female students. Padhi found that there exist no significant relationship between classroom environment and academic achievement. Upadhyaya found that order and teacher support dimensions of classroom environment are not related to achievement. However, contradictory findings were of Dubey (2010d), Baek and Choi (2002), Upadhyaya (1984), and Haertel, Walberg and Haertel (1981). Dubey found positive relationship between achievement in English and competition perceived in learning environment of the classroom. Baek and Choi reported that competition, involvement and order dimensions of classroom environment are related to achievement in English. Upadhyaya found that involvement and competition dimensions of classroom environment are positively related to achievement in English. Haertel, Walberg and Haertel concluded that gains in learning outcome are consistently associated with classroom which was perceived as having greater cohesiveness.

Speed, difficulty and apathy dimensions of classroom environment have been found to be negatively related to achievement in English among both male and female students. In other words, it can be said that as speed, difficulty and apathy in classroom environment increases student's achievement in English decreases. It indicates that students' perception of doing things in short time; difficulty in understanding or executing ideas or things; and absence of sympathy/interest and existence of indifference of persons involved in teaching-learning process decreases students' achievement in English. Finding of Tripathi (1978) lends indirect support to our finding. Findings of Yadav (2006) and Dwivedi (2005) are contrary to the above finding. Yadav found that speed, difficulty and apathy in classroom environment are not related to achievement in Mathematics while Dwivedi reported that these dimensions of classroom environment are not related to Environmental Cognition.

Diversity, goal direction and encouragement dimensions of classroom environment has been found to be positively related to achievement in English among female students, while in case of male students the above mentioned dimensions were not found to be related to achievement in English. In other words, it can be said that diversity, goal direction and encouragement dimensions of classroom environment are conducive to achievement in English among female students. It indicates that female student's perception of variety in the classroom; understanding and acceptance of achievable and appropriate goals of the class and performance of goal oriented behaviours; and teachers' behaviour to stimulate learning of students by encouraging their behaviour can increase their achievement in English. Perception of goal direction leads to enhanced performance in several ways. It helps students to focus their attention. This will reduce distraction (Kalat, 2000). The felt need to perform goal directed behaviour demands motivation to study and learn English. It will help the students to perform better in English. A classroom environment that encourage pupils to have confidence in their abilities and make efforts, to find successful solutions can improve the motivation of individuals even when they face failure. This can increase their achievement. These inferences do not hold true in the case of boys. It seems that as compared to girls, boys are less sensitive to variations in diversity, goal direction and encouragement. As a result, these dimensions of classroom environment have idiosyncratic effects on achievement in English among male and female students. The findings of Yadav (2006) and Dwivedi (2005) are contrary. The former states that perceived diversity, goal direction and encouragement dimensions of classroom environment are not related to achievement in Mathematics, while the latter states that perceived encouragement in classroom environment is not related to Environmental Cognition among both male and female students. Zareen (2001) is of the view that achievement in mathematics is not related to encouragement dimension of the classroom environment. However, Baek and Choi (2002) found that task orientation is related to achievement in English. Dubey (2010d) also found that goal direction is positively related to achievement in English. It has been found that students who perceive their teachers as supportive of learning, enjoy their studies, feel competent, set mastery goals and utilise adaptive study strategies. Upadhayaya (1984) and Haertel, Walberg and Haertel (1981) reported that goal orientation is related to achievement. In a study done by GCPI (1981) it was reported that encouragement to students is effective in improving the examination results. All these findings lend direct support to our finding. It reflects that girls' achievement in English increases when they are goal oriented.

Favouritism dimension of classroom environment has been found to be negatively related to achievement in English among female students, while in the case of male students no such relationship was found. It means that if teachers have the tendency to favour some and reject others then female students' achievement in English will be retarded. It can be inferred that girls' perception of practice of favouring persons in the classroom by the teachers decreases their achievement in English. This may be due to the reason that female students are more sensitive towards social discrimination and perception of favouritism in teachers' behaviour will make them stressful and adversely affect their achievement in English. However, boys seem to remain indifferent to the practice of favouritism in the class by the teachers. Perhaps they have learned to accept it as a reality of the classroom. Yadav (2006) and Zareen (2001) found that favouritism is not related to achievement in Mathematics.

Friction, a dimension of classroom environment is negatively related to achievement in English among male students but it is not related with achievement in English among female students. Achievement in English is negatively related to cliqueness among male students but it shows no relation in case of female students. Disorganization is negatively related to achievement in English among male students, while for the female students, it is not related to achievement in English. Thus, it can be said that boys perception of occurrence of difference of opinion in class leading to argumentation and quarrelling; tendency of class members to form cliques in the class; and upset working of the class disturbs the student and adversely affects their achievement in English. In other words, it can be said that boys' perception of above mentioned dimensions of classroom environment decreases their achievement in English. However, the same was not true in case of female students. Tripathi (1978) reported that academic achievement and disruptive classroom behaviour yields a negative relationship. The finding draws indirect support from the findings of Yadav (2006), Dwivedi (2005) and Zareen (2001). Yadav and Dwivedi reported that perceived friction, cliqueness and disorganization in classroom are not related to achievement in Mathematics and Environmental Cognition respectively. Zareen also found that achievement in Mathematics is not related to friction dimension of classroom environment.

To sum up it can inferred that girls' perception of diversity, goal direction and encouragement is positively related to achievement in English while speed, favouritism, difficulty and apathy are negatively related to achievement in English. Boys' perception of speed, friction, difficulty apathy, cliqueness and disorganization are negatively related to achievement in English. As compared to girls, boys are less sensitive to diversity, goal direction, favouritism and encouragement and as compared to boys, girls are more immune to friction, cliqueness and disorganization. So, perceptions of these dimensions of classroom environment have idiosyncratic effects on achievement in English of male and female students.

**Study of Achievement in English among Students with Different Levels of Intelligence**

Results of ANOVA have shown that there is significant difference in achievement in English among both male and female students with low, moderate or high intelligence. As compared to students with low intelligence, students with moderate or high intelligence have high achievement in English and as compared to students with moderate intelligence, students with high intelligence have high achievement in English. This indicates positive relationship between intelligence and achievement in English. The present study has revealed that male and female students' achievement in English is positively related to their intelligence. Intelligent students are able to grasp new tasks more quickly, have access to more effective problem-solving strategies, find it easier to identify relevant rules and have a greater processing capacity and more elaborated memory strategies (Gustafsson and Undheim, 1996). The present finding is in direct accordance with the finding of Dubey (2010a). She also reported that students with high intelligence have high achievement in English than their low intelligent counterparts. The finding of Singh (2007), Panigrahi (2005) and Behera (2002) that students with high intelligence level have high academic achievement as compared to students with low intelligence, lends indirect support to our finding. The finding of Dixit (1985) is in contradiction with our finding. He found that there is no difference in the academic achievement of intellectually very superior and superior boys and girls.

**Study of Achievement in English among Students with Different Levels of Emotional Intelligence**

Results have shown that there is significant difference in achievement in English among male students with low or moderate and high emotional intelligence. Male students with low and moderate emotional intelligence do not differ from one another on achievement in English. As compared to male students with low or moderate emotional intelligence, male students with high emotional intelligence have high achievement in English. This finding gets support from our previous finding that has revealed positive relationship between boys' achievement in English and emotional intelligence. Ediger

(1997) opined that quality emotions help students to give their best potential in the classroom, because ability to control and manage emotions helps to reduce stress, anxiety and depression during examination. The above finding draws indirect support from the findings of Srivastava (2007) and Singh (2007). The former found that as compared to high achievers in Environmental Studies, low achievers in the same subject exhibit less emotional intelligence. The latter found that general category students with high emotional intelligence achieve better than their counterparts with low emotional intelligence. The effect of emotional intelligence on academic success is well documented in literature (Lal, Sharma and Sharma, 2010; Marquez *et al.* 2006; Petrides *et al.* 2004a; Parker, Summerfeldt *et al.* 2004; Bar-On, 2003; Farook, 2003; Jaegar, 2002). This result is easily explainable bearing in mind that emotional intelligence competencies, such as ability to regulate ones' feelings, problem solving, intrapersonal and interpersonal skills are highly germane to academic success. An emotionally competent student can ward off stress and anxiety associated with test-taking and examination. Further more, ability to display interpersonal skills may assist students to seek academic help from teachers, peers and resource persons. As indicated by Bar-On (2006), emotionally intelligent people are goal-oriented and optimistic. These attributes are facilitative of academic achievement. In case of female students it was found that girls with low, moderate or high emotional intelligence do not differ from one another on achievement in English. This indicates existence of no relationship between emotional intelligence and achievement in English. The present study has revealed existence of no significant relationship between achievement in English and emotional intelligence among female students. The present finding draws indirect support from the finding of Singh (2007) who reported that there is no significant difference in the achievement of high and low emotionally intelligent SC female students.

**Study of Achievement in English among Students with Different Levels of Formal Reasoning**

Results of ANOVA have shown that male students with moderate and high formal reasoning do not differ from one another on achievement in English. Female students with high formal reasoning have high achievement in English as compared to those with moderate formal reasoning. As compared to students with low formal reasoning, students with moderate or high formal reasoning have high achievement in English. This indicates that there exists positive relationship between achievement in English and formal reasoning. The present study has also revealed that students' achievement in English is positively related to formal reasoning. However (Dubey, 2010a) reported that students with high and low formal reasoning have equal achievement in English. This finding corroborates the finding of Dubey (2007) who found that students with high formal reasoning ability achieve higher in Environmental Studies than those with low formal reasoning. The findings of Srivastava (2005), Singh (1983) and Singh (1983) that reasoning ability has a positive influence on achievement in Mathematics, Chemistry and overall achievement respectively, lends indirect support to our finding.

**Study of Achievement in English among Students with Different Levels of Academic Motivation**

Results of ANOVA have shown that as compared to female students with low academic motivation, female students with moderate or high academic motivation have high achievement in English and as compared to female students with moderate academic motivation, female students with high academic motivation have high achievement in English. This indicates positive relationship between academic motivation and achievement in English. The present study has revealed such a relationship between girls' achievement in English and academic motivation. The present findings draws support from the findings the Tella (2007), Behera (2002) and Yuthim (2001) who found that highly motivated students perform better academically than the low motivated students. The finding is in favour of the study done by Prakash (1981). Results of the study by Prakash revealed that the performance of high achievement motivation students was higher than that of average and low achievement motivation students. The average achievement motivation students had higher achievement than those with low achievement motivation. This finding also corroborates the findings of Bank and Finalapson (1980) who stressed that successful students have higher motivation for achievement than unsuccessful students. In case of male students it was found that male students with low, moderate or high academic motivation do not differ from one another on achievement in English. This may be due to the lack of interest and unfavourable attitude towards English.

**Study of Achievement in English among Students Differing with Respect to Causal Attributions**

Results of ANOVA have shown that there is no significant difference in achievement in English among both male and female students with low, moderate or high task difficulty, ability, effort, spiritual and support attribution. This indicates existence of no relationship between achievement in English and task difficulty, ability, effort, spiritual and support attribution as has been revealed by the present study in case of both male and female students. The findings of Deary, Strand, Smith and Fernandes (2007) and Chou (2005) are in contradiction with our finding. In case of luck attribution, male students with low, moderate or high luck attribution and female students with low or moderate luck attribution have equal achievement in English. Female students with high luck attribution have low achievement in English as compared to female students with low or moderate luck attribution. This means that female students who attribute their success more to luck have low achievement in English.

**Study of Achievement in English among Students Perceiving Different Levels of Stimulation in Classroom Environment**

Results of ANOVA have shown that male students perceiving low, moderate or high formality, facilitation, friction, democratic orientation, cliqueness, disorganization, competition, encouragement, involvement and conformity in classroom environment do not differ from one another on achievement in English. The findings also holds true in case of female students. The findings of no significant relationship between achievement in English on one hand and perceived formality, facilitation, democratic orientation, competition, involvement and conformity on the other hand among both male and female students lends support to this inference. The finding of no relationship between achievement in English and perceived friction, cliqueness, and disorganization among female students, and perceived encouragement among male students also lends support to our finding. Finding of Dubey (2010d) is also in conformity with the above finding. Findings of Kulshrestha (1992) and GCPI (1981) are contradictory to our finding. Kulshrestha found that students group formed on the basis of encouragement differed significantly in their achievement. GCPI reported that encouragement to students is effective in improving the examination results.

Male students perceiving low, moderate or high level of diversity in classroom environment do not differ from one another on achievement in English. As compared to female students perceiving low diversity, female students perceiving moderate or high diversity have high achievement in English. The present study has also revealed existence of positive relationship between achievement in English and perceived diversity in classroom environment among female students and existence of no relationship between achievement in English and diversity in classroom environment among male students.

Female students perceiving low, moderate or high level of cohesiveness in classroom environment do not differ from one another on achievement in English and male students perceiving high cohesiveness do not differ from those perceiving low or moderate cohesiveness in classroom environment. Male students perceiving low cohesiveness exhibit higher achievement in English than their counterparts with moderate perception of cohesiveness. This means that male students who perceive their class members to be less friendly to each other, have high achievement in English in comparison to those who perceive moderate amount of cohesiveness in their class. The present study has also revealed existence of no relationship between achievement in English and perceived cohesiveness. This lends support to our finding.

Female students who perceived low, moderate or high level of speed in classroom environment and male students who perceived moderate or high level of speed in classroom environment do not differ from one another on achievement in English. Male students perceiving low speed in classroom environment have high achievement in English than those who perceive high or moderate speed in classroom environment. It indicates that for male students negative relationship exists between speed and achievement in English. Study of correlation between achievement in English and perceived speed in classroom environment has also revealed existence of such a negative relationship between these variables. In other words, it can be said that as male students' perception of doing things in short time increases their achievement in English decreases. Thus, it can be inferred that male students are unable to cope with the high speed of the class and therefore, their performance in English is adversely affected. However, the behaviour of teacher and student of doing thing in short time do not influence the achievement in English of female students.

Male as well as female students perceiving high goal direction in classroom environment have high achievement in English than their counterparts perceiving low or moderate goal direction. Both male and female students perceiving low or moderate level of goal orientation do not differ from one another on achievement in English. It can be inferred that as students' perception of goal orientation in classroom environment increases their achievement in English also increases. In other words, it can be said that, as understanding and acceptance of achievable goals of the class and performance of goal oriented behaviours of students increases they exhibit high achievement in English because clear and specific goals leads to enhanced performance while vague goals are ineffective. Evidence of academic motivation can be seen in the amount of goals set and achieved (Phillips and SteinKomp, 1995). According to Singh (1976), clear and definite educational goals are expected to have motivational effects on the performance of the students and are conducive for high academic achievement. It has already been established in the previous findings of this study that academic motivation is positively related to achievement in English among both male and female students. Thus, it can be inferred that perception of goal direction leads to academic motivation and as academic motivation of students' increases, their achievement in English also increases. Finding of existence of positive relationship between achievement in English and perceived goal direction lends support to this inference. The finding corroborates with the finding of Dubey (2010d).

Male students perceiving low, moderate or high favouritism and apathy in classroom environment do not differ from one another on achievement in English. It means that, teachers' practice of favouring persons unequally and absence of sympathy or interest and existence of indifference of teacher and students towards each other do not influence male students' achievement in English. The finding of existence of no relationship between achievement in English and favouritism supports this finding. However, female students perceiving low favouritism or apathy in classroom environment have exhibited high achievement in English than their counterparts perceiving moderate or high level of favouritism and apathy. It means that, lesser the perception of practice of favouring persons unequally, higher is the achievement in English among female students. As female students' perception of absence of sympathy or interest in the classroom and existence of indifference of teacher and students towards each other increases their achievement in English is adversely affected. Thus, it indicates that for female students negative relationship exists between achievement in English on one hand and perception of favouritism and apathy on the other. Study of correlations between achievement in English and these two dimensions of classroom environment have also revealed existence of negative relationship.

Both male and female students perceiving low level of difficulty in classroom environment have higher achievement in English than their counterparts perceiving moderate or higher level of the same dimension of classroom environment. It means that when students find less things or ideas that are hard to understand, their achievement in English is more and as students perceive that there exists ideas or things in the class that are difficult to understand or execute, their achievement in English decreases. The finding that there exists negative relationship between achievement in English and difficulty supports this finding.

Female students perceiving low, moderate or high creative stimulation in classroom environment have equal achievement in English. This means that teachers' activities to stimulate creative thinking of students do not influence female students' achievement in English. This also holds true in case of male students perceiving low, moderate or high creative stimulation. The finding that there exists no relationship between achievement in English and creative stimulation lends support to this finding.

**Prediction of Achievement in English among Students**

Out of 28 independent variables, intelligence, emotional intelligence, formal reasoning, and perceived friction, goal direction, democratic orientation and conformity in classroom environment emerged as the best predictors of achievement in English among male students. Among male students, achievement in English has been found to be positively related to intelligence, emotional intelligence and formal reasoning and these variables also appeared as best predictors of achievement in English. Brown (2000) reported that the major purpose of intelligence tests is to predict academic performance. Scores of intelligence tests do correlate with scholastic achievement as measured by grades and standardised achievement tests. The more the cognitive abilities of the students, higher is their achievement in English. Past researches have also established that intelligence is the predictor of academic achievement in general (Trama, 1998; diSibio, 1993; Kumar, 1989; Das, 1986; Mitra, 1985; Ghosh, 1985; Shivappa, 1980; Reddy, 1973) and achievement in English in particular (Laidra, Pullman and Allik, 2007; Chandy, 1991; Kaile, 1988; Patel, 1987). However, the study done by Naderi, Abdullah, Hamid and Sharir (2008) does not reveal intelligence as predictor of students' academic achievement.

Male students who have high emotional intelligence are better able to manage and control their emotions during examinations. Fear of examination give rise to stress, tension and anxiety which adversely affects their performance. Emotional intelligence helps the students to control and overcome their stress, tension and anxiety which in turn enhance their achievement. According to Mayer and Salovey (1997), ability to discriminate amongst and manage emotions may assist with the decision-making and planning which could contribute to greater academic performance. The present finding is in accordance with the findings of Salami and Ogundokun (2009), Downey *et al.* (2008), Berenson, Boyles and weaver (2008), Grace (2004), Parker *et al.* (2004), Robert (2003), Bar-on (2003), Vander-zee *et al.* (2002), Weitazzen-Ski (2001), Mayer, Salovey and Caruso (2000), Pool (1997), Bar-On (1997) and Swart (1996). They have also established that emotional intelligence can predict academic achievement. Sucoromana (2004) reported that emotional intelligence can predict achievement in English. This finding lends direct support to our finding. However, contrary findings are of Newsome, Day and Catano (2000) who found no support for claims that emotional intelligence can predict academic achievement. Grace (2004) also indicated that emotional intelligence is not a significant predictor of GPA.

Formal reasoning of male students can predict their achievement in English. High formal reasoning ability of male students helps them to analyse logically and apply the rules of grammar while dealing with English language. Chikara (1985) found that it is possible to predict achievement in Life Sciences on the basis of the reasoning ability tests. Bhatnagar (1982) found that abstract reasoning ability is the best predictor of achievement in case of student-teachers and medical students. The findings of Chikara and Bhatnagar lend indirect support to the present finding.

Perceived friction in classroom environment have been found to be negatively related to achievement in English and it also appeared as one of the best predictors of achievement in English. Perception of friction increases stress which contributes to lower achievement in English. Difference in opinion and quarrelling between the class members seems to have an adverse effect on achievement in English among male students. It can also be inferred that their achievement in English is adversely affected by argumentation in the classroom.

Among male students, achievement in English can also be predicted by perceived goal direction in classroom environment. Male students who understand and accept the achievable and appropriate goals can have high achievement in English. The felt need to perform goal directed behaviour demands inner motivation to study and learn English which will help male students to perform better in English. Ho and Hau (2008) also found that goal orientation is a significant predictor of achievement.

Perceived democratic orientation also emerged as one of the best predictors of achievement in English. This may be due to the reason that equal treatment to male students gives mental satisfaction, stimulates them and helps them in channelizing their potential in the right direction. Democratic environment provides opportunity to utilise abilities to maximum extent. When male students feel satisfied, they remain relaxed, happy and temperamentally independent which provides them conducive environment to study and learn English.

Achievement in English among male students can be predicted on the basis of conformity in classroom environment too. If male students remain in agreement with what is required by their teachers then their achievement can increase. The present study has shown that among male students intelligence, emotional intelligence, formal reasoning, and perceived friction, goal direction, democratic orientation and conformity can predict 35.49 per cent of variance in achievement in English. Verma (1977) found that socio-emotional climate of the classroom predicts and influence pupil's academic achievement. Dwivedi (2005) found that among male students goal direction and conformity can predict environmental concept development ability.

For female students, intelligence and formal reasoning emerged as cognitive determinants of achievement in English. Misra (1999) also found that formal reasoning can predict achievement among female students. Among female students, achievement in English can also be predicted by academic motivation of students. Patel (1987) reported that academic motivation can predict achievement in Oriya, Hindi and Sanskrit. Sontakey (1986) and Ghosh (1985) found that academic motivation can predict achievement in Biological Science and Chemistry respectively. Mitra (1985) reported that academic motivation accounted 3/5th of the variance in academic achievement. Benno (1995) and Srivastava (1974) also found that academic motivation can predict academic achievement.

Two dimensions of classroom environment namely friction and favourtisim have emerged as the predictors of achievement in English among female students. The present study has shown that 52.89 per cent of variance in achievement in English among female students can be explained by intelligence, formal reasoning, academic motivation and perceived friction and favouritism.

CHAPTER

5

# FINDINGS, IMPLICATIONS AND SUGGESTIONS

THE PRESENT STUDY was undertaken to study achievement in English among class XI students in relation to intelligence, emotional intelligence, formal reasoning, academic motivation, causal attributions and classroom environment. The sample consisted of 439 students from six schools of Allahabad city. The preceeding chapter was devoted to analysis of data, results and discussion. In the present chapter, an attempt has been made to enumerate the findings of the study, describe implications of the study and suggest problems for future research.

## FINDINGS

The findings of the present study are as follows:

### Study of Intelligence, Emotional Intelligence, Formal Reasoning, Causal Attribution, Academic Motivation, Classroom Environment and Achievement in English among Male and Female Students

1. Male and female students do not differ from one another on achievement in English, formal reasoning, academic motivation, task difficulty, ability, effort and spiritual attribution and on cohesiveness, formality, facilitation, friction, goal direction, favouritism, difficulty, apathy, democratic orientation, disorganization, competition, creative stimulation, encouragement, involvement and conformity in classroom environment.
2. As compared to female students, male students have more intelligence, emotional intelligence, and luck and support attributions.
3. As compared to male students, female students perceive more diversity, speed and cliqueness in classroom environment.

**Study of Relationship between Achievement in English and Intelligence**

1. For male students, intelligence is positively related to achievement in English.
2. For female students, intelligence is positively related to achievement in English.

**Study of Relationship between Achievement in English and Emotional Intelligence**

1. Emotional intelligence is positively related to achievement in English among male students.
2. Emotional intelligence is not related to achievement in English among female students.

**Study of Relationship between Achievement in English and Formal Reasoning**

1. Formal reasoning is positively related to achievement in English among male students.
2. Formal reasoning is positively related to achievement in English among female students.

**Study of Relationship between Achievement in English and Academic Motivation**

1. Academic motivation is positively related to achievement in English among male students.
2. Academic motivation is positively related to achievement in English among female students.

**Study of Relationship between Achievement in English and Causal Attributions**

1. Task difficulty attribution is not related to achievement in English among male as well as female students.
2. Ability attribution is not related to achievement in English among male as well as female students.
3. Effort attribution is not related to achievement in English among male as well as female students.
4. Luck attribution is not related to achievement in English among male students but for female students luck attribution is negatively related to achievement in English.
5. Spiritual attribution is not related to achievement in English among male as well as female students.
6. Support attribution is not related to achievement in English among male as well as female students.

**Study of Relationship between Achievement in English and Classroom Environment**

1. Cohesiveness is not related to achievement in English among male as well as female students.
2. Diversity is positively related to achievement in English among female students while for male students diversity is not related to achievement in English.

3. Formality is not related to achievement in English among male as well as female students.
4. Speed is negatively related to achievement in English among male and female students.
5. Facilitation is not related to achievement in English among male as well as female students.
6. Friction is negatively related to achievement in English among male students but for female students, it is not related to achievement in English.
7. Goal direction is positively related to achievement in English among female students while for male students, it is not related to achievement in English.
8. Favouritism is negatively related to achievement in English among female students but for male students, favouritism is not related to achievement in English.
9. Difficulty is negatively related to achievement in English among male as well as female students.
10. Apathy is negatively related to achievement in English among male as well as female students.
11. Democratic orientation is not related to achievement in English among male as well as female students.
12. Cliqueness is negatively related to achievement in English among male students but it is not related to achievement in English among female students.
13. Disorganization is negatively related to achievement in English among male students while for female students, disorganization is not related to achievement in English.
14. Competition is not related to achievement in English among male as well as female students.
15. Creative stimulation is not related to achievement in English among male as well as female students.
16. Encouragement is positively related to achievement in English among female students while for male students, encouragement is not related to achievement in English.
17. Involvement is not related to achievement in English among male as well as female students.
18. Conformity is not related to achievement in English among male as well as female students.

**Study of Achievement in English among Students with Different Levels of Intelligence**

1. As compared to students with low intelligence, students with moderate or high intelligence have high achievement in English.
2. As compared to students with moderate intelligence, students with high intelligence have high achievement in English.

**Study of Achievement in English among Students with Different Levels of Emotional Intelligence**

1. As compared to male students with low or moderate emotional intelligence, male students with high emotional intelligence have high achievement in English.
2. Male students with low or moderate emotional intelligence do not differ from one another on achievement in English.
3. Female students with low, moderate or high emotional intelligence do not differ from one another on achievement in English.

**Study of Achievement in English among Students with Different Levels of Formal Reasoning**

1. As compared to male students with low formal reasoning, male students with moderate or high formal reasoning have high achievement in English.
2. Male students with moderate and high formal reasoning do not differ from one another on achievement in English.
3. As compared to female students with low formal reasoning, female students with moderate or high formal reasoning have high achievement in English.
4. As compared to female students with moderate formal reasoning, female students with high formal reasoning have high achievement in English.

**Study of Achievement in English among Students with Different Levels of Academic Motivation**

1. Male students with low, moderate or high academic motivation do not differ from one another on achievement in English.
2. As compared to female students with low level of academic motivation, female students with moderate or high academic motivation have high achievement in English.
3. As compared to female students with moderate academic motivation, female students with high academic motivation have high achievement in English.

**Study of Achievement in English among Students Differing with Respect to Causal Attribution**

1. Students with low, moderate or high task difficulty attribution do not differ from one another on achievement in English.

2. Students with low, moderate or high ability attribution do not differ from one another on achievement in English.
3. Students with low, moderate or high effort attribution do not differ from one another on achievement in English.
4. Male students with low, moderate or high luck attribution do not differ from another on achievement in English.
5. As compared to female students with high luck attribution, female students with low or moderate luck attribution have high achievement in English.
6. Female students with low or moderate luck attribution do not differ from one another on achievement in English.
7. Students with low, moderate or high spiritual attribution do not differ from one another on achievement in English.
8. Students with low, moderate or high support attribution do not differ from one another on achievement in English.

**Study of Achievement in English among Students Perceiving Different Levels of Stimulation in Classroom Environment**

1. As compared to male students perceiving moderate cohesiveness in classroom environment, male students perceiving low cohesiveness have high achievement in English.
2. Male students perceiving high cohesiveness in classroom environment do not differ from those perceiving low or moderate cohesiveness on achievement in English.
3. Female students perceiving low, moderate or high cohesiveness in classroom environment do not differ from one another on achievement in English.
4. Male students perceiving low, moderate or high diversity in classroom environment do not differ from one another on achievement in English.
5. As compared to female students perceiving low diversity in classroom environment, female students perceiving moderate or high diversity have high achievement in English.
6. Female students perceiving moderate or high diversity in classroom environment do not differ from one another on achievement in English.
7. Both male and female students perceiving low, moderate or high formality in classroom environment do not differ from one another on achievement in English.
8. As compared to male students perceiving low speed in classroom environment, male students perceiving moderate or high speed have low achievement in English.

9. Male students perceiving moderate or high speed in classroom environment do not differ from one another on achievement in English.
10. Female students perceiving low, moderate or high speed in classroom environment do not differ from one another on achievement in English.
11. Both male and female students perceiving low, moderate or high facilitation in classroom environment do not differ from one another on achievement in English.
12. Both male and female students perceiving low, moderate or high friction in classroom environment do not differ from one another on achievement in English.
13. As compared to male students perceiving moderate goal direction in classroom environment, male students perceiving high goal direction in classroom environment have high achievement in English.
14. Male students perceiving moderate or high goal direction in classroom environment do not differ from male students perceiving low goal direction in classroom environment on achievement in English.
15. Female students perceiving high goal direction in classroom environment have high achievement in English in comparison to female students perceiving low or moderate goal direction in classroom environment.
16. Female students perceiving low or moderate goal direction in classroom environment do not differ from one another on achievement in English.
17. Male students perceiving low, moderate or high favouritism in classroom environment do not differ from one another on achievement in English.
18. As compared to female students perceiving low favouritism in classroom environment, female students perceiving moderate or high favouritism in classroom environment have less achievement in English.
19. Female students perceiving moderate or high favouritism in classroom environment do not differ from one another on achievement in English.
20. As compared to students perceiving low difficulty in classroom environment, students perceiving moderate or high difficulty in classroom environment have less achievement in English.
21. Both male and female students perceiving moderate or high difficulty in classroom environment do not differ from one another on achievement in English.
22. Male students perceiving low, moderate or high apathy in classroom environment do not differ from one another on achievement in English.
23. As compared to female students perceiving low apathy in classroom environment, female students perceiving moderate or high apathy in classroom environment have less achievement in English.

24. Both male and female students perceiving low, moderate or high democratic orientation in classroom environment do not differ from one another on achievement in English.
25. Female students perceiving moderate or high apathy in classroom environment do not differ from one another on achievement in English.
26. Both male and female students perceiving low, moderate or high cliqueness in classroom environment have equal achievement in English.
27. Both male and female students perceiving low, moderate or high disorganization in classroom environment do not differ from one another on achievement in English.
28. Students perceiving low, moderate or high competition in classroom environment have equal achievement in English.
29. As compared to male students perceiving moderate creative stimulation in classroom environment, male students perceiving high stimulation of the same have high achievement in English.
30. Male students perceiving low creative stimulation in classroom environment do not differ on achievement in English from those perceiving moderate or high creative stimulation in classroom environment.
31. Female students perceiving low, moderate or high creative stimulation in classroom environment do not differ from one another on achievement in English.
32. Both male and female students perceiving low, moderate or high encouragement in classroom environment do not differ from one another on achievement in English.
33. Both male and female students perceiving low, moderate or high involvement in classroom environment have equal achievement in English.
34. Students perceiving low, moderate or high conformity in classroom environment do not differ from one another on achievement in English.

**Study of Intelligence, Emotional Intelligence, Formal Reasoning, Academic Motivation, Causal Attribution and Classroom Environment as Predictors of Achievement in English**

1. For male students, intelligence, emotional intelligence, formal reasoning, and friction, goal direction, democratic orientation and conformity in classroom environment emerged as the best predictors of achievement in English.
2. For female students, intelligence, formal reasoning, academic motivation, and friction and favouritism in classroom environment emerged as the best predictors of achievement in English.

## EDUCATIONAL IMPLICATIONS

### Implications for Guidance

Personal and educational guidance is crucial for adolescents, because adolescent students have to face extensive pressure to perform well in examination and if they fail to do so they sink into depression. Thus, proper guidance and counselling facilities should be made available to students. The present study revealed that achievement in English is positively related to intelligence, emotional intelligence, formal reasoning and academic motivation. Thus, the study has an implication for the work of the counsellors in schools. It provides an empirical basis for suggesting that educators and counsellors can try to find out how intelligence, emotional intelligence, formal reasoning, academic motivation influence the academic performance of the students. While giving counselling to low achievers in English, the counselor may take into consideration the above variables also. He may test students' level of intelligence, emotional intelligence formal reasoning and academic motivation to identify the variable which may be responsible for low achievement in English. This will provide students with increased awareness of interdependence of personal responsibility for choices and consequential thinking (Salami and Ogundokun, 2009). Madsen (1922) opine that students should be given guidance in accordance with their capacities and talents. This information may help in making the students aware of their own drawbacks and will provide them an opportunity to overcome them. Training in self-counselling may be given to low achievers in English to improve their marks. The study also revealed that female students with high luck attribution have low achievement in English as compared to the students with low or moderate luck attribution. It implies that tendency to depend upon luck should be discouraged and instead of it tendency to have faith in one's own ability and effort should be encouraged.

### Implications for Curriculum

Achievement in English has been found to be positively related to emotional intelligence, formal reasoning and academic motivation. It implies that English curriculum should be such that it should develop the formal reasoning ability, emotional intelligence and academic motivation of the students. For this, such literature content should be included in the English curriculum that emphasise and develops such abilities. As emotional intelligence has been found to be a teachable construct (Jaeger, 2002), conscious efforts should be made to integrate emotional intelligence into school curriculum. Emotional intelligence can also be inculcated through co-curricular activities related to English. Dramatising, role playing, story writing etc., may be incorporated in the English curriculum to develop emotional awareness, emotional sensitivity and emotional maturity of the students. According to Singaravelu (2008), inspirational subjects like poetry and literature help in developing an appreciation of the beautiful and sublime emotions in life. Reflective learning and group activity programmes can be included in the school curriculum to enhance IQ and emotional maturity of the students. In schools many things are taught to children through stories. Story characters have their own emotion and the ways to express, understand and control them. Children learn unconsciously the meaning, analysis and control of many emotions through the characters of the stories. English reading curriculum may be designed to train students to think better and help them understand and perceive emotional informations in a better way to inculcate emotional intelligence (Chu, 2005). In English literature such stories should be included which have the message of improving the academic motivation of the students. Exercises like vocabulary enrichment, word-formation through given letters may be given to the English students to foster their formal reasoning ability.

**Implications for English Language Teacher Educators**

The objective of teachers training programme is to develop in prospective teachers an understanding of the psychology of students, develop skills of guidance and counselling and to acquaint them with factors and forces affecting classroom situations. But, our efforts and programmes for preparing prospective teachers are far from being satisfactory. The emphasis on ceremonial completion of practice teaching and related co-curricular activities seldom motivate student-teachers to prepare lesson plans in accordance with students' cognitive and motivational characteristics. The English language teacher educators may acquaint English language teacher-trainees with the fact that intelligence, emotional intelligence, formal reasoning, and academic motivation of the students may positively effect their achievement in English. This would help the English language teacher trainees to give due importance to these psychological variables also while teaching English to the students. The study had revealed that diversity, goal direction and encouragement in classroom are positively related to students' achievement in English. So, efforts are needed to train student-teachers in understanding the characteristics of the learning environment and create environment that may facilitate learning of English language. They may also be trained as to where, when and how to deal with children of different dispositions, needs and cognitive preferences. The English language teacher-trainees should be taught how to maintain variety in the classroom to break monotonous teaching and encourage students' behaviour which will stimulate learning of students. In addition to this, the English language teacher-trainees should also be taught that their speed of teaching English should not be fast and the method should be according to the students' mental level. Such practice may lead to better achievement in English among students. The findings of the present study revealed that speed and difficulty dimension of the learning environment are negatively related to achievement in English. English language teacher educators must realise that it is their responsibility to prepare confident, committed and accountable English teachers who while teaching and evaluating students, must take into account the finding that English achievement is a function of intelligence, emotional intelligence, formal reasoning and friction, goal direction, democratic orientation and conformity in learning environment among male students and intelligence, formal reasoning, academic motivation, perceived friction and favouritism in classroom environment among female students. According to Sarojini (2006), the teacher education institutions may extend their programme to train the teachers to attain proficiency and efficiency in English language teaching and learning skills. English teacher-trainees may also be trained in stress-relief technique so that they can exhibit balanced expression of emotion and present a role model for students to develop emotional intelligence.

**Implications for Teachers**

English is a foreign language and students generally have fear and anxiety related to this language. It is the duty of the English teacher to remove such fear and anxiety regarding English. It is an acceptable goal of language learning that the teachers should be able to express with clarity and correctness the various aspects of language forms as well as they must keep in mind that individual students have distinct characteristics of their own. To educate effectively, attention has to be given to individual differences (Sutherland, 1990b). In the present study, significant effect of intelligence, emotional intelligence, formal reasoning has been found on achievement in English among male students. Intelligence, formal reasoning, academic motivation, luck attribution had significant effect on English achievement among female students. Thus, the teachers should realise that achievement in English is effected by several factors among which intelligence, emotional intelligence, formal reasoning, academic motivation and learning environment of the classroom are critical components. Therefore, it becomes imperative for the teachers to develop these cognitive abilities and boast motivational level of students who lack in it to raise the level of English achievement. Many researchers have shown that teachers are an important factor in enhancing students' learning and students' achievement. The teacher may use various strategies to develop emotional intelligence of the students. It is the teacher who may help to keep the lamp of emotional understanding burning among students by spreading emotional contagion. Teacher themselves may present good role models by exhibiting and showing a restrained and balanced expression of emotions. This shall have a healthy impact on the emotional development of the students and they may learn how to analyse and cope with life. Monitoring self-talk to catch negative messages, talking about feelings effectively, listening as well as asking questions, spontaneous sociability on the part of teachers may expand the light of emotional fitness among students (Singh, 2008b). For motivating students, individual differences in ability and causal attributions must be taken into consideration by the teachers. The present study has also revealed that male and female students differ from one another on mental ability, therefore, all the students cannot be taught by one single method. Thus, it becomes imperative for the teacher to provide education to the students according to their mental level. While planning curriculum, efforts should be made to base it on students' cognitive abilities. Since, luck attribution has been found to have significant effect on achievement in English among female students, the teacher must try to discourage female students to attribute their performance to luck because it may develop the tendency to believe on fate more than their own ability and effort. As a result of this girls will not undermine their performance. Teachers can try to develop in the students an attitude to internalise success or failure by accepting the cause of success or failure, for internal cause may improve the achievement of student (Gupta, 1994).

**Implications for Schools**

Cognitive factors like intelligence, emotional intelligence, formal reasoning and academic motivation as a motivational factor emerged as predictors of achievement in English in the study. It implies that schools also have to share the responsibility to enhance students' achievement in English by providing congenial environment in the classrooms to develop such cognitive and motivational aspects of the students. Academic motivation of the student depends upon his attitude towards school. In this regard, the schools may provide such an educational environment in the institution including facilities and resources that students appreciate them and make use of all the available opportunities for their growth. This will lead to interest and attention for school activities and help the students in his determination to get success in academic arena. Sports, games, dramatics and similar co-curricular activities are of great value for sublimation of emotions. So, schools may organize such constructive activities to foster emotional intelligence of students. Recent studies have shown that social-emotional programme (SEL) significantly improve socio-emotional skills and academic performance (Guil, Mestre and Gil-Olarte, 2004). Initiatives taken by the school administration to integrate SEL and academic programme may provide training in these skills to both teacher and students. Schools shall also take into consideration that the classrooms are not overcrowded because it creates hurdle for English teachers while dealing with students individually and in providing remedial instruction to them (Gupta, 2010). Schools may also organize short term cognitive training programme to improve students' cognitive abilities.

**Implications for Parents**

Asian parents often set very high standards for achievement of their children (Stevenson and Lee, 1990). They use harsh disciplinary methods to achieve compliance (Ho, 1981) and often express negative attitude towards the poor performance of their children (Hess, Chang and McDevitt, 1987). In the present social and educational scenario, parents suffer from psychological limitations so severely that they are unable to initiate an emotional cognitive learning process among their wards. Parents are very anxious about the results of their children. Due to excessive competition in the academic arena, English has become the need of the hour. To be successful in any professional field command over English is an added advantage. So, since childhood parents pressurise their wards to score good marks in English. The findings of the present study can help the parents to understand that intelligence, emotional intelligence, formal reasoning and academic motivation of students may affect students' achievement in English. So, while analysing students' achievement in English, such factors may also be taken into consideration by parents. Parents may foster formal reasoning ability of the students by providing them enough opportunities to use their hypothetical, deductive, reflective and combinatorial thinking. Parents may also foster emotional intelligence of their children by exhibiting emotionally intelligent behaviour on their own part. When young people embody the social-emotional competencies of self-awareness, discovery, respect and empathy for others, academic achievement soar (Keister, 2006). There is need to educate parents to realise the importance of home and provide an environment which is balanced and also congenial for the development of individual potential of students. The findings in the study justify the importance of motivation to academic performance in English. Thus, parents may motivate the students to improve their academic performance in English.

**Implications for Development of Academic Motivation among Students**

An important finding of the study is the significant contribution of academic motivation to achievement in English. The positive relationship between the two variables is probably due to the fact that highly academically motivated students work harder or persistently and thus, acquire or produce more. So, it becomes imperative to give some suggestions concerning the primary problem of arousing and maintenance of academic motivation. Intrinsic academic motivating properties such as English reading, writing, note taking, concentrating over a point, developing a healthy attitude towards school or education, critical and creative thinking may be developed among students for enhancing academic motivation and achievement in English. The educational administrators, teachers, counsellors, and parents shall concentrate their attention not only on intrinsic motivation but also on extrinsic motivation because extrinsic motivation plays an important role in the development of academic motivation (Hilgrad and Rusell, 1950; Ryans, 1942). Teachers and administrators may give rewards, praise, prizes or stars which impel the students to develop academic aspiration, study habits and favourable attitude towards school in order to get better achievement in English. Students' initial discouragement due to poor performance in English may be avoided and prevented by judicious use of external incentives. This may also help in maintaining academic motivation of students. Teachers may make English teaching interesting by shifting to novel methods of teaching instead of resorting to the use of chalk and talk in order to increase students' motivation to learn. The efforts of the student must be recognised and rewarded and the teacher should not discourage or punish the pupils for their inadequate performance or lack of comprehension of even the most rudimentary concept. Teachers should lead students to attribute failing performance to low effort. This may also help in maintaining academic motivation of the students because the failing student who believes that he or she did not try hard enough can be bolstered by the expectation that failure need not reoccur again (Graham, 2003). In the English classroom students may be given constant information concerning their level of performance in English. This feedback has the greatest motivational value (Tollefson, 2000). In order to keep the students motivationally oriented, teachers should try to enhance their learning goals. It is because when learning-oriented students encounter obstacles, they tend to keep trying and their motivation and performance actually increases (Pentrich. 2000; Schunk, 1996).

**Implications for Development of Positive Learning Environment**

The conditions, processes and psychological stimuli which influence the educational achievement of the child constitute educational environment (Dave, 1963). Researches have highlighted the importance of positive classroom learning environment created by students (Borich, 2000; Kauchak and Eggen, 1998). A positive learning environment is one in which all students feel comfortable, wanted, valued, accepted and secure (Madhavi and Kishan, 2009). In the present study, goal direction, democratic orientation and conformity emerged as the best predictors of achievement in English among male students. Male students' understanding and acceptance of the achievable and appropriate goals in classroom situations helps them to try to perform goal oriented behaviour. They properly channelize their energy in positive work performance. Similarly perception of democratic orientation and conformity in the classroom has positive effect on academic performance of students. The present study also reveals that friction and favouritism dimension of learning environment emerged as the best predictors of achievement in English among female students.

The study also highlights that perception of high diversity, goal direction and creative stimulation in the classroom leads to high achievement in English, while perception of high speed, favouritism, difficulty and apathy in classroom leads to low achievement in English. Thus, every possible effort needs to be made by the teacher to sets the climate for the learning of the students (Pandey and Lal, 2002). According to Ladylit (2008), in classroom teachers' tone is extremely important in establishing a positive classroom environment. The teachers must introduce variety in the classroom and this may be achieved by using ICT, multimedia and audio-visual aids for teaching English. Use of audio-visual aid will stimulate the interest of pupils in learning English (Bhargava and Tripathi, 1976) and provides the greatest support for vocabulary acquisition in English (Hernandez, 2004). English teachers also opine that utilising active learning method is crucial as it makes student participate in the discussion, integrate their learning experiences and raise their interest of learning English (Latchanna and Dagnew, 2009). Adams and Brindley (2008) stress the potential of ICT to become a part of the collaborative force of English lessons. Teachers should also make students understand and accept goals of the class. Teachers can create goal structure that affects students' personal goals and achievement in classroom. While teaching English teachers should keep in mind the specific objectives of learning English and clarify to the students the behavioural changes that are expected from them. Various activities may also be arranged in the classroom by the teachers to stimulate creative thinking ability of the students. In addition to this, teachers may also see that the speed of their teaching should not be fast. They should not practice favouritism because the effect of unequal treatment by teachers on English achievement is negative and apathy in classroom situation should be avoided.

Results pertaining to relationship between achievement in English and various dimensions of learning environment imply that more diversity, goal direction and encouragement and less speed, friction, favouritism, difficulty, apathy, cliqueness and disorganization may help in building a congenial atmosphere in the classroom. Such positive environment will contribute to achievement in English. The study has revealed differential effect of various dimensions of the learning environment on achievement in English. So, teachers of boy's school should pay more attention to avoid speed, friction, difficulty, apathy, cliqueness and disorganization in the classroom while teachers of girls' school should pay more attention to ensure diversity, goal direction and encouragement in the classroom.

Teachers while teaching English may also give encouragement to students responses to stimulate learning. A classroom environment that encourages the pupils to have confidence in their abilities, to increase effort and to search for successful solutions when confronted with initial failure can increasingly improve the motivation of those individuals (Rogers, 1990).

**Implications for Understanding the Dynamics of the Effect of Intelligence, Emotional Intelligence, Formal Reasoning and Causal Attributions**

The implication of attribution theory for the understanding of classroom behaviour suggests that the way educational success and failure are attributed by the student will markedly affect future educational behaviour. Effective learning in an educational setting will be more likely if the student attributes his success and failure to himself *i.e.,* his success to high ability and effort and his failure to modifiable factor *i.e.,* lack of effort. It has been convincingly demonstrated that causal attributions influence the likelihood of undertaking achievement activities and the degree of persistence in the face of failure. The present study has revealed that task difficulty, ability, effort, spiritual and support factors of causal attribution have no significant effect on achievement in English. The only exception is luck attribution which had significant effect on achievement in English among female students. It was found that female students with high luck attribution have low achievement in English. However, the same was not true in case of male students. It implies that female students should be trained not to attribute their success to their luck because if they do so then they will attribute their low achievement also to their luck and there will be no future expectancy of success. Causal attributions and their dimensions have their effect on future expectancy of success and affective reaction towards success and failure. Success attributed to an internal cause such as effort produces a sense of pride and attribution of success to stable factors (ability) affects future expectation of success and failure (Salili, 1996).

In the present study, male students were found to be more emotionally intelligent as compared to female students and among them there exists positive relationship between emotional intelligence and achievement in English. Male students with high emotional intelligence have high achievement in English. Emotional intelligence also emerged as one of the best predictor of achievement in English. Emotional intelligence is characterised by a comprehensive grouping of individual skills and dispositions which make up the competency profile of a person. Expression of emotions, management of emotions, knowing other's feeling well and dealing effectively with other people's feelings are very necessary in one's life. They are regarded as the prime factors that influence an individual's chances of success in life. Suppressed emotions and too much control over them lead to immobilising depression, overwhelming anxiety, rage, anger and manic agitation (Goleman, 1995). It is the duty of the teacher to develop the emotional intelligence through various strategies. It can be inculcated through curricular and co-curricular activities. Fostering emotional intelligence can assist students in adapting to the environmental demands and pressures of the school environment. According to Goleman (1995), emotional literacy programme improve children's academic achievement and school performance. EQ training increases focus, learning collaboration, improves classroom relationship and decreases negative put downs and violence. Teaching of emotional intelligence can lead to enhanced academic performance (Chopra, 2009). School children can also be trained to improve their level of emotional maturity through various interventions using cognitive therapy as well as behaviourable therapy.

Intelligence emerged as one of the best predictors of achievement in English among both male and female students. Level of intelligence had a significant positive effect on achievement in English. Students with high intelligence have high achievement in English than their counterparts with low or moderate intelligence. It implies that students shall be given training to capitalize on their capacities and talents. According to Sternberg (2002), by teaching for successful intelligence, students can be taught more effectively. Teaching for successful intelligence involves instructing and assessing analytically, creatively and practically for memory. Such teaching helps students recognise and capitalize on strengths and at the same time recognise and correct or compensate for weaknesses. Thus, teaching for successful intelligence really works in the classroom in raising students' achievement.

**SUGGESTIONS FOR FURTHER RESEARCH**

The present study was conducted on a sample of students of Allahabad city. It may be replicated on a sample of students studying in urban and rural areas.

Use of various teaching strategies may influence students' achievement in English. So, study may be undertaken to find out predictors of English achievement among students taught by different methods of teaching.

Besides these, the following studies may also be undertaken to find answers to following research questions:

- Do determinants of achievement in English among students studying in different board schools differ from one another?
- Does family environment contributes to prediction of achievement in English?
- How can intelligence, emotional intelligence, formal reasoning, academic motivation, causal attributions and various dimensions of classroom environment contribute to prediction of achievement in English among students of general, OBC, SC and ST categories?
- How are self-concept, self-efficacy, aptitude and personality traits related to achievement in English?
- How do academic aspiration, test anxiety, stress and study habits influence achievement in English.?

# REFERENCES

Abdullah, S. (2007). Emotional Intelligence and Academic Achievement: A Study in Kolej Matrikulasi Perlis. Doctoral Dissertation, Utara University, Malaysia.

Abdullahi, O. E. (1996). Student Responsibility in Poor Academic Performance in Kwara State Secondary Schools. *IFE Psychologia: An International Journal*, 4 (1), 64-79.

Abedi, J. (2004). The No Child Left behind Act and English Language Learners: Assessment and Accountability Issues. *Educational Researcher*, 33 (1), 4-14.

Abrol D. N. (1977). A Study of Achievement Motivation in Relation to Intelligence, Vocational Interest, Achievement, Sex and Socio-Economic Status. Doctoral Dissertation, Delhi University.

Adams, S. and Brindley, S. (2008). *Teaching Secondary English with ICT*. Maiden Head: Open University Press.

Adeoye, H. (2010). Emotional Intelligence and Self-Efficacy as Determinants of Academic Achievement in English Language among Students in Oyo State Senior Secondary Schools. www.faqs.org.

Adey, P. S. and Shayer, M. (1994). *Really Raising Standards: Cognitive Intervention and Academic Achievement*. London: Routledge.

Adeyemo, D. A. and Adetona, O. (2007). A Path Analytic Study of the Factors Affecting Student Learning Outcomes in Mathematics. *European Journal of Scientific Research*. In D. A. Adeyemo (2007). Moderating Influence of Emotional Intelligence on the Link between Academic Self-Efficacy and Achievement of University Students. *Psychology and Developing Societies*, 19 (2), 199-213.

Adeyemo, D. A. (2007). Moderating Influence of Emotional Intelligence on the Link between Academic Self-Efficacy and Achievement of University Students. *Psychology and Developing Societies*, 19 (2), 199-213.

Adeyemo, O. A. (2004). Patterns of Emotional Intelligence among Counselling Psychology Students in a Nigerian University. *Sokota Educational Review*, 7, 194-203.

Agarwal, T. (1993). An Analytical Study of Psycho-social Cognitive and Non-cognitive Factors of Academic Achievement of Special Group. Doctoral Dissertation, Dayalbagh Educational Institute.

Aghasafari, M.(2006). On The Relationship between Emotional Intelligence and Language Learning Strategies. Doctoral Dissertation, Allameh Tabataba' ii University, Tehran.

Ahluwalia, I. (1985). A Study of Factors Affecting Achievement Motivation. Doctoral Dissertation, Agra University.

Alam, M. (2010). Effect of Emotional Intelligence and Academic Stress on Academic Success among Adolescents. *Journal of Community Guidance and Research*, 27 (1), 53-61.

Alam, M. M. (2001). Academic Achievement in Relation to Socio-Economic Status, Anxiety Level and Achievement Motivation: A Comparative Study of Muslim and Non-Muslim School Children of Uttar Pradesh. Doctoral Dissertation, Aligarh Muslim University.

Allen, D. and Fraser, B. J. (2007). Parent and Student Perceptions of Classroom Learning Environment and Its Association with Student Outcomes. *Learning Environment Research*, 10 (1), 67-82.

Alloway, B. M. (2004). Emotional Intelligence and Extrinsic Career Success: A Comparison of Gender and Management. *Dissertation Abstracts International*, 66 (1), 601-B.

Anandmani, A. (2006). A Study of General Intelligence and Emotional Intelligence in Relation to Achievement among IX Class Students. *Journal of Educational Studies*, 14 (1 - 2), 47-49.

Anderson, C. S. (1982). The Search for School Climate: A Review of the Research. *Review of Educational Research*, 52, 368-420.

Anderson, L. W. and Burns, R. B. (1989). *Research in Classroom*. Oxford: Pergamon Press.

Areepattamannil and Freeman (2008). Academic Achievement, Academic Self-Concept and Academic Motivation of Immigrant Adolescents of Greater Toronto area Secondary School. *Journal of Advanced Academics*, 19 (4), 700-743.

Arkin , A. M. and Maruvama, G. M. (1979). Attribution Affect and College Exam Performance. *Journal of Educational Psychology*, 71, 85-93.

Armstrong, W. H. (1956). Study is Hardwork. *Psychological Abstracts*, 30.

Aruna, N. S. (1981). A Study of the Factors Influencing the Achievement of Standard VII Students Belonging to Scheduled Castes and Scheduled Tribes whose Medium of Instruction is Kannada. Doctoral Dissertation, Mysore University.

Aswal, G. S. (2001). Intelligence as Acorrelate of Achievement in Mathematics across Different Levels of SES. *Psycho-Lingua*, 31, 127-130.

Atkinson, J. W. (1957). Motivation Determinants of Risk Behaviour. *Psychological Review*, 64, 359-372.

Atkinson, J. W. (1964). *An Introduction to Motivation*. Princeton, N J: Van Nostrand.

Atkinson, J. W. (1967). Implications of Curvilinearity in the Relationship of Efficiency of Performance to Strength of Motivation for Studies of Individual Differences in Achievement Related Motives. Paper presented at National Academy of Sciences Meeting on October 24, 1967, University of Michigan.

Atkinson, S. W. and Feather, N. T. (Eds.) (1966). *A Theory of Achievement Motivation*. New York: John Wiley.

Austin, E. I., Evans, P., Goldwater, R. and Potter, V. (2005). A Preliminary Study of Emotional Intelligence, Empathy and Exam Performance in First Year Medical Students. *Personality and Individual Differences*, 39 (8), 1395-1405.

Avinashilingam, N. A. V. and Sharma, G. (2005). Identification of Factors Influencing the Students' Academic Performance. *Journal of Educational Research and Extension*, 42 (1), 25-32.

Ayishabi, T. C. (1990). A Study of Group Difference in Certain Achievement – Related Personality Variables of College Students. Doctoral Dissertation, University of Calicut.

Baek, S. and Choi, H. (2002). The Relationship between Students' Perceptions of Classroom Environment and their Academic Achievement in Korea. *Asia Pacific Education Review*, 3 (1), 125-135.

Bag, A. (1990. A Cross-sectional Study on the Differential Aptitude of the Students in English. Doctoral Dissertation, University of Kalyani.

Bailey R. C., Helm B. and Glandstone, R. (1975). The Effects of Success and Failure in a Real-Life Setting: Performance, Attribution, Affect and Expectancy. *Journal of Psychology*, 89, 137-147.

Balasubramanian, N. (1989). A Study of Classroom Climate in Relation to Pupils Achievement in English at Higher Secondary Stage. *Indian Educational Abstracts*, 2, 21.

Balasubramanian, N. (1993). A Study of Pupils' Academic Achievement in English in Relation to their Intelligence. *The Journal of English Language Teaching*, 28 (5), 128-137.

Balasubramanian, N. (1994). A Study of Academic Achievement in Relation to Achievement Values and Anxiety. *Perspectives in Education*, 10 (2), 109-113.

Bano, A. (1995). A Study of Mis-conceptions Concerning Genetics and Evolution in Biology at High School Level in Relation to Formal Reasoning Ability, Cognitive Style and Achievement. Doctoral Dissertation, Baraktullah University.

Bano, R. (2010). Emotional Intelligence in Relation to Academic Achievement of Secondary School Students. *Souvenir* of National Seminar on Emotional Intelligence: A Key to Human Well-being, held on 4-5 March, 2010 at Amity University, Lucknow.

Barchard, K. A. (2003). Does Emotional Intelligence Assist in the Prediction of the Academic Success? *Educational and Psychological Measurement*, 63 (5), 840-858.

Barnett, M. and Kaiser, D. (1978). The Relationship between Intellectual Achievement Responsibility Attributions and Performance. *Child Study Journal*, 8, 209-215.

Bar-On, R. (1997). *EQ-I Technical Manual*. Canada: Multi-Health System.

Bar-On, R. (2000). Emotional and Social Intelligence: Insights from the Emotional Quotient Inventory. In R. Bar-On and J. D. A. Parker (Eds.) *Handbook of Emotional intelligence*. San Francisco: Jossey Bass.

Bar-On, R. (2003). How Important is to Educate People to be Emotionally and Socially Intelligent and can it be done? *Perspectives in Education*, 21 (4), 3-13.

Bar-On, R. (2006). The Baron Model of Emotional-Social Intelligence. *Psichotema*, 18, 13-25.

Bar-Tal, D. (1978). Attributional Analysis of Achievement Related Behaviour. *Review of Educational Research*, 48, 259-271.

Barton, K., Dielman, T. E. and Cattell, R. B. (1972). Prediction of School Achievement from Motivation, Personality and Ability Measures. *Psychological Reports*, 30, 35-43.

Baskaran, K. (1991). Achievement Motivation, Attitude towards Problem-Solving and Achievement in Mathematics of Standard X Students in Devakottai Educational District. Doctoral Dissertation, Alagappa University.

Bastian, V. A., Burns, N. R., and Nettelbeck, T. (2005). Emotional Intelligence Predicts Life Skills but not as well as Personality and Cognitive Abilities. *Psychological Abstracts*, 93, 7473.

Bates, E. (1976). Pragmatics and Sociolinguistics in Child Language. In D.M. Morehead and A.E. Morehead (Eds.) *Directions in Normal and Deficient Child Language*. Baltimore: University Park Press.

Beharwal, S. (1986). Locus of Control and Attribution of Responsibility for Success and Failure. Doctoral Dissertation, University of Allahabad.

Behera, A. K. (2002). Intelligence, Achievement Motivation and Personality of Vocational Students in Relationship to Academic Achievement. Doctoral Dissertation, Punjab University.

Benno, M. A. (1995). A Study of Certain Correlates of Academic Achievement among Scheduled Castes Students in the Union Territory of Pondicherry. Doctoral Dissertation, University of Mysore.

Berenson, R., Boyles, G. and Weaver, A. (2008). Emotional Intelligence as a Predictor for Success in Online Learning. *The International Review of Research in Open and Distance Learning*, 9 (2).

Bernstein, B. (1961). Social Class and Linguistic Developmwnt: A Theory of Social Learning. In A. H. Halsey, J. Floud and C. A. Anderson (Eds.), *Education, Economy, and Society*. London: Collier Macmillan.

Bernstein, B. (1970). Language and Social Class. *British Journal of Sociology*, 5 (11).

Bernstein, B. (1971). *Class, Codes and Control: Theoretical Studies towards Sociology of Language*, Vol. 1. London: Routledge Kegan Paul.

Bernstein, W. M., Stephan, W. G. and Davis, M. H. (1979). Explaining Attributions for Achievement: A Path Analytic Approach. *Journal of Personality and Social Psychology*, 37, 1810-1821.

Besharat, M. A., Rezazadeh, M. R., Firozi, M. and Habibi, M. (2005). The Study of the Impact of Emotional Intelligence on the Psychological Health and Academic Success in a Transitional Period from the High School to the University. *Journal of Psychological Science*, 4 (1), 27-42.

Bhalla, A. (2010). Scholastic Achievement in Relation to Emotional Intelligence of Science Students of Senior Secondary Classes. *The CTE National Journal*, 7 (2) and 8 (1), 118-120.

Bhargava, M. and Tripathi, O. P. (1976). The use of Audio-Visual Aids in Teaching of English as a Foreign Language. *Psycho-Lingua*, 6 (1-2), 29-36.

Bhatnagar, A. (1999). A Comparative Study of the Achievement in Language of the X Class Students in Government and Public Schools in Relation to Certain Non-cognitive Attributes. Doctoral Dissertation, M. D. University.

Bhusari, C. V. (1988). Intelligence of SC and ST Students and Its Correlation with their Scholastic Achievement in Vidarbha. Doctoral Dissertation, Nagpur University.

Biehler, R. F. and Snowman, J. (1986). *Psychology Applied to Teaching*. Boston: Houghton Mifflin Company.

Borich, G. D. (1988). *Effective Teaching Methods*. Columbus: Ohioan Merrill Publication Company.

Borich, G. D. (2000). *Effective Teaching Methods*. Upper Saddle River: Merrill.

Boruchovitch, E. (2004). A Study of Causal Attributions for Success and Failure in Mathematics among Brazilian Students. *Interamerican Journal of Psychology*, 38 (1), 53-60.

Bose, K. (2002). *Teaching of English: A Modern Approach*. DOABA House: New Delhi.

Brackett, M. and Mayer, J. D. (2003). Convergent, Discriminant and Incremental Validity of Competing Measures of Emotional Intelligence. *Personality and Social Psychology Bulletin*, 29, 1147-1158.

Brackett, M. A., Mayer, J. D. and Warner, R. M. (2004). Emotional Intelligence and Its Relation to Everyday Behaviour. *Personality and Individual Differences*, 36 (6), 1387-1402.

Brackett, M. A., Warner, R. M. and Bosco, J. S. (2005). Emotional Intelligence and Relationship Quality among Couples. *Psychological Abstracts*, 92 (7-8), 2758.

Brahmabhatt, J. C. (1983). A Study of Preparation of Language Programme in English for Pupils of Class VIII and Its Effect on Achievement in Relation to Some Psycho-social Factors. Doctoral Dissertation, Sardar Patel University.

Brenner, E. and Salovey, P. (1997). In P. Salovey and D. Sluyter (Eds.) *Emotional Development and Emotional Intelligence for Educators*. New York: Basic Books.

Bridgeman, B. and Shipman, V. C. (1978). Pre-school Measures of Self-Esteem and Achievement Motives as Predictors of third Grade Achievement. *Journal of Educational Psychology*, 70, 17-28.

Brookover, W. B., Schweitzer, J. H. and Schneider, J. M. (1978). Elementary School Social Climate and School Achievement. *American Educational Research Journal*, 15, 301-318.

Broussard, S. C. and Garrison, M. E. (2004). The Relationship between Classroom Motivation and Academic Achievement in Elementary School-aged Children. *Family Consumer Science Research Journal*, 33 (2), 106-120.

Brown, J. D. and Rogers, R. J. (1991). Self-Serving Attributions: The Role of Psychological Arousal. *Personality and Social Psychology Bulletin*, 17 (5), 501-506.

Brown, R. and Fraser, C. (1963). The Acquisition of Syntax. In U. Bellugi and R. Brown (Eds.) The Acquisition of Language. *Monographs of the Society for Research in Child Development*, 29, 43-79.

Buch, M. B. (1979). *Second Survey of Research in Education*. Baroda: Society for Educational Research and Development.

Buch, M. B. (1987). *Third Survey of Research in Education 1978-1983*. New Delhi: NCERT.

Buch, M. B. (1988). In M. B. Buch (Ed.) (1991). *Fourth Survey of Research in Education* 1983-88. New Delhi: NCERT.

Buch, M. B. (1991). *Fourth Survey of Research in Education 1983-88*, Vol. 1, New Delhi: NCERT.

Buch, M. B. (1991). *Fourth Survey of Research in Education 1983-88*, Vol. 2, New Delhi: NCERT.

Buch, M. B. (2000). *Fifth Survey of Educational Research 1988-92*, Vol. 1. New Delhi: NCERT.

Buch, M. B. (2000). *Fifth Survey of Educational Research 1988-92*, Vol. 2. New Delhi: NCERT.

Buch, M. B., Patel, J. M. and Kotwal, S. D. (1960). Achievement Tests for Standard VIII of Secondary Schools in Gujrat. Ministry of Education Financed Project, Maharaja Sayaji Rao University.

Burgner, D. and Hewstone, M. (1993). Young Children's Causal Attributions for Success and Failure: Self-financing Boys and Self-derogating Girls. *British Journal of Developmental Psychology*, 11, 125-129.

Byrne. D. B., Hattie, J. A. and Fraser, B. J. (1986). Student Perception of Preferred Classroom Learning Environment. *Journal of Educational Research*, 80 (1), 10-18.

Carroll, J. B. (1963). A Model of School Learning. *Teacher's College Record*, 64, 723-733.

Carroll, J. B. (1969). In R. L. Ebel. V.H. Noll and R.M. Bauer (Eds.) Encyclopedia of Educational Research. USA: McMillan Company.

Carroll, J. B. (1974). Learning Theory for the Classroom Teacher. In G.A. Jarvis (Ed.), *The Challenge of Communicatio*, Vol. 6. Skokie FLL: National Textbook Company.

Cattell, R. B. and Butcher, J. (1968). *The Prediction of Achievement and Creativity*. Indian Polis, Ind.: Bobbs-Merrill.

Cattell, R. B. and Horn, J. L. (1966). Refinement and Test of the Theory of Fluid and Crystallized General Intelligence. *Journal of Educational Psychology*, 57, 253-270.

Cattell, R. B. (1971). *Abilities: Their Structure, Growth and Action*. Boston: Houghton Mifflin.

Cattell, R. B. S. and Cattell, A. K. S. (1973). *Measuring Intelligence with the Culture Fair Tests: Manual for Scales 2 and 3*. New Delhi: Psycho Centre.

Chadha, N. K. and Chandna, S. (1990). Creativity, Intelligence and Scholastic Achievement: A Residual Study. *Indian Educational Review*, 25 (3), 31-85.

Chakrabarti, S. (1988). A Critical Study of Intelligence, Socio-Economic Background of the Family, Educational Environment in the Family and Quality of Schools in Children of Standard V – A Case Study of Some Schools in and Around Pune. Doctoral Dissertation, Poona University.

Chalfont, J. (2000). School Failure. In C.R. Reynolds and E. Fletcher-Janzen (Eds.) *Encyclopedia of Special Education*, Vol. 3. USA: John Wiley and Sons.

Chamundesweri, S. and Vaidharani, S. (2006). General Mental Alertness and Intelligence in Relation to Academic Achievement of Students at the Secondary Level. *Journal of Educational Research and Extension*, 43 (2), 32-46.

Chan, L. K. and Youlden, A. (1995). Motivation Orientations, Strategic Learning and Achievement in English in years 5, 7 and 9 Students: Prelimainary findings. Paper presented at the Australian Association for Research in Education. Annual Conference, Hobart, Nov. 1995.

Chandra, J. G. (1988). Correlates of Written English at the Plus Two Stage. Doctoral Dissertation, University of Madras.

Chandy, S. (1991). Application of Certain Pupil Deficit Models to Differential Achievement in English. Doctoral Dissertation, University of Kerala.

Charles, E. A. (1993). A Study of the Factors Affecting the Academic Performance of Standard X Students of Greater Bombay at the SSC Examination of March 1989 Conducted by the Bombay Divisional Board. Doctoral Dissertation, University of Bombay.

Chatterji, B. (1987). An Investigation into Interdependence of Cognitive Development and Language Development in the Middle School Children. Doctoral Dissertation, Rajasthan University.

Chatterji, S. and Mukherjee, M. (1970). Construction and Development of a Test of English Knowledge and Comprehension at the Higher Secondary Level. Psychometric Research and Service Unit, ISI, Calcutta.

Chaturvedi, M. G. and Mohale, B. U. (1976). *Position of Language in School Curriculum in India.* New Delhi: NCERT.

Chauhan, S. (2008). Relationship between Emotional Intelligence and Adjustment among College going Students. *Shikshak-Shiksha Shodh Patrika*, 2 (4), 16-25.

Chauhan, V. L. and Bhatnagar, T. (2003). Assessing Emotional Maturity, Emotional Expression and Emotional Quotient of Adolescent Male and Female Students. *Journal of Community Guidance and Research*, 20 (2), 157-167.

Chawla, S. (1992). Standardisation of a Multiple-choice Vocabulary Test: Pre-test and Analysis. *Indian Educational Review*, 27 (3), 49-68.

Chhikara, M. S. (1985). An Investigation into the Relationship of Reasoning Abilities with Achievement of Concepts in Life Sciences. Doctoral Dissertation, Jamia Milia Islamia University.

Chico, C. (1999). Evaluation Psicometrea de una Escala de Intelligence Emotional. Psychometric Evaluation of an Emotional Intelligence Scale *Boletin de Psicologie*, 62.

Chitra, J. U., Thiagarajan, A. P. and Krishnan, S. S. (1995). Psycho-social Educational Factors of SC Students in Higher Secondary Schools. *The Progress of Education,* LXX (4), 87-89.

Chomsky, N. A. (1959). *Syntactic Structures*. Hague: Mouton.

Chomsky, N. A. (1965). *Aspects of the Theory of Syntax.* Cambridge: MIT Press.

Chopra, V. (2009). Educational Implications of Emotional Intelligence for better Teacher and Student Performance. *MERI Journal of Education,* 4 (1), 51-58.

Chou, A. (2005). Factors Affecting the Learning of English: A Study of the Attitudes toward and Motivations for Learning English as a Foreign Language among University Students in Taiwan. *Dissertation Abstracts International,* 66 (6), 2137-A.

Chouhan, V. L. and Bhatnagar, T. (2003). Assessing Emotional Maturity, Emotional Expression and Emotional Quotient of Edolescent Male and Female Students. *Journal of Community Guidance and Research,* 20 (2), 157-167.

Chu, Y. (2005). Celebrating Self-Actualization: Improving Emotional Intelligence through a Cognitive-based English Reading Curriculum. *Dissertation Abstracts International,* 66 (6), 2137-A

Ciarrochi, J. C. A. and Bajgar, J. (2001). Measuring Emotional Intelligence in Adolescents. *Personality and Individual Differences,* 28.

Ciarrochi, J. V., Chan, A. Y. and Caputi, P. (2000). A Critical Evaluation of the Emotional Intelligence Construct. *Personality and Individual Differences,* 28, 539-561.

Clement, B. A. and Singh, B. K. M. (1993). Medium of Instruction – Its Effect on Learning English. *Indian Psychological Abstracts and Reviews,* 1 (2), 330-331.

Click, H. S. (2002). An Exploration of Emotional Intelligence Scores among Students in Educational Administration Programme. Doctoral Dissertation, East Tennessee State University.

Cloutier, R. and Goldschmid, M. L. (1976). Individual Differences in the Development of Formal Reasoning. *Child Development,* 47 (4), 1097-1102.

Codaty, J. (2008). *Understanding Emotional EQ*. Delhi: Pustak Mahal.

Cole, K. N., Dale, P. S. and Thal, D. J. (Eds.) (1996). *Assessment of Communication and Language.* Baltimore: Brookes.

Commons, M., Miller, P. and Kuhn, D. (1979). In D. Kuhn, V. Ho and C. Adams (1979). Formal Reasoning among pre-and Late Adolescents. *Child Development,* 50 (4), 1128-1135.

Constantino, R., Lee, S. and Krashen, S. (1997). Free Voluntary Reading as Apredictor of TOEFL Scores. *Applied Language Learning,* 8, 111-118.

Crandall, V., Katkovsky, W. and Crandall, V. (1975). Children's Belief in their own Control of Reinforcements in Intellectual and Academic Achievement Situations. *Child Development*, 36, 91-109.

Cronbach, L. J. (1954). *Educational Psychology.* New York: Harcourt Brace and Co.

Dalal, A. K. (1988). *Attribution Theory and Research.* New Delhi: Wiley Eastern Limited.

Dart, B., Burnett, P., Boulton-Lewis, G., Campbell, J., Smith, D. and McCrindle, A. (1999). Classroom Learning Environment and Students' Approaches to Learning. *Learning Environments Research*, 2 (2), 137-156.

Das, S. (1986). Peer Influence and Educational Aspiration of Secondary School Students: A Study in Relation to their Academic Achievement. Doctoral Dissertation, Maharaja Sayajirao University.

Dash, B. N. (2004). *Teaching of English.* Dominant Publishers and Distributors. New Delhi.

Daudi, M. A. R. and Yahya, R. (2008). Importance of English in Knowledge Society. *Gyanodaya*, 1(1), 8-12.

Dave, R. H. (1963). The Identification and Measurement of Environment Process Variables that are Related to Educational Achievement. Doctoral Dissertation, University of Chicago.

Deary, I. J., Strand, S., Smith, P. and Fernandes, C. (2007). Intelligence and Educational Achievement. *Intelligence*, 35, 13-21. www.sciencedirect.com

Deaux. K. and Farris, E. (1977). Causal Attributions for Performance: Approaching Substance via Method. In T. W. Elig and I. H. Freize (1979). Measuring Casual Attribution for Success and Failure. *Journal of Personality and Social Psychology*, 37 (4), 621-634.

DeCarcer, I. A., Gabel, D. L. and Staver, J. R. (1978). Implications of Piagetian Research for High School Science Teaching: A Review of the Literature. *Science Education*, 62, 571-583.

Deci, E. L., Vallerand, R. J., Pelletier, L. G. and Ryan, R. M. (1991). Motivation in Education: The Self-Determination Perspectives. *Educational Psychologist*, 26, 325-346.

DeMarrais, K. B. and LeCompte, M. D. (1995). *The Way Schools Work: A Sociological Analysis of Education*. New York: Longman.

Desai, S. B. (1979). A Study of Classroom Ethos, Pupils Motivation and Academic Achievement Ph.D. (Edu.), Maharaja Sayaji Rao University, Baroda.

Deshpande (1972). In M. B. Buch (Ed.) (1986). *Third Survey of Research in Education 1978-1983*. New Delhi: NCERT.

Deshpande, M. U. (1971). An Analytical Study of some Scholastic Conditions and Practices and Contributing Factors to Creative Ability. Unpublished Doctoral Dissertation, Nagpur University.

Devanesan, P. P. (1990). Socio-Economic Status, Achievement – Motivation and Scholastic Achievement of Higher Secondary Students in Pasumpon Thevar Thirumagan District. M. Phil. Dissertation, Alagappa University.

Devi, U. A. (1990). Pupil's Academic Achievement in Relation to their Intelligence, Neuroticism and Locus of Control. M.Phil. Dissertation, Annamalai University.

Dewal, O. S. (1974). A Study of Difficulties in Teaching English and Effectiveness of Programmed Teaching. Doctoral Dissertation, Maharaja Sayaji Rao University, Baroda.

Dey, S. (1991). A Critical Appraisal of the Abilities of the Students in some Aspects of English as a Second Language and Finding out some Linguistic Factors. Doctoral Dissertation, University of Kalyani.

Dhaka, M. S. (2008). English Language and Communication Skills. *University News*, 46 (18), 5-10.

Dhall, S. and Thukral, P. (2010). Intelligence as Related to Self-Confidence and Academic Achievement of School Students. *Journal of All India Association for Educational Reseach*, 21 (2), 80-84.

Dhami, G. S. (1974). Intelligence, Emotional Maturity and Socio-Economic Status as Factors Indicative of Success in Scholastic Achievement. Doctoral Dissertation, Punjab University.

Dhar, R. N. (1989). Effect of School Environment and Approval Motive on Memory and Achievement. Doctoral Dissertation, University of Gorakhpur.

Dipti and Sharma, I. (2008). The Effect of Emotional Intelligence and Academic Anxiety on Academic Achievement. M.Ed. Dissertation, Dayalbagh Educational Institute, Agra.

DiSibio, M. (1993). Conjoint Effects of Intelligence and Adaptive Behaviour on Achievement in a Non-referred Sample. *Journal of Psycho-Educational Assessment*, 11 (4), 304-313.

DiVesta, F. J. (1982). Cognitive Development. In H. E. Mitzel (Ed.) (1982). *Encyclopedia of Educational Research*, Vol. I. New York: The Free Press.

Dixit, M. K. (1985). A Comparative Study of Intelligence and Academic Achievement of Adolescent Boys and Girls Studying in Class IX and XI. Doctoral Dissertation, Kanpur University.

Dixit, S. K. (1989). The Effect of Personality Factors and Self-Concept on Educational Achievement. Doctoral Dissertation, Agra University.

Doctor, Z. N. (1984). A Study of Classroom Climate and the Psyche of Pupils and their Achievement. Doctoral Dissertation, South Gujrat University.

Downey, L. A., Mountstephen, J., Lloyd, J., Hansen, K. and Stough, C. (2008). Emotional Intelligence and Scholastic Achievement in Australian adolescents. *Australian Journal of Psychology*, 60 (1), 10-17.

Drago, J. M. (2004). The Relationship between Emotional Intelligence and Academic Achievement in Non-Traditional College Students. Doctoral Dissertation, Walden University.

Dubey (2009a). Emotional Intelligence among Undergraduate Students: A Survey. *Experiments in Education*, 37 (5), 25-28.

Dubey, R. (2007). A Study of Relationship between Achievement in Environmental Studies and Formal Reasoning among IX Class Students. *Journal of Educational Studies*, 5 (1), 14-16.

Dubey, R. (2008a). Cognitive Determinants of Academic Achievement among Socially Deprived. *Journal of Educational Studies*, 6 (2), 30-33.

Dubey, R. (2008b). A Study of Relationship between Emotional Intelligence and Achievement among Under-graduate Students. *Journal of Educational Studies*, 6(1), 46-50.

Dubey, R. (2009). Causal Attribution Patterns among High and Low Achievers in English. *Journal of Educational Studies*, 7 (2), 12-17.

Dubey, R. (2010a). Study of Achievement in Language in Relation to Intelligence, Emotional Intelligence and Formal Reasoning. *MERI Journal of Education*, 5 (1), 76-81.

Dubey, R. (2010b). Impact of Academic Motivation on Achievement in English. *Journal of Educational Studies*, 8 (1), 13-17.

Dubey, R. (2010c). Academic Motivation of High and Low Achievers of English. *Shikshamitra*, 2 (3), 36.

Dubey, R. (2010d). Learning Environment for Quality Teaching of English Grammar. *Journal of Education and Indian Perspectives*, 2 (1), 54-58.

Dubey, R. N. D. (1989). Effect of School Environment and Approval Motive on Memory and Achievement. Doctoral Dissertation, Gorakhpur University.

Dwivedi, A. N. (2005). Paryavaran Sangyan par Adhigam Shailey, Kaksha Vatavaran Tatha Vanchan ka Prabhav. Doctoral Dissertation, University of Allahabad.

Ebel, R. L., Noll, V. H. and Bauer, R. M. (Ed.) (1969). Encyclopedia of Educational Research. USA: The Macmillan Company.

Ediger, M. (1997). *Affective Objectives in the Science Curriculum*. Montgomery, AL: Arbun University.

Ehman L. H. (1980). Change in High School Students' Political Sttitudes as a Function of Social Studies Classroom Climate. *American Educational Research Journal*, 17, 253-265.

Elias, H., Mahyuddin, R., Abdullah, M. C., Roslan, S., Noonlin, N. and Fauzee, O. (2008). Emotional Intelligence of at Risk Students in Malaysian Secondary Schools. *The International Journal of Learning*, 14 (8), 51-56.

Ellekkakumar, B. and Elankathirselvan, N. (2001). Achievement Motivation of Higher Secondary Students and their Achievement in Physics. *Indian Educational Abstracts*, 6 (2), 45-46.

Emeke, E. A. and Adeoye, H. (2009). The Relative Effect of Emotional Intelligence and Self-Efficacy Training on the Scholastic Achievement of some Nigerian Secondary School Students. *Perspectives in Education*, 25 (3), 186-195.

Emeke, E. A., Adeyeo, A. and Torubelli, V. A. (2006). Locus of Control, Self-Concept and Emotional Intelligence as Correlates of Academic Achievement among Adolescents in Senior Secondary Schools in Oyo State, Nigeria. *Journal of Clinical and Counselling Psychology*, 12 (2), 122-139.

Entwistle, N. J. (1968). Academic Motivation and School Attainment. *British Journal of Educational Psychology*, 38(2), 181-188.

Eppler, M. A. and Harju, B. J. (1997). Achievement Motivation Goals in Relation to Academic Performance in Traditional and Non-Traditional College Students. *Researches in Higher Education*, 38, 557-573.

Eysenck, H. J. (1979). *The Structure and Measurement of Intelligence*. Berlin: Springer-Verlag.

Faether, N. T. and Simon, J. G. (1971). Causal Attributions for Success and Failure to Expectations of Success based upon Selective and Manipulative Control. *Journal of Personality*, 39 (1-4), 527-541.

Fahim, M. and Pishghadam, R. (2007). On The Role of Emotional, Psychometric and Verbal Intelligences in the Academic Achievement of University Students Majoring in English Language. *Asian EFL Journal*, 9 (4). www.asian_efl_jpurnal.com/Dec_2007_mfandrp.php

Fakeye, D. O. (2010). Students' Personal Variables as Correlates of Academic Achievement in English as a second language in Nigeria. *Journal of Social Sciences*, 22 (3), 205-211.

Farmer, S. S. (2000). Language Assessment. In C.R. Reynolds and E. Fletcher-Janzen (Eds.). *Encyclopedia of Special Education*, Vol. 2. USA: John Wiley and Sons.

Farook, A. (2003). The Effect of Emotional Intelligence on Academic Performance. Doctoral Dissertation, University of Karachi, Karachi.

Faroqui, M. A. (1974). Some Studies on Progressive Matrices test. In B. Krishnan (Ed.), *Studies in Psychology*. Mysore: University of Mysore.

Fatt, J. P. T. and Howe, J. C. K. (2003). Emotional Intelligence of Foreign and Local University Students in Singapore: Implications for managers. *Journal of Business and Psychology*, 17 (3), 345-367.

Feather, N. T. (1969). Attribution of Responsibility and Valence of Success and Failure in Relation to initial Confidence and Task Performance. *Journal of Personality and Social Psychology*, 13, 129-144.

Feldman, D. H. (1982), A Developmental Framework for Research with Gifted Children. In D. H. Feldman (Ed.). *Developmental Approaches to Giftedness and Creativiyt.* San Francisco: Jossey Bass.

Fernandez – Ballesteros, R. (Ed.) (2003). *Encyclopedia of Psychological Assessment,* Vol. 1. New Delhi: Sage Publication.

Finger, J.A. and Schlesser, G.E. (1965). Non-Intellectual Prediction of Academic Success in School and College. *School Review,* 73, 14-29.

Flescher, I. (1963). Anxiety and Achievement of Intellectually Gifted and Creative Children. *Journal of Psychology,* 56, 251-263.

Fontana, D. (1981). *Psychology for Teachers.* London: MacMillan Press Ltd.

Fowler, L. M. and Watford, L. J. (2000). Formal Reasoning and Academic Performance in College Mathematics and Psychology Courses. *Educational Research Quarterly.* www.highbeamresearch.com.

Fraser, B. J. and O'Brien, P. (1985). Student and Teacher Perceptions of the Environment of Elementary School Classrooms. *The Elementary School Journal,* 85, 567-580.

Fraser, B. J. and Walberg, H. J. (1991). *Educational Environments: Evaluation, Antecedents and Consequences.* Oxford: Pargamon Press.

French, J. W. (1965). New Tests for Predicting the Performance of College Students with High-Level Aptitude. *Journal of Educational Psychology,* 55, 184-194.

Frieze, I. H. (1976). Causal Attributions and Information Seeking to Explain Success and Failure. *Journal of Research in Personality,* 10, 293-305.

Gama, E. M. P. and deJesus, D. M. (1991). School Achievement and Causal Attribution Patterns among Low Income Students. Paper presented at the Annual Convention of the American Psychological Association, San Francisco on Aug. 16-20, 1991.

Gandhi, P. (1982). Academic Achievement in Relation to Achievement Motive, Affiliation Motive and Power Motive. Doctoral Dissertation, Banaras Hindu University.

Garfinkel, A. and Tabor, K. E. (1991). Elementary School Foreign Languages and English Reading Achievement: A New View of the Relationship. *Foreign Language Annuals,* 24(5), 375-382.

Garg, C. (1992). A Study of Family Relations, Socio-Economic Status, Intelligence, and Adjustment of Failed High School Students. Ph.D. (Edu.), Hemvati Nandan Bahuguna Garhwal University.

Garg, V. P. and Chaturvedi, S. (1992). Intelligence and Socio-Economic Status As Correlates of Academic Performance: Some Field Evidences. *Indian Educational Review,* 27 (3), 107-10.

Garrett, H. E. (2004). *Statistics in Psychology and Education.* Delhi: Paragon International Publishers.

Gaur, P. K. (1982). A Psychological Study of Reading Ability in Relation to Achievement. Doctoral Dissertation, Agra University.

Gautam, R. (2000). Self-Concept and Academic Achievement as Related to Emotional Intelligence of Adolescents. M.Ed Dissertation, Panjab University.

Gawande, E. N. (1988). A Study of the Relationship between Achievement Motivation and Scholastic Achievement of Higher Secondary Students of Class XI of Amaravati District of Maharashtra State. M. Phil. Dissertation, University of Poona.

GCPI (1981). A Study of the Factors Responsible for Good Examination Results in Allahabad. In M.B. Buch (Ed.) (1987). *Third Survey of Research in Education*. New Delhi: NCERT.

George, M. (1969). Personality Patterns of College Students Specialising in Different Fields. Doctoral Dissertation, Kerala University.

Gesinde, A. M. (2000). In Z. A. A. Omideyi (Ed.), *Fundamental of Guidance and Counselling*. Ibadan: Kanead Publishers.

Ghahbazi, P. (1956). The Use of Projective Test in Predicting College Achievement. *Educational and Psychological Measur*ement, 16, 538-542.

Ghanshyam, G. A. and Chakravarti, D. (2008). Colonial to Global: Changing Perspectives of English. *University News*, 46 (27), 10-13.

Ghosh, G. P. (1983). A Study of the Achievement of the Students in Chemistry and Finding Relation with Some of Its Determinants. Doctoral Dissertation, Kalyani University.

Girad, D. (1977). Motivation: The Responsibility of the Teacher. *Journal of English Language Teaching*, 31.

Girija, P. R. and Bhadra, B. R. (1976). Personal and Environmental Factors Related to Academic Performance of College Students. *Asian Journal of Psychology and Education*, 1 (3), 5-10.

Girja, P. R. (1980). A Study of Intellectual and Non-Intellectual Factors in Academic Achievement of Advantaged and Disadvantaged Students from Professional Colleges. Doctoral Dissertation, Karnataka University.

Goh, S. C. and Fraser, B. J. (1997). Teacher Interpersonal Behaviour, Classroom Environment and Student Outcomes in Primary Mathematics in Singapore. *Learning Environments Research*, 1 (2), 199-229.

Goh, S. C., Young, D. J. and Fraser, B. J. (1995). Psychosocial Climate and Student Outcomes in Elementary Mathematics Classrooms: A Multilevel Analysis. *Journal of Experimental Education*, 64, 29-40.

Goldenberg, C., Rueda, R. S. and August, D. (2006). Social and Cultural Influences on the Literacy Attainment of Language-Minority Children and Youth. In D. August and T. Shanahan (Eds.). *Developing Literacy in*

*Second Language Learners: Report of the National Literacy Panel on Language Minority Children and Youth*. Mahwah, NJ: Lawrence Erlbaum.

Goleman, D. (1995). *Emotional Intelligence*. New York: Bantam Books.

Goleman, D. (1998). *Working with Emotional Intelligence*. New York: Bantam Books.

Goswami, D. (2009). Emotional Intelligence of the Post-graduate Students of Gauhati in Relation to Certain Variables. *Experiments in Education*, 37 (5), 25-28.

Gottfried, A. E. (1990). Academic Intrinsic Motivation in Young Elementary School Children. *Journal of Educational Psychology*, 82 (3), 525-538.

Government of India (1948). University Education Commission (1948). New Delhi: Ministry of Education.

Government of India (1953). Conference of Professors of English (1953). Proceedings of the Conference of Professors of English held on Jan. 23-24, 1953. New Delhi: Ministry of Education.

Government of India (1953). Proceedings of the Conference of Professors of English, Jan 23-24, 1953. New Delhi: Ministry of Education.

Government of India (1964-66). Indian Education Commission (1964-66). New Delhi: Ministry of Education.

Grace, F. R. (2004). The Relationship between Student Satisfaction and Emotional Intelligence among Under-graduate Students Enrolled in Nursing Programmes. *Dissertation Abstracts International*, 65 (10), 3717-A.

Graham, S. (2003). Motivation. In J. W. Guthrie (Ed.) (2003). *Encyclopedia of Education*, Vol. 5. New York: Thomsom Gale.

Green-Demers, I., Legault, L., Pelletier, L. G. (2008). Factorial Invariance of the Academic Amotivation Inventory Across Gender and Grade in a Sample of Canadian high School Students. *Educational and Psychological Measurement*, 68 (5), 862-880.

Griffith, W. T. (1985). Factors Affecting Performance in Introductory Physics Courses. *American Journal of Physics*, 53 (9), 839-842.

Gudadur, S. S. (2009). A study of Academic Achievement among Students with High and Low School Adjustment. *Journal of Educational Studies*, 7 (1), 24-26.

Guil, R., Mestre, J. M. and Gil-Olarte, P. (2004). Inteligencia Emocionaly Rendimiento Academico. In F. Miras, N. Yuste and F. Valls (Eds.), *Actas del IV Congreso Internacional de Psocologia y Education: Calidad Educativa*. Almeria: Servicio de Publicaciones de la Universidad de Almeria.

Gupta, N. (1994). A Study of Some Non-Intellective Factors Related to Achievement Differences in Gifted Children. Doctoral Dissertation, University of Allahabad.

Gupta, P. C. (1990). Contribution of Memory and Speed Factors to the Intermediate Examination Scores. Doctoral Dissertation, Utkal University.

Gupta, R., Mukerjee, M. and Chatterji, S. (1993). A Comparative Study of the Factors Affecting Academic Achievement among Four Groups of Adolescents. *Indian Journal of Applied Psychology*, 30 (1), 30-38.

Gupta, S. (1983). Factors Underlying Achievement in first Language (Hindi), Related Classical Language (Sanskrit) and Foreign Language (English) with their Implications for Instructional Methods. Doctoral Dissertation, Jammu University.

Gupta, S. B. (2009). Emotional Intelligence of Senior Secondary Students in Relation to their Reasoning Ability. *Journal of Educational Studies*, 7 (2), 27-29.

Gustafsson, J. E. and Undheim, J. O. (1996). Individual Differences in Cognitive Functions. In D. C. Berlines and R. C. Calfee (Eds.) *Handbook of Educational Psychology*. New York: Macmillan.

Guthrie, J. W. (2003). *Encyclopedia of Education*. New York: Thomson Gale.

Gyanani, T. C. and Agarwal, T. (1998). Effect of Classroom Climate, Teacher's Leadership Behaviour and Expectations on Student's Scholastic Achievement. *Psycho-Lingua*, 28 (1), 61-66.

Haertel, G. D., Walberg, H. J. and Haertel, E. H. (1981). Socio-Psychological Environments and Learning: A Quantitative Synthesis. *British Educational Research Journal*, 7, 27-36.

Hakutta, K., Butler, Y. G. and Witt, D. (2000). *How Long Does it Take English Learners to Attain Proficiency?* Santa Barbara: University of California, Linguistic Minority Research Institute.

Halpern, D. F. and LaMay, M. L. (2000). The Smarter Sex: A Critical Review of Sex Difference in Intelligence. *Educational Psychology Review*, 12 (2), 229-246.

Hamachek, D. (1990). *Psychology in Teaching, Learning and Growth*. Boston: Allyn and Becon.

Hamachek, D. (2000). Dynamics of Self-Understanding and Self-Knowledge: Acquisition, Advantages and Relation to Emotional Intelligence. *Journal of Humanistic Counselling Education and Development*, 38 (4), 230-243.

Haq, N. (1988). A Study of Certain Personality Correlates of Over-Under-Achievement in Different School Subjects. Doctoral Dissertation, Aligarh Muslim University.

Harikrishnan, M. (1992). A Study of Academic Achievement of the Students of the Higher Secondary Stage in Relation to Achievement Motivation and Socio-Economic Status. M. Phil. Dissertation, Annamalai University.

Harry, B., Klinger, J., Cramer, E. P. and Sturges, K. M. (2007). *Case Studies of Minority Students Placement in Special Education*. New York: Teachers College Press.

Hassan, A., Sulaiman, T. and Ishak, R. (2009). Philosophy Underlying Emotional Intelligence in Relation to Level of Curiosity and Academic Achievement of Rural Area Students. *Journal of Social Sciences*, 5 (2), 95-103.

Haynes, W. O., Pindzola, R. H. and Emerick, L. L. (1992). *Diagnosis and Evaluation in Speech Pathology*. Engle-wood Cliffs, NJ: Prentice Hall.

Henry, J. W. and Campbell, C. (1995). A Comparison of the Validity, Predictiveness and Consistency of a Trait *vs.* Situational Measure of Attributions. In M. J. Marinok (Ed.). *Attribution Theory: An Organizational Perspective*. Delray Beach FL: St. Lucie Press.

Hernandez, S. S. (2004). The Effects of Video and Captioned Text and the Influence of Verbal and Spatial Abilities on Second Language Listening Comprehension in a Multimedia Learning Environment. Doctoral Dissertation, New York University.

Hernstein, R. J. and Murray, C. (1994). *The Bell Carve: Intelligence and Class Structure in American Life*. New York: Free Press.

Hernstein, R. J. (1973). *IQ in the Meritocracy*. Boston: Little Brown.

Hess, R. D., Chang, C. M. and McDevitt, T. M. (1987). Cultural Variations in Family Beliefs about Children's Performance in Mathematics: Comparisons among People's Republic of China, Chinese-American and Caucasian-American families. *Journal of Educational Psychology*, 79 (2), 179-188.

Hilgrad, E. R. and Rusell D. H. (1950). Motivation in School Learning. *Learning and Instruction*, 1, 36-68.

Hill, J. K. (1967). Recent Articles on Language Acquisition. *International Journal of Linguistics*, 33, 65-73.

Hills, J. R. (1958). Needs for Achievement, Aspiration and College Criteria. *Journal of Educational Psychology*, 49 (1) 156-61.

Hiruwal, A. (1980). A Study of Pupils' Self-Concept, Academic Motivation, Classroom Climate and Academic Performance. Doctoral Dissertation, Maharaja Sayaji Rao University, Baroda.

Ho, D. Y. F. (1981). Traditional Patterns of Socialisation in Chinese Society. *Acta Psychologica Taiwanica*, 23 (2), 81-95.

Ho, G. H. Y., Bennett, S. M. and Cox, D. (2008). Brief Report: Cognitive Functioning and Academic Achievement in Children and Adolescents with Chronic Pain. *Journal of Pediatric Psychology*, 34 (3), 311-316.

Ho, I. T. and Hau, K. T. (2008). Academic Achievement in the Chinese Context: The Role of Goals, Strategies and Effort. *International Journal of Psychology*, 43 (5), 892-897.

Holt, S. S. (2008). Emotional Intelligence and Academic Achievement in Higher Education. Paper presented at Higher Education Symposium on Emotional Intelligence, held on Oct. 2-3, 2008 at Georgetown University.

Hubley, A. M. (2003). In R. Fernandez – Ballesteros, (Ed.) (2003). *Encyclopedia of Psychological Assessment*, Vol. 1. Sage Publication. New Delhi.

Hundal, P. S. (1969). Sex Differences in Verbal and Performance Tests of Intelligence of Different Class Grades VII, IX and X. *Psychologia*, 12, 115-120.

Hutchinson, C. (1990). Communicative Competence in Language Teaching. In N. Entwistle (Ed.) *Handbook of Educational Ideas and Practices*. New York: Routledge.

Jaegar, A. J. (2002). Job Competencies and the Curriculum: An Inquiry into Emotional Intelligence in Graduate Professional Education. *Researches in Higher Education*, 44, 615-639.

Jain, D. K. (1979). A Study of Significant Correlates of High School Failures in Mathematics and English with Special Reference to Jammu Division. Doctoral Dissertation, Jammu University.

Jain, S. P. (1995). An Investigation into the Relationship of Achievement in Sanskrit with Intelligence, Study Habits, Vocabulary, Comprehension and Grammar of Sanskrit. Doctoral Dissertation, Jamia Milia Islamia. In *Indian Educational Abstracts*, 4, 34-35.

Jensen, A. R. (1969). Environment, Heredity and Intelligence. *Harvard Educational Review*, 39 (1), 1-50.

Jerath, J. M. (1979). A Study of Achievement Motivation and Its Personality, and Ability Correlates. Ph. D. Punjab University.

Jesa, M. (2005). *Efficient English Teaching*. APH Publishing Corporation. New Delhi

Jha, D. D. (2008). A Study of Causal Attribution Pattern among the Undergraduate University Students in the Context of Academic Achievement. M.Ed. Dissertation, University of Allahabad.

Jindal. O. R. (1976), A Comparative Study of Some Personality Variables and Affective Reactions toward Examination of Superior and Failing College Students. Doctoral Dissertation, Kurushetra University.

John (1996). In A. Tella (2007). The Impact of Motivation on Student's Academic Achievement and Learning Outcomes in Mathematics among Secondary School Students in Nigeria. *Eurasia Journal of Mathematics, Science and Technology*, 3 (2), 149-156.

Johnson, J. O. (1996). *Child Psychology*. Calabar: Wusen Press Limited.

Johnston, C. G. (2006). Predictors of College Success among African-American, Caucasian and Hispanic Students. Dissertation, Texas Technical University. http://hdl.handle.net/2346/1100.

Joseph, T. M. (2008). Language and Politics in South India. *Man and Development*, 30 (2), 29-42.

Joshi, A. N. (1984). Factors Influencing English Language Abilities. Doctoral Dissertation, Meerut University.

Joshi, J. N. and Passi, B. K. (1968). The Role of Intelligence and Levels of Instruction on the Development of Numerical Ability in Pupils at the Junior Secondary Stage. *Journal of Psychological Researches*, 12, 57-62.

Judy, S. N. (1981). *Explorations in the Teaching of English.* New York: Harper and Row.

Kafetsios, K. (2004). Attachment and Emotional Intelligence Abilities Across the Life Course. *Personality and Individual Differences*, 37 (1), 129-145.

Kaile, H. S. (1988). Intelligence and Creativity as Predictors of Scholastic Achievement in Mother Tongue and Foreign Language at Different Levels of Socio-Economic Status. Doctoral Dissertation, Punjab University.

Kakkar, S. B. (1970). Popularity, Intelligence, Economic Status and Academic Achievement. *Indian Journal of Psychology*, 45, 233-237.

Kakkar, U. (1975). A Comparative Study of Achievement in Hindi and English. *Researches and Studies*, 26, 15-17.

Kalat, J. M. (2000). Motivation. In C.R. Reynolds and E. Fletcher-Janzen (Eds.) *Encyclopedia of Special Education*, Vol. 2. USA: John Wiley and Sons.

Kanderian, S. S. (1969). Study of the Relationship between School Achievement and Measures of Intelligence and Creativity for Students in Iraq. Doctoral Dissertation, University of Southern California.

Kanoy, B. C., Johnson, B. W. and Kanoy, K. (1980). Locus of Control and Self-Concept in Achieving and under Achieving bright Elementary Students. *Psychology in the Schools*, 7, 395-399.

Karabenick, S. A. and Youssef, Z. I. (1968). Performance as a Function of Achievement Motive Level and Perceived Difficulty. *Journal of Personality and Social Psychology*, 10, 414-418.

Kashiwagi, K., Azuma, H. and Miyake, K. (1982). Early Maternal Influences upon Later Cognitive Development among Japanese Children: A follow-up Study. *Japanese Psychological Research*, 24, 90-100.

Katiyar (1979). In M. B. Buch (Ed.) (1991). *Fourth Survey of Research in Education*, Vol. 1. New Delhi: NCERT.

Katyal, S. and Awasthi, E. (2005). Gender Differences in Emotional Intelligence among Adolescents of Chandigarh. *Journal of Human EOI*, 17 (2), 153-155.

Kauchak, D. P. and Eggen, P. D. (1998). *Learning and Teaching: Research Based Methods*. Boston: Allyn and Bacon.

Kaur, D. (1991). A Study of the Effects of Test Anxiety, Belief in Control of Reinforcement and Intellectual Achievement of Two School Population. Doctoral Dissertation, Punjab University.

Kaur, K. and Meenakshi (2010). Social and Emotional Intelligence of School going Adolescents and Working Status of Mothers. *Journal of Community Guidance and Research*, 27 (3), 299-309.

Kaur, M. (2001). A Study of Emotional Maturity of Adolescents in Relation to Intelligence, Academic Achievement and Environmental Catalysts. Doctoral Dissertation, Punjab University, Chandigarh.

Kaur, P. (1992). Relationship among Creativity, Intelligence and Academic Achievement in Different Subjects of X Graders. Doctoral Dissertation, Punjab University.

Keister, S. C. (2006). Fostering caring Character and Responsibility in Schools. In M. J. Elias and H. Arnold (Eds.), *The Educator's Guide to Emotional Intelligence and Academic Achievement*. Thousand Oaks: Corwin Press.

Kerlinger, F. N. (1973). *Foundations of Behavioural Research*. Surjeet Publications. New Delhi.

Khan I. A. (1996). Factors Affecting the Learning of English as a Second Language: The Indian Socio-Linguistic Context. *The Progress of Education*, LXX (7), 152-155.

Khan, Y. (1989). Construction and Standardisation of Diagnostic Tests in English for Standard VIII with Regard to Structures. Doctoral Dissertation, Nagpur, University.

Khare, M. (1986). A Comparative Study of Traditional and Structural Approaches to Teaching of English with Reference to their Learning Outcomes. Doctoral Dissertation, Gorakhpur University.

Kim, S. E. (2001). Meta-analysis of Gender Differences in Test Performance using HLM. Paper presented at the Annual Meeting of the American Educational Research Association, Seattle.

Klinger, E. (1966). Fantasy need Achievement as a Motivational Construct. *Psychological Bulletin*, 66, 291-308.

Koh, B. H. (1999). A Study of Relationship between Emotional Intelligence, Academic Achievement and Vocational Choice. Doctoral Dissertation, University of Utara, Malaysia.

Kovacs, R. (1981). The Relationship between Student Achievement Motivation and Student Attributions for Examination Performance. *Dissertation Abstracts International*, 42 (2), 614-A.

Kovenklioglu, G. and Greenhaus, J. H. (1978). Causal Attributions, Expectations and Task Performance. *Journal of Applied Psychology*, 63, 698-705.

Kulshrestha, P. (1993). Relationship of Educational Achievement of Adolescents with Intelligence, Adjustment and Achievement Motivation. Doctoral Dissertation, Agra University.

Kulshrestha, P. K. (1992). The Effect of School Environment on Adjustment, Study Habits and Achievement of High School Students. Doctoral Dissertation, Agra University.

Kumar and Bhatia (2005). In K. S. Misra (2007). *Emotional Intelligence: Concept, Measurement and Research.* Allahabad: Association for Educational Studies.

Kumar, A. (1986). A Study of Ego-involvement, Level of Aspiration and Associated Factors in Relation to Achievement at Graduation Level. Doctoral Dissertation, Gorakhpur University.

Kumar, D. V. (2007). Errors in oral Expression of English Language by Secondary Students. *Journal of All India Association for Educational Research,* 19 (3 - 4), 59-60.

Kumar, R. (1989). Children's Curiosity, Intelligence and Scholastic Achievement. Doctoral Dissertation, Agra University.

Kumar, R. K. and Ambedkar, V. (2005). A Study on Effectiveness of Computer Assisted English Language Learning. *Indian Journal of Teacher Education,* 2 (2), 68-77.

Kunzru Committee (1959). http://www.education.nic.in/cd50years/g/12/21/12210A01.htm

Kusche, C. A. and Greenberg, M. T. (1994). *The PATHS (Promoting Alternative Thinking Strategies) Curriculum.* South Ceerfield: Channing-Bete.

Ladson-Billings, G. (1994). *The Dreamkeepers: Successful Teachers of African American Children.* San Francisco: Jossey-Bass.

Ladylit (2008). Establishing and Maintaining the Tone of your Classroom. http:// www.brighthub.com/education/k-12/articles/16774-aspx.

Laidra, K, Pullman, H. and Allik, J. (2007). Personality and Intelligence as Predictors of Academic Achievement: A Cross Sectional Study from Elementary to Secondary School. *Personality and Individual Differences,* 42 (3), 441-451.

Laidra, K., Pullman, H. and Allik, J. (2007). Oersonality and Intelligence as Predictors of Academic Achievement: A Cross-Sectional Study from Elementary to Secondary School. Personality and Individual Differences, 42 (3), 441-451.

Lal, C., Sharma, A. K. and Sharma, S. K. (2010). A Study of Emotional Intelligence of SC Students in Relation to Academic Achievement. *Journal of Teacher Education and Research,* 5 (1), 26-32.

Lam, L. T. and Kirby, S. L. (2002). Is Emotional Intelligence an Advantage? An Exploration of Emotional Intelligence and General Intelligence on Individual Performance. *Journal of Social Psychology,* 142 (1), 133-145.

Lane, V. W. and Molyneaux, D. (1992). *The Dynamics of Communicative Development.* Englewood Cliffs, NJ: Prentice Hall.

Larson, V. L. and McKinely, N. (1995). *Language Disorders in Older Students: Preadolescents and Adolescents.* Eauclaire, W.I.: Thinking Publications.

Latchanna, G. and Dagnew, A. (2009). Attitude of Teachers towards the use of Active Learning Methods. *Journal of All India Association for Educational Research,* 21 (1), 70-73.

Lavin, D. E. (1967). *The Prediction of Academic Performance.* New York: John Wiley and Sons.

Lawson, A. E. (1982). Formal Reasoning, Achievement and Intelligence: An Issue of Importance. *Science Education,* 66, 77-83.

Lawson, A. E. (1985). A Review of Research on Formal Reasoning and Science Teaching. *Journal of Research in Science Teaching,* 22, 569-617.

Lawson, A. E. *et al.* (1975). Relationship of Formal Reasoning to Achievement, Aptitudes and Attitudes in Preservice Teachers. *Journal of Research in Science Teaching,* 12 (4), 423-42.

Lazarus (1966). In Poonam (2007). *Effect of Stress on Job-Satisfaction and Work-Values among Teachers.* New Delhi: Adhyayan Publishers and Distributors.

Lei, C. (2009). On The Causal Attribution of Academic Achievement in College Students. *Asian Social* Science, 5 (8), 87-96.

Leopold, W. F. (1948). The Study of Child Language and Infant Bilingualism. *Word,* 4, 1-17.

Lepage, L. and Pamela (1997). Exploring Patterns of Achievement and Intellectual Development among Academically Successful Women from Disadvantaged Backgrounds. *Journal of College Student Development,* 38 (15), 468-478.

Levine, R., Reis, H. T., Turner, E. S. and Turner, G. (1976). Fear of Failure in Males: A More Salient Factor than fear of Success in Females? *Sex Roles,* 2, 389-398.

Lewis, M. K. (2003). Differences in Emotional Intelligence and Related Construct among Academically Resilent and Academically Non-resilient African American Under-graduate Students. Dissertation, Microfiche.

Lightbody, P., Siann, G., Stocks, R. and Walsch, D. (1996). Motivation and Attribution at Secondary School: The Role of Gender. *Educational Studies,* 22 (1), 13-25.

Linn, M. C. (1982). Theoretical and Practical Significance of Formal Reasoning. *Journal of Research in Science Teaching,* 19, 727-742.

Lori, L. (2003). An Examination of Emotional Intelligence Factors: Their Relationship to Academic Achievement and the Implications for Retention of the at Risk Community Collage Student. Dissertation, Capella University.

Lynn, R., Hampson, S. L., and Magee, M. (1983). Determinants of Educational Achievement at 16 Plus: Intelligence, Personality, Home Background and School. *Personality and Individual Differences*, 4, 473-81.

Mabekoje, S. O. and Ogunyemi, B. (2003). Emotional Intelligence within Classroom Context: The Influence of Gender and Sociometric Status. *Journal of Research in Counselling Psychology*, 9 (1), 94-103.

MacGinite, W. M. (1969). In R.L. Ebel, V.N. Noll and R.M. Bauer (Eds.) *Encyclopedia of Educational Research*. USA: The MacMillan Company.

Mackintosh, N. J. (1998). *IQ and Human Intelligence*. Oxford: Oxford University Press.

Madhavi, G. and Kishan, N. R. (2009). Development of Positive Learning Environment. *Edutracks*, 9 (3), 17-18.

Madhubala (1990). Classroom Learning Behaviour of Students of Different Intelligence Levels and their Problems Related to Achievement in Economics at 10+2 Stage. Doctoral Dissertation, Maharishi Dayanand University.

Madsen, I. N. (1992). The Contribution of Intelligence Tests to Educational Guidance in High School. *The School Review*, 30 (9), 692-701.

Mahapatra, R. (1998). Meta-cognitive Correlates of Efficient and Deficient Learners. Doctoral Dissertation, M. L. Sukhadia University.

Makhija, G. K. (1973). Interaction among Values, Interests and Intelligence and Its Impact on Scholastic Achievement. Doctoral Dissertation, Agra University.

Malviya, S. (2007). A Study of Emotional Intelligence in Relation to Moral Judgment of the Secondary School Students. M.Ed. Dissertation, University of Allahabad.

Malviya, S. (2008). A Study of Effect of Socio-Economic Status and Sex on the Emotional Intelligence of Under-graduate Professional Students. M. Phil Dissertation, C.S.J.M University, Kanpur.

Manhas, K. (2004). Cognitive and Non-Cognitive Correlates of Emotional Entelligence of Adolescents. Doctoral Dissertation, Punjab University.

Manhas, K. D. and Gakhar, S. C. (2005). Non-Cognitive Correlates of Emotional Intelligence of Adolescents. *Journal of Educational Research and Extension*, 43 (1).

Manhas, K. D. and Gakhar, S. C. (2006). Non-Cognitive Correlates of Emotional Intelligence of Adolescents. *Journal of Educational Research and Extension*, 43 (1), 1-9.

Marjoribanks, K. (2003). Learning Environment, Family Contexts, Educational Aspirations and Attainment: A Moderation-mediation Model Extended. *Learning Environments Research*, 6 (3), 247-265.

Marquez, P. G., Martin, R. P. and Brackett, M. A. (2006). Relating Emotional Intelligence to Social Competence and Academic Achievement in High School Students. *Psicothema,* 18, 118-123.

Marsh, H. W. (1984). Relations among Dimensions of Self-Attribution Dimensions of Self-Concept and Academic Achievement. *Journal of Educational Psychology,* 6, 1291-1308.

Marsh, H., Cairns, L., Relich, J., Barnes, J. and Debus, R. (1982). The Relationship between Dimensions of Self-Attributions and Dimensions of Self-Concept. Unpublished Manuscript, University of Sydney.

Mason, B. and Krashen, S. (1997). Can Extensive Reading Help Unmotivated Students of EFL Improve? *ITL Review of Applied Linguistics,* 9 (2), 78-84.

Mavi, N. S. and Patel, I. (1997). A Study of Academic Achievement in Relation to Selected Personality Variables of Tribal Adolescents. *Experiments in Education,* 25 (7-8), 155-162.

Mayer, J. D., Caruso, D. and Salovey, P. (2000). Emotional Intelligence Meets Traditional Standards for Intelligence. *Intelligence,* 27, 267-298.

Mayer, J. D., Salovey, P. and Caruso, D. (2002). *The Mayer-Salovey-Caruso Emotional Intelligence Test MSCEIT Version* 2. Toron: Multi-Health Systems.

Mayer, J. D., Salovey, P. and Caruso, D. R. (2000). Models of Emotional Intelligence. In R. J. Sternberg (Ed.). *Handbook of Human Intelligence.* New York: Cambridge.

Mazumdar, A. (1992). A Study of the Relationship between Attitude towards and Achievement in English of Standard IX Students in Guwahati City. M.Phil. Dissertation, North-Eastern Hill University.

McCarthy, D. (1954). Language Development in Children. In C. Leonard (Ed.). *Manual of Child Psychology,* 492-630.

McClelland, *et al.* (1953). *The Achievement Motive.* New York: Appleton.

McRobbie, C. J. and Fraser, B. J. (1993). Associations between Student Outcomes and Psycho-social Science Environment. *Journal of Educational Research,* 87, 78-85.

Meenakshi (2003). Effect of Achievement Motivation on the Academic Motivation of Students. In R. Sharma (2008). A Study of Art Competencies of B.Ed. Pupil-Teachers as Correlates of Emotional Intelligence, Creativity and Achievement Motivation. *Journal of Teacher Education and Research,* 3 (1), 15-18.

Meena Rani (1992). A Study of Locus of Control, Self-Esteem, Academic Responsibility, Academic Motivation and Scholastic Achievement of Advantaged and Disadvantaged Students. Doctoral Dissertation, University of Allahabad.

Meera, K. P. and Remya, P. (2010). Effect of Extensive Reading and Creativity on Achievement in English Language. *Journal of All India Association for Educational Research*, 22 (1), 16-22.

Mehrotra, A. and Nigam, V. (2008). Shaikshik Samprapti Par Vidyalayi Vatavaran Ka Prabhav. *DEI-FOERA*, 2, 54-55.

Mehrotra, S. (1986). A Study of the Relationship between Intelligence, Socio-economic Status, Anxiety, Personality, Adjustment and Academic Achievement of High School Students. Doctoral Dissertation, Kanpur University.

Mehta, P. (1968). Achievement Motivation Training for Educational Development. *Indian Educational Review*, 3 (1) 46-74.

Meijer, A. M. *et al.* (2004). The Joint Contribution of Sleep, Intelligence and Motivation to School Performance. *Personality and Individual Differences*, 37, 95-106.

Mian, S. (1988). Intelligence, Neuroticism, Scholastic Achievement and Need Achievement – A Comparative Study between Boys and Girls. Doctoral Dissertation, University of Kashmir.

Miles, C. C. (1954). Gifted Children. In L. Carmichael (Ed.) *Manual of child Psychology*. New York: Willey.

Miller, P. T. and Ross, M. (1975). Self-Serving Biases in the Attribution of Causality: Fact or Fiction? *Psychological Bulletin*, 82, 213-225.

Mishra, R. and Ranjan, P. (2008). Emotional Intelligence as Related to Self-Esteem of Adolescents. *Indian Journal of Human Relations*, 34, 13-17.

Misra, G. (1983). Situational and Personal Determinants of Attributions for Achievement Outcomes in India. Paper Presented at the 3rd Asian Regional Conference of IACCP, Malaysia.

Misra, K. S. (1999). *Manual for Test of Cognitive Processes*. Kanpur: Sangyanalaya.

Misra, K. S. (2001). *Measuring Learning Enviornment*. Kanpur: Sangyanalaya.

Misra, K. S. (2002). Impact of Learning Environment on Science Processes and Achievement. Report of the UGC Sponsored Minor Research Project. Department of Education, University of Allahabad.

Misra, K. S. (2007). *Emotional Intellignece: Concepts, Measurement and Research*. Allahabad: Association for Educational Studies.

Misra, M. (1986). A Critical Study of the Influence of Socio-Economic Status on Academic Achievement of Higher Secondary Students in Rural and Urban Areas of Kanpur. Doctoral Dissertation, Kanpur University.

Misra, S. (1982). Effect of Socio-Economic Background, Gender and Achievement Outcome on Attribution, Affect and Expectation. Dissertation, University of Allahabad.

Misra. G. and Misra S. (1986). Effect of Socio-Economic Background on Pupils Attributions. *Indian Journal of Current Psychological Research,* 1, 77-88.

Mitra, R. (1985). Some Determinants of Academic Performance in Pre-Adolescent Children. Doctoral Dissertation, Calcutta University.

Mitzel, H. E. (Ed.) (1982). *Encyclopedia of Educational Research,* Vol. 2. New York: The Free Press.

Mohan, E. A. (2006). High-Stakes Testing and English Language Learners: Questions of Validity. *Bilingual Research Journal,* 30 (2), 479-497.

Mohan, S. (1991). A Study on the Role of Aptitude, Attitude and Motivation in English Acquisition. Doctoral Dissertation, University of Delhi.

Moreano, G. (2004). The Relationship between Academic Self-Concept, Causal Attribution for Success and Failure and Academic Achievement in Pre-Adolescents. www.self.ox.ac.uk/conferences/2004_Moreano.pdf

Morris, E. A., Brooks, P. R. and May, J. L. (2003). The Relationship between Achievement Goal Orientation and Coping Style: Traditional *vs.* Non-Traditional College Students. *College Student Journal,* 37 (1), 3-9.

Mukalel, J. C. (2003). *Approaches to English Language Teaching.* Discovery Publishing House Pvt. Ltd., New Delhi.

Murray, S. R. and Mednick, M. T. S. (1975). Perceiving the Causes of Success and Failure in Achievement: Sex, Race and Motivational Comparisons. *Journal of Consulting and Clinical Psychology,* 43, 881-885.

Muthumanickam, R. (1972). A Study of Academic Achievement of Students of Higher Secondary Commerce Group in Relation to their Reasoning Ability, Socio-Economic Status and Interest in Commerce. M. Phil. Dissertation, Annamalai University.

Naderi, H., Abdullah, R., Hamid, T. A. and Sharir, J. (2008). Intelligence and Gender as Predictors of Academic Achievement among Under-graduate Students. *European Journal of Social Sciences,* 7 (2), 199-207.

Namrata (1992). The Relationship of Personality Traits, Situational Stress and Anxiety Factors to Student Achievement. Doctoral Dissertation, University of Lucknow.

National Knowledge Commission (2005). http://www.knowledgecommission.gov.in/recommendations.

National Research Council (2000). In K. Hakuta and A. Beatty (Eds.), *Testing English Language Learners in U.S. Schools: Report and Workshop Summary.* Washington D C: National Academy Press.

Nelson, D. W. and Nelson, K. (2003). Emotional Intelligence Skills: Significant Factors in Freshmen Achievement and Retention. (ERIC Document No. 476121).

Neugebauer, S. R. (Ed.) (2008). Editor's Reviews. *Harvard Educational Review,* 78 (1), 252.

Newsome, S., Day, A. L. and Catano, V. M. (2000). Assessing the Predictive Validity of Emotional Intelligence. *Personality and Individual Differences*, 29, 1005-1016.

Ngailiankim, C. (1991). A Study of Selected Variables Associated with Achievement in Mathematics. Doctoral Dissertation, North-Eastern Hill University.

Nicholls, J. G. (1975). Causal Attributions and Other Achievement Related Cognitions: Effects of Task Outcome, Attainment Value and Sex. *Journal of Personality and Social Psychology*, 31, 377-389.

Nicholls, J. G. (1978). The Development of the Concepts of Effort and Ability Perception of Academic Attainment and the Understanding that Difficult Task Require more Ability. *Child Development*, 49, 800-814.

Niebuhr, K. (1995). The Effect of Motivation on the Relationship of School Climate, Family Environment and Students Characteristics to Academic Achievement (ERIC Document Reproduction Service Ed 393202).

Nikose, R. L. (2010). Academic Achievement of Secondary School Tribal Students in Relationship to Mental Health and Intelligence: A Correlational Study. *C T E National Journal*, 8 (2), 99-104.

O'Connor, R. M. and Little, I. S. (2003). Revisiting the Predictive Validity of Emotional Intelligence: Self-Report *vs.* Ability-Based Measures. *Personality and Individual Differences*, 35, 1893-1902.

O'Sullivan, J. T. and Howe, M. L. (1996). Causal Attributions and Reading Achievement: Individual Differences in Low-Income Families. *Psychological Abstracts*, 84 (4), 1808.

Olatoye, R. A., Akintunde, S. O. and Yakasai, M. I. (2010). Emotional Intelligence, Creativity and Academic Achievement of Business Administration students. *Electronic Journal of Research in Educational Psychology*, 8 (2), 763-786.

Oller, J. W. (1980). A Comment on Specific Variance *vs.* Global Variance on Certain EFL Tests. *Teachers of English to Speakers of other Languages Quarterly*, 14, 527-530.

Omoluabi, P. F. (1993). Relationship between Performance in Intelligence Tests and Achievement in School Examinations. *IFE Psychologia: An International Journal*, 1 (2), 48-58.

Padhi, J. S. (1991). The Effects of Creativity and Classroom Environment on Pupil's Academic Self-Concept and Academic Achievement. Doctoral Dissertation, Barkatullah Vishwavidayalaya.

Palta Singh, S. (2008). Relationship among Creativity, Intelligence and Achievement Scores of Secondary School Students. *Journal of Teacher Education and Research*, 3 (2), 54-60.

Pan, W. D. (1993). Causal Attributions and Affective Reactions of Chinese Students in Hong Kong. Doctoral Dissertation, Thr Chinese University of Hong Kong Graduate School. http://www.fed.cuhk.edu.hk

Pandey, A. (2008). +2 Star par Vidyarthiyo ki Samvegatmak Budhi Avam Shikshik Uplabdhi ke Madhya Sambandh ka Adhyan. M.Ed. Dissertation, University of Allahabad.

Pandey, R. and Tripathi, A. N. (2004). Development of Emotional Intelligence: Some Observations. *Psychological Studies*, 49 (2-3), 147-150.

Pandey, R. S. (1982). A Study of the Factors Relating to Low Achievement in English. *Researches and Studies*, 33, 28-30.

Pandey, R. S. (1992). *National Policy on Education in India*. Allahabad: Horizon Publishers.

Pandey, S. and Lal, K. (2002). A Study of Behaviour Patterns of Language Teaching in Relation to Class-climate and Elicitation-Response Modes. *APEAR Journal of Education*, 1 (2), 10-13.

Pandey, S. and Lal, K. (2002). A Study of Behaviour Patterns of Language Teaching in Relation to Class Climate and Elicitation Response Modes. *APEAR Journal of Education*, 1 (2), 10-13.

Pandey, T. C. (2002). Emotional Intelligence and Attitude towards Modernisation of Kumaoni Adolescents in Relation to Some Socio-Familiar and Educational Factors. Doctoral Dissertation, Kumaon University.

Panigrahi, M. N. (2005). Academic Achievement in Relation to Intelligence and SES. *Edutracks*, 5 (2), 26-27.

Pant, N. and Prakash, A. (2004). Multifactor Emotional Intelligence Scale (MEIS) in India – An Evaluation. *Psychological Studies*, 49 (2-3), 128-135.

Parker, J. D. A. (2002). Emotional Intelligence and Academic Success: Examining the Transition from High School to University. www.MHS. Com.

Parker, J. D. A. *et al.* (2001). Emotional Intelligence and Academic Achievement. Presentation of the Canadian Psychological Association Quebec City, Quebec.

Parker, J. D. A., Summerfeldt, L. J., Hogan, M. J. and Majeski, S. (2004). Emotional Intelligence and Academic Success: Examining the Transition from High School to University. *Personality and Individual Differences*, 36, 163-172.

Parker, J. D., Creque, R. E., Barnhart, D. L., Harris, I. J., Majeski, S. A., Wood, L. M., Bond, B. J. and Hogan, M. J. (2004). Academic Achievement in High school: Does Emotional Intelligence Matter? *Personality and Individual Differences*, 37, 1321-1330.

Parkerson, J. H., Schiller, D. P., Lomax, R. G. and Walberg, H. J. (1984). Exploring Causal Models of Educational Achievement. *Journal of Educational Psychology*, 76, 638-46.

Parmane, S. S. (1999). A Study of Psychological Barriers Encountered by Adolescents during Classroom Communication of Algebra in Relation to their Achievement in the Subject. Doctoral Dissertation, Shivaji University.

Patel D. (1987). Academic Achievement in Relation to Cognitive and Personality Differentials of Socially Disadvantaged and Advantaged Secondary School Children of Orissa. Doctoral Dissertation, Punjab University.

Pathak, P. (1962). Exploratory Study of Creativity, Intelligence and Scholastic Achievement. *Psychological Studies*, 7, 1-9.

Patil, D. K. (1985). The English Language Achievement of Shivaji University arts graduates. Doctoral Dissertation, Shivaji University.

Pau, A. K. H. and Croucher, R. (2003). Emotional Intelligence and Perceived Stress in Dental Under-graduates. *Journal of Dental Education*, 67, 1023-1028.

Paul, S. (1982). Achievement Motivation. In H.E. Mitzel (Ed.) (1982). *Encyclopedia of Educational Research*, Vol. 4. New York: The Free Press.

Pearl, R., Brayon, T. and Donahue, M. (1980). Learning Disabled Children's Attributions for Success and Failure. *Learning Disabled Quarterly*, 13, 242-246.

Peck, R. F. and Rickek, H. (1969). Cognitive Development. In R.L. Ebel, V.H. Noll and R.M. Bauer (Eds.) (1969). *Encyclopedia of Educational Research.* USA: The MacMillan Company.

Peterson, C. and Barrett, L. (1987). Explanatory Style and Academic Performance among University Freshmen. *Journal of Personality and Social Psychology*, 53, 603-607.

Petrides, K. V. and Furnham, A. (2000). On The Dimensional Structure of Emotional Intelligence. *Personality and Individual Differences*, 29, 313-320.

Petrides, K. V., Fredrickson, N. and Furnham, A. (2004a). The Role of Emotional Intelligence in Academic Performance and Deviant Behaviour at School. *Personality and Individual Differences*, 36, 163-217.

Petrides, K. V., Furnham, A. and Martin, G. N. (2004b). Estimates of Emotional and Psychometric Intelligence: Evidence for Gender Based Stereotypes. *Journal of Social Psychology*, 144, 149-162.

Phillips L. and Steinkomp, M. (1995). *Improving Academic Performance*. Action Research Project, Illinois: Saint Xavier University.

Phillips, M. (2005). An Analysis of Emotional Intelligence and Faculty Qualities Necessary for Success in A Non-Traditional Classroom Setting. *Dissertation Abstracts International*, 66 (7), 2465-A.

Piaget, J. and Inhelder, B. (1958). *The Growth of Logical thinking from Childhood to Adolescence*. In R. L. Ebel, V. H. Noll and R.M. Bauer (Eds.) (1969). *Encyclopedia of Educational Research*. USA: The MacMillan Company.

Piaget, J. (1926). *The Language and Thought of the Child.* New York: Harcourt, Brace and World.

Pillai, K. S. and Salimkumar, C. (1995). Achievement Motivation: A Multifactorial Approach Scale. *The Progress of Education,* LXIX (8), 153-155.

Pishghadam, R. (2007). On The Influence of Emotional and Verbal Intelligence on Second Language Learning. Ph.D. Thesis, Allameh Tabataba'ii University, Tehran.

Pishghadam, R. (2009). A Quantitative Analysis off the Relationship between Emotional Intelligence and Foreign Language Learning. *Electronic Journal of Foreign Language Teaching,* 6 (1), 31-41.

Pool, C. R. (1997). Up with Emotional Health. *Educational Leadership,* 54(8), 40-42.

Power, S., Douglas P., Cool, B. A. and Gose, K. F. (1987). Achievement Motivation and Attributions for Success and Failure. *Psychological Abstracts,* 74 (3).

Pradhan, D. (1997). Effect of Socio-Economic Status and Intelligence on Scholastic Achievement of Girls. *Praachi Journal of Psycho-Cultural Dimensions,* 13 (1), 41-44.

Prakash, B. (1981). An Experimental Study of Achievement Motivation and Confirmation of Results on the Performance in a Linear Programme on Hindi Vocabulary Building. Doctoral Dissertation, Himachal Pradesh University.

Pramod, S. (1996). Future Time Perspective, Cognitive Efficiency, Achievement Motivation, Anxiety and Academic Performance among XI Standard Boys and Girls. *Indian Journal of Applied Psychology,* 33 (1), 34-38.

Pressley, M. and McCormick, C. B. (1995). *Advanced Educational Psychology: For Educators, Researchers and Policy-makers.* New York: Harper Collins.

Prieto, M. D., Fernandiz, C., Ferrando, M., Sainz, M., Bermejo, R. and Hernandez, D. (2008). Emotional Intelligence in High-Ability Students – A Comparative Study between Spain and England. *Electronic Journal of Research in Educational Psychology,* 6 (2), 297-320.

Priyadarshini, R. P. G. (2005). A Study of Emotional Intelligence among Academic Professionals. *Prestige Journal of Management and Research.*

Radha Rani (1992). A Study of Intelligence, Socio-Economic Status, Achievement Motivation and Academic Achievement with Reference to Pupil's Behaviour in Classroom. Doctoral Dissertation, Agra University.

Rajput, A. S. (1984). A Study of Academic Achievement of Students in Mathematics in Relation to their Intelligence, Achievement Motivation and Socio-Economic Status, Doctoral Dissertation, Punjab University.

Ramachandran, R. (1990). A Study on the Relationship between Performance and other Psychological Variables – Reasoning, Anxiety and Adjustment. M.Phil. Dissertation, Annamalai University.

Ramamani (1990). Home Language, School Language and Educational Performance – An Empirical Study of SC Children of Different Social Classes. Ph.D. (Edu.), University of Mysore.

Ramasamy, R. (1988). An Inquiry into the Correlates of Achievement. Doctoral Dissertation, South Gujarat University.

Rangaswamy and Feroze (1957). In M.B. Buch (Ed.) (1986). *Third Survey of Research in Education* 1978-1983. New Delhi: NCERT.

Rani, S. and Kaushik, N. (2005). A Comparative Study of Achievement Motivation, Home Environment and Parent Child Relationship of Adolescents. *Journal of Psychological Research,* 49 (2), 89-94.

Rao, S. and Murthy, V. N. (1984). Psycho-Social Correlates of Locus of Control among College Students. *Psychological Studies,* 29 (1), 51-56.

Rao, S. N. (1971). A Prognostic Study of Achievement in Relation to Academic Adjustment. *Indian Educational Review,* 6, 196-213.

Rastogi, K. G. (1974). Intelligence, Achievement and Value System of Students in Different Professional Courses. *Teacher Education,* 9, 29-36.

Rathbone. C. H. (1972). Examining the Open Education Classroom. *School Review,* 80, 521-542.

Raviv, A. and Bar-Tal, D. (1980). Causal Perceptions of Success and Failure by Advantaged, Integrated and Disadvantaged Pupils. *British Journal of Educational Psychology,* 50, 137-146.

Ray, A. (1996). The Responsive Classroom Approach: Its Effectiveness and Acceptability in Promoting Social and Academic Competence. In K. S. Misra (2007). *Emotional Intelligence: Concept, Measurement and Research.* Allahabad: Association for Educational Studies.

Reddy, B. S. K. and Venu, P. (2010). Impact of Gender and Locality on Emotional Intelligence of Secondary School Students. *Journal of Community Guidance and Research,* 27 (3), 331-336.

Reddy, V. L. N. (1973). A Study of Certain Factors Associated with Academic Achievement at the First Year Degree Examination. Doctoral Dissertation, Maharaja Sayajirao University of Baroda.

Reeve, J., Bolt, E. and Cai, Y. (1999). Autonomy-Supportive Teachers: How they Teach and Motivate Students. *Journal of Educational Psychology,* 91, 537-548.

Reif, H. B. *et al.* (2001). The Relation of Learning Disability and Gender with Emotional Intelligence in College students. *Dissertation Abstracts International,* 34 (1), 66-78.

Roberts (2002). In K. S. Misra (2007). *Emotional Intelligence: Concept, Measurement and Research.* Allahabad: Association for Educational Studies.

Roebken, H. (2007). The Influence of Goal Orientation on Student Satisfaction, Academic Engagement and Achievement. *Electronic Journal of Research in Educational Psychology,* 5 (3), 679-704.

Rogers, C. (1990). Teacher's Expectations and Pupils' Achievement. In N. Entwistle (Ed.) (1990). *Handbook of Educational Ideas and Practices.* New York: Routledge.

Ronis, D. L., Hansen, R. D. and O'leary, V. E. (1983). Understanding the Meaning of Achievement Attributions: A Test of Derived Locus and Stability Scores. *Journal of Personality and Social Psychology,* 44, 702-711.

Rosen, B. C. (1956). The Achievement Syndrome: A Psycho-Cultural Dimension of Social Stratification. *American Sociological Review,* 21, 203-211.

Rosenfield, D. and Stephan, W. G. (1978). Sex Differences in Attributions for Sex – Typed Tasks. *Journal of Personality,* 46, 244-259.

Rouhani, A. (2008). An Investigation into Emotional Intelligence, Foreign Language Anxiety and Empathy through a Cognitive – Affective Course in EFL Context. *Linguistic Online,* 34, 41-57.

Rusillo, M. T. C. and Arias, P. F. C. (2004). Gender Difference in Academic Motivation of Secondary School Students. *Electronic Journal of Research in Educational Technology,* 2 (1), 97-112.

Ryans, D. G. (1942). Motivation in Learning. *Psychology of Learning,* 2, 289-331.

Sabath, A. (2010). Emotional Intelligence: Key to Performance Excellence. Souvenir of National Seminar on Emotional Intelligence: A Key to Human Well Being, held on 4-5 March 2010 at Amity University, Lucknow.

Sahay, N. (1991). Familial Correlates of Academic Achievement in Rural Hindu School Students. Doctoral Dissertation, Ranchi University.

Salami, S. O. and Ogundokun, M. O. (2009). Emotional Intelligence and Academic Self-Efficacy as Predictors of Academic Performance among Senior Secondary School Students in Oyo State, Nigeria. *Perspectives in Education,* 25 (3), 175-185.

Salili, F. (1996). Learning and Motivation. *Psychology and Developing Societies,* 8 (1).

Sandra, D. (2002). Mathematics and Science Achievement: Effects of Motivation, Interest and Academic Engagement. *Journal of Educational Research.* http://www.findarticles.com

Sankarappan, R. (1992). A Study of Some Variables Related to Achievement in English of Standard IX Pupils in Madurai District in Tamil Nadu. M.Phil. Dissertation, Annamali University.

Santha, K. M. (1998). Influence of Classroom Climate and Approaches to Studying on Achievement in Physics of Secondary School Pupils. Doctoral Dissertation, University of Allahabad.

Saricaolu, A. and Arikan, A. (2009). A Study of Multiple Intelligence, Foreign Language Success and Some Selected Variables. *Journal of Theory and Practice in Education*, 5 (2), 110-122.

Sarode, V. B. (1995). A Study of Impact of SES, Study Habits and Academic Motivation on Academic Achievement of Higher Secondary Students of Rural Areas. Doctoral Dissertation, University of Pune.

Sarojini, N. B. (2000). English Methodology in the Pre-Service Teacher Education Programme. *Teacher Education*, 34 (2), 22-27.

Sarojini, S. (1971). Personality Problems of Pupils of Age Group 16-18 Years. Doctoral Dissertation, Madras University.

Saville-Trioke, M. (1982). Language Development. In H.E. Mitzel (Ed.) *Encyclopedia of Educational Research*, Vol. 2. New York: The Free Press.

Saville-Troike, M. (1982). Language Development. In H. E. Mitzel (Ed.). *Encyclopedia of Education Research*. New York: The Free Press.

Schlesser, G. E. and Finger, J. A. (1965). Non-Intellective Predictors of Academic Success in School and College. *School Review*, 73-14-29.

Schunk, D. H. (1996). Goal and Self-Evaluative Influences during Children's Cognitive Skill Learning. *American Educational Research Journal*, 33 (2), 359-382.

Schutte, N. S., Malouff, J. M., Hall, L. E., Haggerty, D., Cooper J. T., Golden, C. J. and Dornheim, L. (1998). Development and Validation of a Measure of Emotional Intelligence. *Personality and Individual Difference*, 25,167-177.

Shah, P. C. (2002). A Study of the Relationship between Educational Achievement and Socio-Economic Status of SC and Non-SC Students of Secondary Schools with Reference to Psychological Variables. Doctoral Dissertation, Gujrat University.

Shanmagusundram, R. (1983). An Investigation into Factors Related to Academic Achievement among Under-Graduate Students under Semester System. Doctoral Dissertation, Madras University.

Shanmughadas, K. K. (2004). Interaction Effect of Learning Style, Approaches to Studying and Classroom Climate on Achievement in Social Sciences of Secondary School Pupils. Doctoral Dissertation, University of Calicut.

Shanwal, V. K. (2003). A Study of Correlates and Nurturance of Emotional Intelligence in Primary School Children. *Indian Educational Abstracts*, 4(1).

Sharma, K. (2007). *Psychological Factors Learning English at School*. New Delhi: Gyan Publishing House.

Sharma, M. (1988). A Study of Factors in Pupil Academic Achievement in Different Streams of Courses of the Higher Secondary Stage. Doctoral Dissertation, Agra University.

Sharma, P. (1981). A Study of Factors Related to Academic Under-Achievent of Girls of Secondary Schools Located in Rural areas of Haryana. Doctoral Dissertation, Mysore University.

Sharma, P. (2008). Effect of Family Environment on Academic Achievement of Students. *Souvenir* of National Seminar on Family – A Stepping Stone in Holistic Development of Child, held on 27-28 Sept. 2008 at Rani Bhagyawati Devi Mahila Mahavidhyalay, Bijnor.

Sharma, R. and Tripathi R. C. (1986). Social Factors and Teacher Expectation. Paper presented in the National Seminar on Human Resource Development: The Challenge for Young Psychologists, held on Nov. 12-14, 1986, Department of Psychology, University of Allahabad.

Sharma, R. (2008). A Study of Art Competencies of B.Ed. Pupil-Teachers as Correlates of Emotional Intelligence, Creativity and Achievement Motivation. *Journal of Teacher Education and Research*, 3 (1), 15-18.

Sharma, S. (2003). A Study of Emotional Intelligence of Pupil-Teachers in Relation to SES, Caste and Gender. M.Ed. Dissertation, Bundelkhand University, Jhansi.

Sharma, S. (2006). Causal Attribution for Performance in B.Ed. Examination M.Ed. Dissertation, University of Allahabad.

Sherman, M. S. (1977). Selective Affective Characteristics and Creative Problem Solving Performance in Gifted Elementary School Children. *Dissertation Abstracts International*, 38-A, 186.

Shipley, K. G. and McAfee, J. G. (1998). *Assessment in Speech Language Pathology: A Resource Manual.* SanDiego: Singular.

Shivappa, D. (1980). Factors Affecting the Academic Achievement of High School Pupils. Doctoral Dissertation, Karnataka University.

Shobhna, N. (2004). A Survey to Identify the Difficulties in written English among Secondary School Learners. *Experiments in Education*, 32 (6), 8-18.

Shukla, A. (1994). Role of Locus of Control in Attributing Cause of Success and Failure. *Psycho-Lingua*, 24 (1), 25-31.

Siana, G., Lightbody, P. S. R. and Walsch, D. (1998). Motivation and Attribution At Secondary Schools: The Rule of Ethic. *Group and Gender Education*, 8 (3) 261-274.

Sibia, A. (1989). Degree of Prediction of Achievement by Field Dependence, Test Anxiety and Intelligence in Females. *Indian Educational Review*, 24 (3), 116-124.

Sibia, A., Misra, G. and Srivastava, A. K. (2005). Assessing Emotional Intelligence in the Indian Context. *Psychological Studies*, 50 (2-3), 263-271.

Sidhu, R. K. and Singh, P. (2005). Comparative Study of Concept Attainment Model, Advance Organizer Model and Conventional Method in Teaching

Physics in Relation to Intelligence and Achievement Motivation of Class IX Students. *Journal of All India Association for Educational Research,* 17 (1-2), 89-92.

Singarvelu, S. (2008). Emotional Maturity: A Significant Predictor of Academic Success of Post-Graduate Students. *University News,* 46 (25), 17-19.

Singh, A. (1978). Construction of a Battery of Objective Test for Assessment of Proficiency in writing English Composition. Doctoral Dissertation, Kurukshetra University.

Singh, A. K. (2008a). National Knowledge Commission Reports to the Nation: Challenges and Opportunities. *University News,* 46 (41), 1-8.

Singh, B. K. (1976). *Non-Intellective Correlates of Academic Achievement.* Allahabad: Indian International Publications.

Singh, D. (2006). *Emotional Intelligence at Work.* New Delhi: Response Books.

Singh, D. (2007). A Study of Achievement among General and SC Students in Relation to Emotional Intelligence. *Souvenir* of National Seminar on Education of the Deprived, held on 19-20 Nov., 2007 at Department of Education, University of Allahabad.

Singh, D. R. (1983). Study of Memory, Symbolic Representation and Some other Mental Abilities in Relation to Achievement in Chemistry at Graduation Level. Ph.D. (Edu.), Gorakhpur University.

Singh, D. R. (1986a). Reasoning Ability – The Best Predictor of Achievement in Chemistry at Graduation Level. *AYRE Journal of Education,* 5 (2), 21-28.

Singh, P. (2008b). A Study of Classroom Climate, Deprivation and Personality as Determinants of Emotional Intelligence. Doctoral Dissertation, University of Allahabad.

Singh, P. (2008c). A Study of Achievement among General and SC Students in Relation to Emotional Intelligence. *Journal of Educational Studies,* 6 (2), 49-52.

Singh, R. and Verma, S. K. (1995). The Effect of Academic Aspiration and Intelligence on Scholastic Success of XI Graders. *Indian Journal of Psychometry and Education,* 26 (1), 43-48.

Singh, T. and Dwivedi, C. B. (1993). Deprivation, Context and Processing of Textual Materials. *Journal of Genetic Psychology,* 154, 73-83.

Singh, V. K. (2007). Apvanchit Varg ke Balako ki Budhi Tatha Samajik Arthik Stithi ka Unki Shaikshik Uplabdhi par Prabhav. *Souvenir* of National Seminar on Education of the Deprived held on 19-20 Nov. 2007 at Department of Education, University of Allahabad.

Singh, V. P. (2008). Effectiveness of Jurisprudential Inquiry Model of Teaching on Verbal Fluency of Ninth Graders. *Perspectives in Education,* 24 (3), 167-179.

Singhal, S. (1991). A Study of Academic Achievement in Relation to Academic Motivation and Classroom Social Climate. *Journal of Psychological Researches*, 35 (2-3), 120-124. In *Indian Psychological Abstracts and Reviews*, 1 (1), 133.

Sinha, A. (1998). Use of Language for Effective Interaction. *The Primary Teacher*, 23 (1), 23-30.

Sinha, D. (1970). *Academic Achievers and Non-Achievers*. Allahabad: United Publishers.

Sinha, H. C. (1967). Factorial Analysis of Different aspects of English Attainment of Hindi Speaking Students. Doctoral Dissertation, Gorakhpur, University.

Sinha, N. (1991). A Social and Psychological Study of Academically Talented and Average Students. Doctoral Dissertation, University of Allahabad.

Sinha, N. C. P. (1967). A Study of Inteligence and Some Personality Factors in Relation to Academic Achievement of School Students. Doctoral Dissertation, Magadh University.

Skaalvik, S. and Skaalvik, E. M. (2004). Gender Differences in Mathematics and Verbal Self-Concept, Performance Exceptions and Motivation. *Sex Roles: A Journal of Research*. http:// www.findarticles.com

Skaalvik, S. and Skaalvik, E. M. (2006). Self-Concept and Self-Efficacy in Mathematics: Relation with Mathematics Motivation and Achievement. *Proceedings of the International Conference on Learning Sciences*. Bloomington, Indiana. http:// www.findarticles.com

Skinner, B. F. (1957). *Social Behaviour*. In J.C. Mukalel (2003). *Approaches to English Language Teaching*. Discovery Publishing House, Pvt. Ltd., New Delhi.

Slobin, D. E. (1970). Universals of Grammatical Development in Children. In W. Level and G.B.F. d'Arcais (Eds.). *Advances in Psycho Linguistic Research*. Amsterdam: North Holland.

Smith, C. P. (1964). Relationship between Achievement Related Motives, Intelligence, Performance Level and Persistence. *Journal of Abnormal and Social Psychology*, 68, 523-532.

Smith, L., Sinclair, K. E. and Chapman, E. S. (2002). Students' Goals, Self-Efficacy, Self-Handicapping and Negative Affective Responses: An Australian Senior School Student Study. *Contemporary Educational Psychology*, 27, 471-485.

Sontakey, V. V. (1986). A Comparative Study of Personality Factors and Achievement Motivation of High and Low Achievers in Natural and Biological Sciences. Doctoral Dissertation, Nagpur University.

Sood, R. (1988). Cattell's Personality Factors as Predictors of Academic Achievement in some Selected Professional Courses. Doctoral Dissertation, Kurukshetra University.

Sorenson, H. (1954). *Psychology in Education.* New York: McGraw Hill.

Srivastava N. (2007). A Study of Emotional Intelligence in Relation to Achievement in Environmental Studies. *Journal of Educational Studies,* 5(1),7-9.

Srivastava, J. E. (1974). A Study of Effect of Academic Motivation and Personality Characteristics on the Academic Achievement of Boys Reading in Class X. Doctoral Dissertation, Rajasthan University.

Srivastava, J. P. (1974). *Non-Cognitive Factors in Academic Achievement*. Meerut: Anu Books.

Srivastava, N. (1980). Intelligence, Interest, Adjustment and Family Status as Predictors of Educational Attainment of High School Students. Doctoral Dissertation, Gorakhpur University.

Srivastava, N. (2009). Dabav ke Sandarbh mai Samvegatmak Budhi ka Adhyan. Paper presented in the the National Seminar on Quality Control in School Education, held at Mahatama Gandhi Kashi Vidyapith, Varanasi on 27-28 Feb., 2009.

Srivastava, N. C. (1992). Prognostic Value of Non-verbal Intelligence Tests for Success in Literary Subjects at the High School Examination. *Indian Journal of Psychometry and Education,* 23 (2), 61-68.

Srivastava, N. C. (1995). Predictive Value of Psychological Tests for Achievement in Literary Subjects at the High School Examination. *Indian Journal of Psychometry and Education,* 26 (2), 91-96.

Srivastava, P. (2005). Study of Some Mental Abilities in the Learning of Mathematics at the Junior High School Level. *Researches and Studies,* 58, 28-29.

Srivastava, R. (1992). A Study of Socio-Psychological Characteristics of Class X Students of Navodaya Vidhyalays. Doctoral Dissertation, University of Lucknow.

Srivastava, Y. V. (1995). Efficacy of Concept Attainment Model in the Teaching of English grammar. *Psycho-Lingua,* 25 (1-2), 69-72.

Steinberg, L. C. (2006). The Graying Freshmen: Examining Achievement Motivation Goals and Academic Performance in Traditional and Non-traditional Under-graduate Students. Doctoral Dissertation, University of Kansas.

Stephan, W. G., Rosenfield, D. and Stephan, C. (1976). Egotism in Males and Females. *Journal of Personality and Social Psychology,* 34, 1161-1167.

Sternberg, R. J. (2002). Raising the Achievement of all Students: Teaching for Successful Intelligence. *Educational Psychology Review,* 14 (4), 383-393.

Stevenson, H. W. and Lee, S. Y. (1990). Context of Achievement. *Monograph of the Society for Research in Child Development,* 55 (122).

Stewart, J. H. (1998). Practical Intelligence: Assessing its Convergent and Discriminant Validity with Social, Emotional and Academic Intelligence. *Dissertation Abstracts International*, 8 (8-B), 4504.

Strahan, D. V. and O' Sullivan, R. G. (1988). Achievement Test Scores in Middle Grades: The Influence of Cognitive Reasoning. *The Journal of Early Adolescence*, 8 (1), 53-61.

Suarez-Orozco, C. and Suarez-Orozco, M. (2001). *Children of Immigration: The Developing Child Series*. Cambridge MA: Harvard University Press.

Sucaromana, U. (2004). The Relationship between Emotional Intelligence and Achievement in English for Thai Students in the Lower Secondary School. *Educating Weaving Research into Practice*. 3, 158-164. http://search.informit.com.au/documentsummary dn = 008030217825449:res = E-LIBRARY.

Sudhir, M. A. and Muraleedharan-Pillai, P. G. (1987). Science Achievement in Relation to Intelligence and SES: A Study of Secondary School Students in Aizawl. *Indian Journal of Psychometry and Education*, 18, 37-44.

Sutherland, M. (1990a). Education and Gender Differences. In N. Entwistle (Ed.), *Handbook of Educational Ideas and Practices*. New York: Routledge.

Sutherland, M. (1990b). Individual Differences and Development. In N. Entwistle (Ed.), *Handbook of Educational Ideas and Practices*. New York: Routledge.

Swart, A. (1996). The Relationship between Well-being and Academic Performance. Doctoral Dissertation, University of Pretoria, South Africa.

Sween (1984). Academic Achievement of High School Students in Relation to the Instructional Design, Intelligence, Self-Concept and Achievement. Doctoral Dissertation, Punjab University.

Szuberia, A. L. (2006). Emotional Intelligence and School Success. *Journal of Developmental Psychology*, 31 (1).

Tachibana, Y., Matsukawa, R. and Zhong, Q. X. (1996). Attitudes and Motivation for Learning English: A Cross-national Comparison of Japanese and Chinese High School Students. *Psychological Reports*, 79 (2), 691-700.

Taliuli, N. and Gama, E. M. P. (1986). Causal Attribution, Self-Concept and Academic Achievement of School Children from Low SES Families. Paper presented at the Annual Meeting of the American Educational Research Association, San Francisco on Aug. 16-20, 1986.

Tella, A. (2007). The Impact of Motivation on Students' Academic Achievement and Learning Outcomes in Mathematics among Secondary School Students in Nigeria. *Eurasia Journal of Mathematics, Science and Technology*, 3 (2), 149-156.

Terman, L. M. and Tyler L. E. (1954). In R. L. Ebel; V. H. Noll and R. M. Bauer (Eds.) (1969). *Encyclopedia of Educational Research*, USA: The Macmillan Company.

Terman, L. M. (1916). *The Measurement of Intelligence: An Explanation for the Use of the Stanford Revision and Extension of the Binet-Simon Intelligence Scale*. New York: Houghton Mifflin Company.

Thejovathi, K. (1995). A Study of the Environmental Factors Affecting the Acquisition of English Language Skills at the High School Stage in Guntur District. *Experiments in Education*, 23 (5), 88-92.

Tiwari A. D. (1986). An Investigation into the Interrelationship between Measures of Selected Guilford's S-I Factors and Set-Concept Achievement of Secondary Level Students of Delhi State. Doctoral Dissertation, Jamia Milia Islamia University.

Tiwari, A. P. (1999). Arthik Drishti se Saksham Tatha Kamjor Chatro ki Shaikshik Abhiprerna Avam Saikshik Uplabdhi ka Tulnatmak Adhyan. Dissertation, University of Allahabad.

Tiwari, P. S. N. and Srivastava, N. (2004). Schooling and Development of Emotional Intelligence. *Psychological Studies*, 49 (2-3), 151-154.

Tiwari, R. (1984). A Study of the Achievement Motivation, Intelligence and Personality Traits of Privileged and Deprived Children. Doctoral Dissertation, R. S. University.

Tollefson, N. (2000). Classroom Applications of Cognitive Theories of Motivation. *Educational Psychology Review*, 12 (1), 63-84.

Tomblin, J. B., Morris, H. L. and Spriesterbach, D. C. (1994). *Diagnosis in Speech Language Pathology*. San Diego: Singular.

Torres, J. L. (2000). Cognitive Development. In C.R. Reynolds and E.F. Janzen (Eds.) (2000). *Encyclopedia of Special Education*, Vol. 1. New York: John Wiley and Sons.

Tourani, P. (2006). Comparative Effectiveness of Jerk Technology and Lecture Method in Terms of Cognitive and Effective Domain Related Variables of Class I-IX Students. Doctoral Dissertation, Devi Ahilya Vishwavidyalaya.

Trama, S. (1998). A Study of Academic Achievement in Relation to Intelligence, Parental Involvement and Children's Motivational Resources at Upper Elementary and Secondary School Levels. Doctoral Dissertation, Punjab University.

Tripathi (1992). In M. Saroj (2006). Muk-Badhir Bacho ki Shaikshik Abhiprerna aur Parivarik Vatavaran ka Adhyan. Dissertation (Edu.), University of Allahabad.

Tripathi, A. (2009). Learning Environment for Quality Primary Education. *Souvenir* of National Seminar on Quality Control in School Education, held at Mahatama Gandhi Kashi Vidyapeeth, Varanasi, on 27-28 Feb. 2009.

Tripathi, B. K. (1978). A Study of Relationship between Personality Patterns, Social Acceptance, Classroom Behaviour and Academic Achievement. Doctoral Dissertation, Rajasthan University.

Tripathi, R. C. (1986). Achievement Motivation and Its Correlates among High School Students of East U. P. Doctoral Dissertation, Gorakhpur University.

Tripathy, S. K, (1990). A Study of the Academic Performance of Tribal and Non-tribal High School Students in Relation to their Self-Concept, Level of Aspiration and Academic Motivation. Doctoral Dissertation, Kurukshetra University.

Upadhyaya, S. (2000). A Study of Creativity in English Language at Plus two Levels in Relation to Achievement Motivation, Imagery and Achievement. Doctoral Dissertation, Baraktullah University.

Upadhyaya, S. K. and Upadhyaya, V. (2004). A Study of Emotional Stability and Academic Achievement of Boys and Girls at Secondary Level. *Indian Journal of Educational Research*, 23(2), 41-46.

Upadhyaya, S. N. (1984). Analysis of Classroom Environments in Tribal Setting with a View to Study Its Effect on Learning and Attainment. Department of Psychology, Ravi Skankar University (NCERT Financed).

Urdan, T. (2004). Using Multiple Methods to Assess Students' Perception of Classroom Goal Structures. *European Psychologist*, 9 (4), 222-231.

Valenzuela, A. (1999). *Subtractive Schooling: US-Mexian Youth and the Politics of Caring*. Albany: State University of New York Press.

Valle Arias *et al.* (1999). Causal Attribution, Self-Concept and Motivation in Students with Low Academic Performance. *Revista Espondade Pedagogia*, 214, 525-546.

Van Rooy, D.L., Alonso, A. and Visvesvaran, C. (2005). Group Difference in Emotional Intelligence Scores: Theoretical and Practical Implications. *Personality and Individual Differences*, 38 (3), 689-700.

Vander Zee, K., Schakel, L. and Thijs, M. (2002). The Relationship of Emotional Intelligence with Academic Intelligence and the Big Five. *European Journal of Personality*, 16, 103-125.

Varma, M. K. (2003). Relationship between Academic Achievement of Middle School Students with their Intelligence, Adjustment and Achievement Motivation. Doctoral Dissertation, Bundelkhand University.

Vazquez. S. M. and deAnglat, H. D. (2009). Academic Achievement and Formal thought in Engineering Students. *Electronic Journal of Research in Educational Psychology*, 7 (2), 653-679.

Veekarchavan, V. and Bhattachayra R. (1989). School Achievement, Student Motivation and Teacher Effectiveness in Different Types of School. *Indian Educational Review*, 25.

Vela, R. H. (2003). The Role of Emotional Intelligence in the Academic Achievement of First Year College Students. Disseratation, Texas University, Kinsville.

Venugopal, G. (1994). Intellect Profile and Achievement of Middle School Pupils. *Experiments in Education*, 22 (7), 141-147.

Verma, B. P. (1996a). Study Habits, Locus of Control and Academic Performance. *Indian Journal of Psychometry and Education*, 27 (2), 1-6.

Verma, B. P. (1996b). Test Anxiety and Study Habits: A Study of their Main and Interaction Effects on Academic Achievement. *Indian Journal of Applied Psychology*, 33 (2), 55-61.

Verma, B. P. (1996d). Intellectual Ability, Test Anxiety and Achievement in Different School Courses. *Indian Journal of Psychology*, 71 (3-4), 115-119. In *Indian Educational Abstracts*, 4, 93.

Verma, M. (1996a). Significant Correlates of Secondary School Failures. Department of Education, Gorakhpur University (NCERT Financed).

Verma, S. K. (1987). Teaching English as a Second Language in India: Focus on Objective. In R. Steele and T. Treadgoled (Eds.), *Language Topics*. Amsterdam: John Benjamins Publishing Co.

Verma, S. K. (1994). Certain Aspects of Second Language Teaching. *Trends in Social Science Researches*, 1 (1), 59-64. In *Indian Psychological Abstracts and Reviews*, 2 (2), 395-396.

Verma. R. P. S. (1977). A Study of School Learning as a Function of Socio-Emotional Climate of the Class. Doctoral Dissertation, Rajasthan University.

Vidler, D. C. (1977). Curiosity. In S. Ball (Ed.) (1977). *Motivation in Education*. New York: Academic Press.

Visvesvaran, H. (1975). Learning of Teaching Items in English in the Upper Primary Classes in Coimbatore District. Doctoral Dissertation, Madras University.

Walberg, H. J. (1968). Structural and Affective Aspects of Classroom Climate. *Psychology in the Schools*, 5, 247-253.

Wallach, G. P. and Miller. L. (1988). *Language Invervention and Academic Success*. Boston: College-Hill/Little Brown and Co.

Wallach, G.P. and Butler, K.G. (1994). *Language Learning Disabilities in School-Age Children and Adolescents: Some Principles and Applications*. New York: Merril/MacMillan College Publishing.

Watkins, D. and Astilla, E. (1980). Causal Attribution of Performance in University Examinations: A Filipino Investigation. *Higher Education*, 9 (4), 443-451.

WEAC (2005). Variables Affecting Student Achievement. http://weac.org/resources/primer/variable.htm

Webster, M. (1981). *Webster's Third New International Dictionary.* U.S.A.: Encyclopedia Britannica, Inc.

Weiner, B. and Potepan, P. A. (1970). Personality Correlates and Affective Reactions towards Exams of Succeeding and Failing College Students. *Journal of Educational Psychology,* 61, 144-151.

Weiner, B. (1971). *Statistical Principles in Experimental Design.* Tokyo: McGraw-Hill, Kogakusha Ltd.

Weiner, B. (1972). Attribution Theory, Achievement Motivation and the Educational Process. *Review of Educational Research,* 42, 203-214.

Weiner, B. (1974). *Achievement Motivation and Attribution Theory.* Morristown: General Learning Press.

Weiner, B. (1979). A Theory of Motivation for Some Classroom Experiences. *Journal of Educational Psychology,* 71, 3-25.

Weiner, B. (1992). *Human Motivation: Metaphors Theories and Research.* Sage Publications: New Delhi.

Weiner, B., Heckhausen, H., Meyer, W. and Cook, R. (1972). Causal Ascriptions and Achievement Behaviour: A Conceptual Analysis and Reanalysis of Locus of Control. *Journal of Personality and Social Psychology,* 21, 239-248.

Weiner, B., Kukla, A., Frieze, I., Reed, L., Rest, S. and Rosenbaum, R. M. (1971). Perceiving the Cause of Success and Failure. In E. E. Jones, D. E. Kanouse, H. H. Kelley, R. E. Nisbett, S. Valins and B. Weiner (Eds.), *Attribution: Perceiving the Causes of Behaviour.* Morristown: General Learning Press.

Weiner, B., Russell, D. and Lerman, D. (1978). Affective Consequences of Causal Ascription. In J. H. Harvey, W. Ickes and R. Kidds (Eds.). *New Directions in Attributional Research,* Vol. 2. Hillsdale NJ: Eribaum.

Weller, C., Crelley, C., Watteyne, L. and Herbert, M. (1992). *Adaptive Language Disorders of Young Adults with Learning Disabilities.* SanDiego: Singular.

Wethington, C. T. (1970). A Study of Relationship between Attitude towards English and Several Selected Variables. *Dissertation Abstract International,* 31, 1637-38A.

Wong, A. F. L. and Fraser, B. J. (1997). Assessment of Chemistry Laboratory Classroom Environment. *Asia Pacific Journal of Education,* 17, 41-58.

Wren, P. C. and Martin, H. (1994). *High School English Grammar and Composition.* New Delhi: S. Chand and Company Ltd.

Yadav, S. (2006). Kaksha XI ke Vidyarthiyo ki Gadit mai Nishpatti par Kaksha Vatavaran, Budhi, Tathaa Adhyan ke Prabhav ka Adhyan. Dissertation (Edu.), University of Allahabad.

Yelle, M., Green-Demers, I. and Pelletier, D. (2005). The Influence of Social Climate, Family Relationships and Negative Peer Influence on Academic

Motivation and Its Consequences. Paper presented at the Annual Meeting of the Canadian Psychological Association, Montreal, Canada.

Yuthim, O. (2001). Evaluation of Academic Achievement in Bloom's Taxonomic Categories in Relation to Instructional Design and Achievement Motivation. Ph.D. (Edu.), Punjab University.

Zareen, S. (2001). Parishadiya Avam Niji Prathmik Vidhyalayo Mai Vidhyarthiyo ki Gadit mai Nishpatti Avam Kaksha Vatavaran mai Sambandh ka Adhyan. M. Ed. Dissertation, University of Allahabad.

Zeitoun, H. H. (1988). The Relationship between Abstract Concept Achievement and Prior Knowledge, Formal Reasoning Ability and Sex among some Egyptian Secondary School Students. Paper presented at the Annual meeting of the National Association for Research in Science Teaching, held at Lake of Ozarks on 10-13 April, 1988. (ERIC # E9292636.)

# INDEX

A



B

C



D



E